THE BHAGAVAD GITA

A Scripture for the Future

THE BHAGAVAD GITA
A Scripture for the Future

Translation and Commentary

by

Sachindra Kumar Majumdar

ASIAN HUMANITIES PRESS
Berkeley, California

ASIAN HUMANITIES PRESS

Asian Humanities Press offers to the specialist and the general reader alike, the best in new translations of major works and significant original contributions, to enhance our understanding of Asian literature, religions, cultures and thought.

Library of Congress Cataloging-in-Publication Data

Bhagavadgita. English.
      The Bhagavad Gītā : a scripture for the future / [translation and commentary] by Sachindra Kumar Majumdar.
          p.   cm.
      Translation of : The Bhagavadgita.
      Includes bibliographical references and index.
      ISBN 0-89581-885-X—ISBN 0-89581-896-5 (pbk.)
      1. Bhagavad Gītā.—Commentaries. I. Majumdar, Sachindra Kumar..
II. Title.
BL 1138.62.E5 1991b
294.5'924—dc20   92-21423
                                                CIP

Printed in the United States of America

To
Shivananda

Table of Contents

TABLE OF CONTENTS

Acknowledgements

THE BOOK WAS WRITTEN AT THE INSTANCE of Mr. Ralph Brockway, a friend of many years. He has done much of the work connected with its preparation and publication. No thanks are enough for his work of love.

Thanks are also due to Mrs. Ivri Patricia Wormser for preparing the Index and Glossary as well as reading through the manuscript and improving it and also to Mrs. Elizabeth Strong-Cuevas, an unfailing friend and patron, for help and encouragement in numerous ways.

Finally our very profound and grateful thanks are due to the Advaita Ashrama of Calcutta for kind permission to quote from the works of Vivekananda and Ramakrishna.

Sachindra Kumar Majumdar
Montrose, New York
September 1991

Forewords

From Arthur Lall, Former Ambassador to the United Nations from India.

SACHINDRA KUMAR MAJUMDAR'S RENDERING of the *Bhagavad Gita*, together with his wise and often brilliant commentary, is like the opening wide of a grand gateway to a beautifully landscaped garden. The result is a truly gripping book that is very difficult to put down in spite of its presentation of an often abstruse philosophy.

There are innumerable sentences in the commentary to ponder over: "There is only one religion of man which may be called man's return to Reality or Truth. The so-called different religions or opinions or creeds are different ways of reaching the one goal... There are infinite ways of reaching the same goal." (The last of the above sentences is taken from Ramakrishna, the great Indian saint of the nineteenth century.) Or. "There is no perfection in history until it winds up." Or, again, "Divine incarnation is a mystery." Majumdar suggests that in each major cycle of time a Teacher will come so that a balance may be preserved between despair and hope.

FOREWORDS

Of this wise book excusably Sachindra Majumdar thinks that its subtle outpourings will make it a scripture of the future. This would seem to be a plausible view, especially in the context of the infinite ways of reaching the goal of reality that he and his teachers propound. For all those interested in puzzling out the nature of that goal, this will be a text they will want to read and re-read. In preparing it Sachin Majumdar has performed an outstanding service.

From Swami Shraddhananda, Vedanta Society of Sacramento.

THIS NEW VERSION OF THE *Bhagavad Gita* by S.K. Majumdar has its unique features. The author has presented the teachings of Sri Krishna in the light of the Sri Ramakrishna-Vivekananda ideal. This standpoint is bound to bring to thoughtful readers a novel understanding of the *Gita*. The *Gita*, like the *Bible,* never gets old. It has the innate potentiality to reveal new healthy directions to our everyday life. It can make simple but powerful syntheses of the secular and the spiritual. Mr. Majumdar deserves our praise and appreciation for producing the present work.

Preface

There are already many editions of the Gita with commentaries in the market. The question naturally arises, why is there any need for a new edition? The main reasons for the present edition are briefly the following:

The Gita is not a book of philosophy or theology. It does not speak in the uncertain voice of intellectuals. It is the scripture which reveals Truth and how to find it in endless ways. I have attempted to point this out in the light of the experience and teachings of those who have realized this Truth and expressed it in our time. Truth is perception and not theory.

I have also attempted to present the Truth of the Gita in the light of modern developments in science and psychology, in history and cosmology.

The comments follow faithfully the teachings of the enlightened of our time who alone can speak with authority in verification of the Gita teachings and who alone can point out the right course of action in the world of today with its special problems. Old coins do not circulate in new times. The ancient metal needs the new imprint of modernity to lead men out of the maya that the world of common perception is.

PREFACE

Further, understanding the Gita needs acquaintance with the analysis of nature which is infinitely more complex and comprehensive than the physical nature of modern science. The evolution and principles of this nature form the background of the Gita's teachings. The Introduction presents such an analysis and also points out how these teachings went out of India in ancient times to form the basis of Pythagorean and Platonic philosophy that have dominated European philosophical and theological thinking down to our time.

The above are a few of the things that distinguish the present edition from others. I have tried to make the translation of the text as clear and faithful as I found it possible, keeping in mind the central teaching of the Gita.

In the last century the German philosopher Schopenhauer was so impressed by reading a Latin translation of a Persian translation of a few of the Upanishads that he predicted that when their teachings would become known in the West they would produce a revolution of thought comparable to the Renaissance in Italy when medieval Europe came into contact with Greek learning. The Gita is the essence of the Upanishads.

The Lord of time is not without a witness in time. Sometimes He is His own witness.

Om Krishnarpanam astu!

Introduction

RIGINS AND SETTING. The *Gita,* or the *Bhagavad Gita,* is the greatest testament of the Eternal Religion *(Sanatana Dharma),* the name by which the Hindus call their spiritual tradition. In it, spiritual wisdom finds its most profound, catholic, clear and modern expression.

Gita means a song and *Bhagavad Gita* means the divine song. It is a small book of seven hundred verses and forms part of the vast and ancient Indian epic, the *Mahabharata,* which has a hundred thousand verses in its present form.

There are uncertainties concerning historical facts about the Mahabharata and the Gita. Several things, nevertheless, are beyond dispute. The truth of scripture or of science does not depend on historical facts, though it is true, as Ramakrishna said, that scriptures generally are a mix of sugar and sand, and that one has to separate sugar carefully from sand.

The Gita, however, is an unusual scripture, the local and temporal coloring in it being minimal. The truth of a scripture is independent of historical circumstances. It is not that important to know when truth was discovered; the important thing is the truth itself, the verified fact, the experience which is not peculiar, but universal.

INTRODUCTION

The Gita belongs to the tradition according to which religion is Truth, a higher truth than science or common experience. It is knowledge not open to the methods of science. It is knowledge more important than the practical knowledge with which we grow food, cook meals, build houses, drive cars, etc., for it is knowledge of life's goals, its ideals and the proper way of living, which is not accessible to sense-observation or intellectual, speculative effort, but without which civilized life disintegrates into the chaos from which it slowly arose.

The Gita is a sermon on the battlefield. It was delivered by Krishna, the Divine Teacher, to Arjuna, his disciple, on the eve of a great battle between two sets of opposing cousins in which were engaged most of the princes and noblemen of India of the time.

The huge epic, the Mahabharata, is built around the battle which was fought, no one knows exactly when, but at least three thousand five hundred years ago according to the most conservative and critical estimate. It could have been earlier. The battlefield came to be known as Kurukshetra or the Field of King Kuru who according to a story in the Mahabharata once ploughed it. The King of Gods, Indra, stopped him from ploughing by giving him the boon he desired; namely, that any one who died in the field practicing austerities or fighting in battle would go to heaven. It is a vast area in a part of which the modern city of Delhi is situated. The field has been the scene of many fateful battles in India's history.

There is no doubt that Krishna was an historical figure and an object of worship several centuries before Christ. He was the friend and guide of Arjuna and his four brothers who were arrayed with their army against their opponents, an army led by one hundred cousins.

Arjuna was the leader on one side. He and his brothers were the Pandavas or sons of Pandu. On the other side were Duryodhana and his brothers who were the Kauravas. Both sides were descendants from their common ancestor Kuru.

The dramatization of the main story of the Mahabharata by Peter Brook and his associates, which is available on video cassette, gives an idea of its vastness, of the great battle and of Krishna.

Krishna was Arjuna's friend and charioteer. He is venerated as a Divine Incarnation by the Hindus. His life and character have been delineated in such a manner in the epic and in other *Puranas*, or historical and religious books, that he has become a most endearing idol, the darling hero of the Hindus.

Arjuna like other Aryan noblemen fought from a chariot as did the aristocratic fighters of Greece in the heroic age. It was the custom of noble warriors in those days to engage opponents openly, face to face and with due ceremonies, some traces of which are still seen in the martial arts of judo and karate.

When Arjuna's chariot was drawn up in front of the opposing army, Arjuna was grief-stricken at the sight of his friends and relatives whom he would have to fight. He was also morally perplexed about his duty as a warrior loyal to king and country because of the prospect of killing his superiors, relatives and friends for the sake of winning kingdoms and wealth. Dismayed and despondent he sank down in his chariot reluctant to fight.

It was at this point that Krishna addressed him with a most stirring call:

> Do not give way to unmanliness, O Son of Partha
> (Arjuna)! It does not befit you. Relinquishing this
> petty weakness of heart arise, O Destroyer of Enemies!

This is the key appeal of *Vedanta* to the innate strength and greatness of man.

Thus began Krishna's sermon and the message of the Gita. The dialogue between Krishna and Arjuna and the battle scene were reported to the blind and old King Dhritarashtra, father of Duryodhana, by Sanjaya, his minister. The king was in his palace remote from the scene of war, but Sanjaya was given the power of distant vision to report the war to the king who was anxious about the fate of the war in which his sons and relatives were engaged.

Krishna's sermon epitomizes the wisdom of Sanatana Dharma (the Eternal Religion). Was the message delivered on the field of battle and in verse? There is only one authentic case in history of a great philosophical text being composed amid the din of battle — the *Meditations* of the Stoic Roman Emperor, Marcus Aurelius.

INTRODUCTION

Probably the Gita was composed by a supremely gifted philosopher-artist. It is a marvel because such an excellent work on religion and ethics has not been written since, nor is it likely to be written again.

APPEAL TO HEAD AND HEART. The Gita has been read daily and recited by millions in India over centuries and across its vast expanse. It has been the source of inspiration to individuals, to seekers of enlightenment and peace and also to leaders of great social and political movements. Gandhi would turn to the Gita for light and guidance in times of crisis just as a child in trouble turns to its mother for comfort and assurance. He would specially recite the verses at the end of the second chapter, which describe the marks of a person of steady wisdom.

The Gita was first translated into English nearly two hundred years ago and since then many other translations in the different languages of the world have appeared. The Gita's appeal and influence will grow as science and education spread and create the demand for an intelligent perspective of life. It will help modern man who is in search of spiritual truth that appeals to both reason and feeling.

The Gita is the noblest gospel of Truth. Its clarion call to the innate divinity and strength of man; its high and unparalleled definition of moral qualities, which is the promised perfection of all devotees of Truth and which inspires all noble hearts; its assurance and promise to man that the Redeemer dwells sleeplessly in the hearts' of all, the eternal Lover and Friend who forsakes none; its gospel of the religion of love and work based on devotion to the Personal Deity, the first manifestation of the Impersonal Wisdom, the Absolute; its identification of all life as religion; its recognition of infinite ways of approaching the Divine; its clear annunciation of the truth of Divine Incarnations in history at times of crises in civilizations; its philosophy of history; its account of creation and dissolution of universes, like the systole and diastole of the heart, of which modern mathematical and physical theories are far distant echoes; its beautiful poetry; its assurance that even the most outrageous character who takes refuge in Krishna, the Lord, is redeemed; its superb delineation of the saint who is established in wisdom and who amongst other things is like the vast ocean, which is ever steady and unperturbed, though water keeps flowing into it endlessly, appealing as it does to man's imagination and feeling — all these qualitites besides many others make the Gita the most marvelous and all-encompassing compendium of spiritual truths and religious inspiration. Its appeal is to the deepest man in us, both to his head and heart. It is the Truth and it is the Way also.

Even before our time, despite difficulties of communication, the Gita inspired many thoughtful men of letters and theologians of the West; several influential and liberal movements like Christian Science and New England Transcendentalism owe their origin to it.

The source of Emerson's inspiration was the Gita. Carlyle presented him with a copy of the Gita, and this little book was responsible for the Concord Movement. "All the broad movements in America," said Vivekananda, "in one way or the other are indebted to the Concord Party."

Thoreau, the Concord sage, said, "The Vedanta teaches how by 'forsaking religious rites' the votary may obtain purification of mind." And, "One sentence is worth the State of Massachusetts many times over."

The poet William B. Yeats, whom T.S. Eliot thought to be the greatest in the English language or in any language so far as he was able to judge, was influenced by the Gita through contact with a Bengali scholar and spiritual person whom he had met in England and whose name was Mohini Mohan Chatterji. Yeats wrote the following in memory of him:

> I asked if I should pray,
>   But the Brahmin said,
> "Pray for nothing, say
>   Every night in bed,
> 'I have been a king,
>   I have been a slave,
> Nor is there anything,
>   Fool, rascal, knave

INTRODUCTION

That I have not been,
And yet upon my breast
    A myriad heads have lain.'"

That he might set at rest
    A boy's turbulent days
        Mohini Chatterji
Spoke these, or words like these,
    I add in commentary,
"Old lovers may yet have
    All that time denied —
        Grave is heaped on grave
That they be satisfied —
Over the blackened earth
    That old troops parade
Birth is heaped on birth
    That such cannonade
    May thunder time away,
Birth-hour and death-hour meet.
    Or, as great sages say,
    Men dance on deathless feet.

The Gita is the diamond among scriptures. Invocatory poems praise it as the essence of all scriptures. Its just appraisal can be made by saints alone; to assimilate its teaching there is no other way but to follow in their foot-steps. A great scripture appeals both to head and heart.

A number of philosophers and theologians have interpreted the Gita according to their own lights. This is natural. But a spiritual seeker, especially of our time, seeking authoritative guidance cannot but depend on the certain voice of the appraiser of the diamond. Here is a story told by Ramakrishna, of whom more later in this introduction, about the appraisal of a diamond:

Once a rich man gave his servant a diamond telling him to go to the market with it and let him know how different people priced it. The servant took the diamond to an eggplant seller. He examined it turning it over in the palm of his hand and said, "Brother, I can give you nine pounds of eggplant for it." "Friend," said the servant, "a little more, say, ten pounds." The eggplant seller replied, "No, I have already quoted above the market price. You may give it to me if that price suits you." The servant laughed. He went back to his master and said, "Sir, he would give me only nine pounds of eggplant and not one more. He said he had offered more than the market price." The master smiled and said, "Now take it to the cloth dealer. The other man deals only with eggplants. What does he know about a diamond? The cloth dealer has a little more capital. Let us see how much he offers for it." The servant went to the cloth dealer and said, "Will you buy this? How much will you pay for it?" The merchant said, "Yes, it is a good thing. I can make a nice ornament out of it. I will give you nine hundred rupees for it." "Brother," said the servant, "offer a little more and I will sell it to you. Give me at least a thousand rupees." The cloth dealer said, "Friend, don't press me for more. I have offered more than the market price. I cannot give a rupee more. Suit yourself." Laughing the servant returned to his master and said, "He won't give me a rupee more than nine hundred. He, too, said he had quoted above the market price." The master said with a laugh, "Now take it to a jeweler. Let us see what he has to say." The servant went to a jeweler. The jeweler glanced at the diamond and said at once, "I will give you one hundred thousand rupees for it."

Vedanta scriptures of which the Gita is the essence have been misunderstood as philosophical or theological texts by several Western thinkers and their followers in the East who have lost touch with the ancient teaching. Vedanta is wisdom, which is the fundamental perception of Reality, and its communication in language to intelligent seekers of the secret truths of life hidden from sense and intellect. The spiritual truths are to be heard, reflected upon and then realized in the heart, The spiritual truths thus discovered through meditation constitute Vedanta.

The underlying truth of existence is a mystery to the intellect and it is therefore called super-science (*paravidya*) or mystery (*rahasya*) as in ancient Greece.

The guidance of the illumined is necessary to assimilate the teachings of the Gita. I have therefore tried to interpret its teachings in the light of the experience and words of those who have in our time manifested them in their own lives. The Gita declares that a spiritual inquirer should approach the enlightened and assimilate the Truth through humility, inquiry and service.

EXPRESSION OF TRUTH. The Gita proclaims that knowledge is the ideal and goal of man. This knowledge is knowledge of Truth or spiritual knowledge or wisdom, but it also recognizes that science or practical knowledge is indispensable for civilization. Higher knowledge is knowledge of the heart. Practical knowledge is knowledge of the brain. Practical knowledge becomes meaningless and destructive without the higher knowledge of the heart. Practical knowledge gives us power over matter while spiritual knowledge makes man the conqueror of nature, external and internal. That is the goal of man and civilization. Without perception of the higher spiritual and moral truth of man, practical knowledge, useful for serving the material needs of man, aborts the promise of human destiny and civilization.

Science does not give us the truth of nature, nor of life. It is clear today that scientific observation does not give us Reality. There are no laws or causality outside ourselves. These are inventions of logic or mathematics or laws of self-identity imposed by the mind on chaotic natural processes outside. Truth is not to be found outside.

Truth, beauty, love and freedom — the values we prize and the values which are reflected momentarily in the passing processes of nature— are found inside of man through inner search. I am reminded in this connection of a conversation I had with a cousin of Albert Einstein who came over to this country in the wake of Nazi dominance in Germany. He told me that Einstein had a sense of the fleeting quality of the glamor of life. Whenever he saw a beautiful woman, Einstein, his cousin said, would think how she would look when she grew old. Persons with spiritual endowments are not impressed by uncertain and fleeting pageantry.

Truth and beauty, etc., belong to substance and not to their shadows in nature. Handsome is as handsome does.

Modern science helps us in our search for substance. Its investigations of the substances or things in nature have reduced them to processes. The only obdurate entity that still resists dissolution is the ego. We do not know what it is! We can never grasp it. But it is the basis of our experience in the world, giving it unity and continuity. It is elusive, while the world and the universe is its construct. It is happy with little things, but its fears are great. It dreams of eternal life and bliss and truth, but can never hope to attain them.

The ego is a limitation of consciousness. Truth lies beyond it. Through worship, prayer, love, humility and meditation we sometimes escape its narrow bonds and have a glimpse of the Reality beyond. When the ego melts down completely through meditation and love of God, when the mind, to borrow an expression from physics, attains a kind of singularity through concentration, Reality stands self-revealed. Upon return the ego is aware of its creatureliness. It realizes itself to be an instrument of a Higher Personality. The world and its many objects are seen as concoctions of ignorance which keep us moving continuously on the tread-mill of the world.

In religion as in science, there are historical developments. Dualistic religions, like nineteenth century science, do not meet the test of reason, the goal of which is Reality beyond mind and imagination. Reality is no speculation of reason or science. Besides, values are never found in the physical process that is nature. All values are in the Great Person who dwells in the hearts of all, in the heart of creation. Religion is a return journey to Reality which is pure consciousness and bliss.

This is the ideal of life and civilization, the motor of history. Reality is Silence; all truths and values issue out of the silence of the heart.

Humanism or love of man is born of religious experience and ideals. It is absurd to say that religion is the opium of the people when it is obvious to a student of history that great political and social revolutions in the world have been inspired by religious ideas. Even in England where Marx lived and wrote *Das Kapital,* there was a peasant revolt in the Middle Ages led by a man named

Wat Tyler, whose slogan was, "When Adam delved and Eve span: Who then was the gentleman?" Wat Tyler lived long before the so-called Age of Reason or Enlightenment, but he drew inspiration from the *Bible*. Religion is rejection of all servitude.

In the poem below, Tagore, the supremely talented poet of India, presents the vision of a society and humanism based on the ideals of Vedanta. Norman Cousins, Editor of *The Saturday Review,* wrote, "I cannot conceive of a modern man as being quite complete without some acquaintance with Tagore..." The poem became the national anthem of India:

> Where the mind is without fear and the head
>   is held high;
> Where knowledge is free;
> Where the world has not been broken up into
>   fragments by narrow domestic walls;
> Where words come out from the depth of truth;
> Where tireless striving stretches its arms toward
>   perfection;
> Where the clear stream of reason has not lost its
>   way into the dreary desert sand of dead habit;
> Where the mind is led forward by Thee into
>   ever-widening thought and action —
> Into that heaven of freedom, my Father, let my
>   country awake.

THE GITA AND ETHICS. The Gita is the world's first and greatest book on ethics. Ethics and religion are not different. The summit of ethical experience and the height of spiritual illumination are one and the same, which is realization of the basic truth of our personality.

The Gita's excellence as a scripture rests chiefly on its identification of self-less performance of duty with the common practice of worship at home or in temples. Both are worship of the Divinity present everywhere. The Gita's ethics are based on the ideal of Wisdom. The unity of ethics, aesthetics and wisdom was hinted at by Plato, but did not develop as a practical and spiritual tradition in Greece.

The Bhagavad Gita

The ethical ideal of man is based on the underlying unity of existence. It is contradicted by the apparent diversity which is the common perception. The task of culture and civilization is the overcoming of this apparent conflict within and without us. When we struggle to overcome the conflict within us between the little self of desires and the ideals of peace and love and balance, we are religious in a restricted sense — in the sense in which Professor Alfred Whitehead defined religion as what a person does with his solitariness; but when we try to achieve this unity or ideal in our relationship with others, this effort is called ethical. Both these efforts aim at Wisdom or Knowledge; they are inspired by the innate drive in us for integrity.

Living in society we advance to the same goal on two fronts: one by overcoming the selfish sense of me and mine through prayer and worship, which is called religion in the narrow sense, and second, by sacrificing the little self to the ideal of service in our dealings with others. The link between the two is provided by faith in the common goal of all, which is the basic truth of our life and which is freedom, peace and eternal existence.

The Gita emphasizes this wisdom-based ethical action (the religion of duty, or the method of karma yoga) as the enlightened pursuit of life's goal. We do not have to run away from the world to be spiritual. We have to run away from the little self only. By changing our attitude to the world we can transform our every day life in the world into a life of worship and prayer. The health of a society is maintained through pursuit of this ideal.

The Gita recognizes different forms of worship, but it does not emphasize the religion of the cloister or the forest, though it does not disparage any sincere spiritual effort.

Forgetting the spiritual goal and his duty to humanity, a person in a modern, developed society becomes dehumanized and a prey to endless incurable psychological troubles, or at the very least falls under the tyranny of likes and dislikes.

The Gita emphasizes that religion is service to man, *lokasamgraha*. Swami Sivananda, a disciple of Ramakrishna, wrote to a devotee, "Dedicate your life to the service of man; there is no other work dearer to the Lord than this." This is the true spirit of civilization.

RAMAKRISHNA AND VIVEKANANDA: EXPRESSIONS OF THE GITA IN LIFE. Information of the historical context of the Gita as presented above, and knowledge of the basic philosophical concepts as discussed below, will be useful for understanding its teachings which have become part of India's spiritual tradition. The Gita, not being a book of theological or philosophical speculation, needs to be understood in the light of the life and teachings of those who embody its truths. Many commentators have turned either to the past or to learned thinkers for explanation of many of its statements. But modern man with questions of faith and direction in life, living in this age of unique historical and scientific development, needs answers which are not old or speculative, but which are relevant to the changed circumstances and which address clearly the problems and perplexities of today.

It is for this reason that I have quoted extensively the words of Ramakrishna and Vivekananda in this introduction and in the comments that appear after the verses. Many readers may not know about them, so I give below a brief introduction to their lives and teachings. Those who want to know more can go to the original sources which are ample.

Ramakrishna is in line with the great teachers and Incarnations of India such as Krishna and Buddha. He was born a Brahmin from Bengal in 1836 and died in 1886. His life was from beginning to end an unparalled odyssey of varied and extraordinary spiritual experiences and power. Romain Rolland, the French Nobel laureate and deep thinker, wrote in his biography of Ramakrishna that he was the consummation of two thousand years of the spiritual life of three hundred million Hindus.

Long before Ramakrishna became known all over the world, Max Muller, the famous Indologist and Sanskrit scholar, wrote about him. Tolstoy came to know about him from a few morsels of his teachings translated into English. Alexander Shifman, author of *Tolstoy and India* and adviser to the Tolstoy Museum, writes,

THE BHAGAVAD GITA

"During the last decade of Tolstoy's life Ramakrishna Parama-hamsa and his pupil Vivekananda occupied his (Tolstoy's) thoughts..." (*World Thinkers on Ramakrishna-Vivekananda.* Ramakrishna Mission Institute of Culture, Gol Park, Calcutta).

The Eternal Religion which the Gita preaches was reincarnated in Ramakrishna in modern times. Vivekananda was his chief apostle, as was St. Paul of Christ.

There are many biographies of Ramakrishna in many languages. The most authoritative is the one by Swami Saradananda who was one of his direct disciples. Originally written in Bengali, it has been translated into English under the title, *Sri Ramakrishna, the Great Master.*

Ramakrishna's sayings, recorded in Bengali by one of his non-monastic devotees have been translated into English under the title, *The Gospel of Ramakrishna* by Swami Nikhilananda of the Ramakrishna-Vivekananda Center of New York. With a foreword by Aldous Huxley, and edited in part by Joseph Campbell, it is a treasure house of spiritual truths in the plainest language, where one finds even the latest conclusions of science and philosophy expressed in the simplest manner.

Ramakrishna said that the essential message of the Gita can be had by repeating the word Gita ten times, until it sounds like the word *tagi* which means renunciation.

Renunciation means renunciation of the little self. An *Upanishad* declares, "Through renunciation alone some have attained immortal life." Through practice of self-denial with faith, the great truth of Spirit becomes manifest. A poem freely translated from Tagore reads:

> I long with all my heart for the fulfilment
>   of a million desires.
> But you have saved me by denying them all to me.
> This severe grace of yours I have garnered
>   all my life.
> And day by day you are making me worthy of your
>   great gifts which you gave me unasked—
> This life, the mind, the light and the sky.

Introduction

Truth is always Truth, but the advance of history demands its expression in the accents of the time. As Ramakrishna himself said, "Old coins do not circulate in modern times." They need the stamp of modern authorities. Ramakrishna speaks the universal spiritual truths relevant to our time. His sayings contain answers to all the spiritual problems of modern man.

Vivekananda was his chief disciple whom he fashioned to spread the message of Eternal Religion in accordance with the spirit and developments of our time.

There are several biographies of Vivekananda in English. Romain Rolland wrote one. He was inspired to write about him by the poet Tagore, who won the Nobel prize in literature in 1914 and who was the idol of the poet William B. Yeats.

When Tagore met Romain Rolland in Europe in the early 1920's, he told the latter, "If you want to understand India, study Vivekananda. In him, everything is positive, nothing negative."

It is the above hint that turned the attention of Romain Rolland, an idealistic student of life and history and a great artist, to Vivekananda and his teacher Ramakrishna.

Vivekananda was born in Calcutta in 1863 to an aristocratic family. He lived for only thirty-nine years. Born with divine endowments he was groomed by Ramakrishna to be the teacher of the new age.

Those who want to know the inspiration behind the birth of modern India have to turn to him. Gandhi said that his love for India increased a thousandfold after reading Vivekananda. C. Rajagopalachari, a close associate of Gandhi in India's struggle for freedom, and free India's first Governor General, wrote, "Swami Vivekananda saved Hinduism and saved India. But for him we would have lost our religion and would not have gained our freedom. We therefore owe everything to Swami Vivekananda." Jawaharlal Nehru admired him so much that he sent the seven volumes of Vivekananda's works to President Sukarno of Indonesia by airmail. Volumes can be filled if we gather together all the tributes to him. But here we can mention only briefly some facts which will indicate the living truths of the Gita, for Vivekananda's life was the perfect expression of the spiritual truth taught in it.

The Bhagavad Gita

Vivekananda came to America in 1893 and represented Hinduism at the Parliament of Religions in Chicago. From the very outset he moved like a conqueror like Caesar who said, "I came, I saw, I conquered (vini, vidi, vici)." He established Vedanta in America. It continues to grow in influence.

William James, the outstanding American philosopher invited Vivekananda to lecture at Harvard and afterwards offered him a chair in philosophy there. He used to address the swami as "Master" and mentioned him in his most famous book, *Varieties of Religious Experience,* as the paragon of Vedantists. Vivekananda, a man of monumental learning, also lectured in England and France and travelled widely in Europe. He founded the Ramakrishna Mission in India which has spread all over the country and abroad as well, and which continues today to do valuable social and spiritual work.

This brief reference to Vivekananda would be very inadequate without some mention of his prophetic vision. He predicted the rise of India and the political and social upheavals in Russia and China in the nineties of the last century when no one dreamed that mass revolutions would happen in such non-industrialized and backward countries. When he travelled through Europe in 1900 he remarked that, "Austria-Hungary was the sick woman of Europe," — a kind of repartee to Gladstone's remark that Turkey was "the sick man of Europe." At the time Gladstone inveighed against Turkey, she was the largest empire in history. Her rule extended over the Middle East including Arabia, and her possessions lay athwart the British Imperial route to India, a source of great annoyance to imperialists who wanted a safe and easy access to the colony and therefore sought Turkey's dismemberment. He also said that Europe was sitting on top of a volcano which was going to erupt in fifty years. The Austro-Hungarian Empire broke up in 1914 and the second world war came in 1939.

Vivekananda said that he had a mission to the West as Buddha had a mission in the East and also, "What I am today and what the world will be tomorrow is due to my Master."

Vedanta, vivified by Ramakrishna and Vivekananda, will increasingly dominate thought in the world and provide a broad

INTRODUCTION

philosophical basis for the different religions. This train of thought brings to mind a momentous prophecy which Vivekananda made in a lecture delivered in London with the title, "The Absolute and Manifestation." He said, "Science and religion will meet and shake hands." Earlier in America, anticipating modern developments in science, he had said, "Science is contemplation of energies." At that time physical science in the West was hardly beyond the table of elements in its analysis of nature.

Nearly thirty years or so later Sir James Jeans, F.R.S., repeated his words almost exactly when he wrote in a popular book on science, "Science and religion are shaking hands." Sir James' view of religion was of course very different, and though he believed in a higher truth than sense-experience, he was still far from the concept of the timeless Reality of pure and universal consciousness which according to modern scientists such as Max Planck and others constitutes the primary fact of existence.

Max Planck (1858-1974) said in an interview: "I do not think consciousness can be explained in terms of matter and its laws. Consciousness I regard as fundamental. I regard matter as derivative from consciousness. We cannot get behind consciousness. Everything that we think about, everything that we regard as existing postulates consciousness" (J.W.N. Sullivan. Interview with Max Planck, *Observer,* January 25, 1931).

Vivekananda presented the Vedantic view of Reality and nature. Today there is excitement among some Western writers of popular science as they compare modern scientific conclusions with Vedantic views. However their picture of reality is not what Vedanta asserts, for nature is infinitely more than the vibrations of physics. Only a few physicists who have delved deeper are hinting at the Vedantic truth; namely, that which we call reality is a kind of projection of consciousness, a kind of "Alice in wonderland" dream. But not having analyzed their own minds and by not being able to look deep enough into themselves, they are still groping for the Truth.

Today's science rests its case for explanation with the theory of randomness, whether it is the evolution of the universe or of life. It finds neither law nor fact in nature. At heart nature is chaos.

The Sanskrit word for the universe is *samsara* or process. The process is so swift that our crude senses can grasp it only by freezing it and thus creating the image of steady and enduring objects, while nature is really changing as rapidly as a waterfall. The fine instruments of scientific observation and also some cameras demonstrate the rapidity of this process called physical nature.

Besides, not only is the physical process faster than scientific instruments can detect, but it is also continuous with the thought-process called mind.

In a lecture delivered in California in 1900 Vivekananda declared, "... there are no such realities as a physical world, a mental world, a spiritual world. Whatever is, is one. Let us say it is a sort of tapering existence, the thickest part is here, it tapers and becomes finer and finer. The finest is what we call spirit, the grossest, the body. And just as it is here in macrocosm, it is exactly the same in the microcosm. The universe of ours is exactly like that; it is the gross external thickness and it tapers into something finer and finer until it becomes God."

It is the range of perceptions that Vivekananda was talking about. The yogi perceives in meditation that the outer energies of the universe melt into the subtler, the inner energies of mind, and finally disappear into the silence of the motionless deep, the Spirit or Pure Consciousness beyond time. It is the living silence, the essential truth of personality, the repository of the dearest values of life for which we all knowingly or unknowingly hanker. The energy of creation is no dead energy of matter; it is the power of a Personal Deity, the first expression of the Impersonal. Religion is search for the highest values of personality epitomized by the idea of God.

In New York in 1896 Vivekananda met the well-known electrician, Tesla, during an interview that the actress Madam Sarah Bernhardt had arranged. It took place at the end of her performance of *Iziel,* a Frenchified drama about Buddha which Vivekananda had gone to see out of curiosity. The actress spied Vivekananda in the audience and sought an interview with him. During the interview with her at which Tesla was present,

INTRODUCTION

Vivekananda presented the Vedantic theory of creation out of *akasa* and *prana,* according to which prana or energy acting on akasa, or the aboriginal emptiness, created the universe. Tesla was fascinated by the account, and he invited Vivekananda to his home for a demonstration of his theory that matter and energy were one.

It is appropriate to mention here another remark of Vivekananda in his first lecture at the Parliament of Religions in Chicago in 1893; namely, that physics would come to an end when it would discover the one energy of which the different energies are various manifestations. Today the scientists have unified the four or five basic forces into two, though the ultimate unity of all the forces is still beyond achievement. To achieve such an unification it is surmised by mathematicians that a cyclotron (accelerator) of the dimension of the Milky Way (10 million light years) would be needed! Maybe a more practicable means will emerge.

The role of reason which Vivekananda emphasized is the role of science, and it cannot be dismissed in our search for religious truth. The Reality that is hinted at by reason and science is reached only through a kind of mental 'singularity' *(ekagrata)* to borrow a term from modern cosmologists; in other words, through meditation. Einstein came close to this perception when he said that pure thought could discover reality. However, to discover it one has to go beyond thinking to the pure mind or intellect which is, as Ramakrishna said, pure Spirit.

Vedanta alone provides justification for dualistic religions which have always been troubled by the conflict between reason and faith, without ever solving it. The different and many religions are ways to Truth but they are not the Truth.

In a lecture on the Gita in Los Angles Vivekananda declared, "Outside of India we will find no further development of religion beyond the idea of God in heaven. That was the highest knowledge ever obtained outside of India... As far as I have seen, we should call it a very primitive idea... Mumbo jumbo in Africa and God in heaven equal the same."

THE ESSENCE OF VEDANTA. The Gita is the essence of Vedanta. Vedanta means literally the end of the *Vedas.* The Vedas are the earliest literature of the Indo-Aryan people. They are books of sacred knowledge and are compositions in prose and verse in archaic Sanskrit. The time of their production is uncertain, but must have extended over centuries. Conservatively the Vedas are assigned to a period from approximately 3,000 B.C. to 800 B.C.

The Vedic literature is divided into several categories. Of these, the *Samhitas* are collections of the hymn portions (*Rik, Sama* and *Yajus*), while the final sections dealing with mystic wisdom are called Vedanta or the Upanishads.

The earlier section of the Vedic literature deals with rituals and ceremonies designed to gain rewards in heaven or on earth. Vedanta is the religion of knowledge and freedom from human bondage due to ignorance. Vedanta is wisdom, not the popular religion of sacrifice to reach heaven or for enjoying prosperity on earth.

Life was simple in those days, the aristocrats and the Brahmins had plenty of leisure to reflect upon existence and seek answers to the ultimate questions of man as the Greeks did in ancient times. Through reflection and meditation they discovered, at the dawn of civilization, the answers they were seeking to the questions of creation, life's meaning and its goal. This discovery is evidenced in some of the very earliest parts of the Vedic literature. We cannot help quoting here one of the most beautiful and profound philosophical hymns that is found in an early section of the Vedic literature. It is the hymn of creation:

> Neither being nor non-being was then.
> There was neither the earth, nor the interspace,
>   nor the heavens above.
> What covered all this? Where and by whom?
> Was there the abyss of fathomless waters?
> Death was not then, nor immortality,
> Night was not yet separate from day,
> Alone, that one breathed without air,
>   self-sustained.
> Beyond that nothing whatever was.
> At first darkness in darkness lay hidden,
> This universe was like a mass of waters
>   undistinguished,

INTRODUCTION

> That which lay secret in the void became
> manifest through the power of his
> contemplation.
> There arose in his mind desire, the primal seed
> of manifestation.
> The wise searching in their hearts discovered
> through intuition the bond that connects
> being with non-being.
> Who knows who can tell truly
> From whom this universe has come and
> From where it has sprung?
> The gods came after creation;
> Who then knows from where it came?
> The source from which the universe has arisen,
> Does it have a support or not?
> He alone knows who is self-luminous and the
> Lord in the supreme heaven of Truth.
> Maybe even He does not know.

"Breathed without air" in the above is an image of motionless existence.

The Upanishads developed the tradition of the discovery of Reality through meditation. The universe has been compared by a Persian poet to an old manuscript of which the first and the last pages have been lost. Philosophers have speculated endlessly about the origin and end of the universe without success. Kant said that philosophical search proceeds on the twin wings of reason and experience. But the bird that flies on the wings of reason and experience never reaches Truth. When, however, it flies on the wings of reason and faith, it reaches home.

The sages of the Upanishads discovered the lost pages not through thinking, but by turning their gaze within. The origin of the universe of time and space is the Reality beyond time. The Reality is called *Brahman;* it is no abstract concept but the self-existing Reality of bliss and consciousness. It is the true Self of all, and it is the goal of life. The universe is a projection of Brahman's power.

This goal of man is difficult to reach. Therefore the Upanishads declare that one should learn this secret (mystery in the religion of Greece) from the teacher who knows; the student must have great moral and intellectual qualifications. The Upanishads also provide some images as aids to meditation, and we find mention of worship of the Teacher and of a Personal God in the later Upanishads. Worship of a Personal Deity, the first manifestation of Spirit, is also taught as a means of realizing the Impersonal Truth.

The Vedas belong to the archaic age. Later society became complex, kingdoms and empires flourished, commerce and wealth developed and people of many races formed part of expanded polities; the need arose for a religion of love directed to a Personal Deity without losing sight of the Deity's Impersonal, universal basis. The need of the time was met by the Gita's religion of love combined with work and wisdom. Society became complex, the web of reponsibilities, duties and relationships became intricate and the traditional scheme of the religion of caste and stages of life became inapplicable to society at large.

It was at this time that the religion of the Gita was taught by Krishna, who was the manifestation of the deity of love and wisdom, and who proclaimed that everyone by doing his duty with understanding and dedication will attain perfection. And for the first time in history, Krishna proclaimed the doctrine of Divine Incarnation, the manifestation in history of the Personality of the Supreme Godhead.

A somewhat similar situation arose in the West when Christ appeared. The Roman Empire had brought under control various races and peoples. The philosophical religions which flourished among the cultivated in Rome, Egypt and Greece were too high and dry for the common masses who needed a god of love and an inspiring leader. Christ came as an answer.

THE GITA, BUDDHISM AND CHRISTIANITY. It will be appropriate here to say a few words about the influence of the Gita and Indian religion on Buddhism and Christianity.

The Gita doctrine of lokasamgraha (good of humanity) and

of Divine Incarnation influenced the Mahayana or the Northern school of Buddhism. The Buddhist scholar Taranath who wrote about the history of Buddhism mentions that the teacher of Nagarjuna, who is regarded as the chief originator of the Mahayana school of Buddhism, was Rahulabhadra who "was much indebted to sage Krishna and still more to Ganesha...This quasi-historical notice, reduced to its less allegorical expression means that Mahayanism is much indebted to the Bhagavadgita and more even to Shaivism" (Dr. Kern's *Manual of Buddhism*).

The origin of Christianity is also due to Buddhist influence. The Hindus venerate Christ as an Incarnation, and they see that his essential message is that of the Sanatana Dharma (the Eternal Religion). The special ethical and religious ideas contained in the teachings of Christ have no antecedents in the religious tradition in which he was born. Non-resistance to evil, love of enemies, monasticism, love of death, the assertion of man's innate perfection (the kingdom of heaven is within you), universalism are principles not to be found in the religion into which he was born.

John the Baptist, who belonged to the monastic sect of the Essenes, was a Buddhist. King Asoka of India (third century B.C.) sent Buddhist missionaries to different parts of the world, from Siberia to Ceylon, from China to Egypt, and for two centuries before the advent of Christ, the Buddhist missionaries preached the ethics of Buddha in Syria, Palestine and Alexandria. The Christian historian, Mahaffi, declared that the Buddhist missionaries were the forerunners of Christ. "Philosophers like Schelling and Schopenhauer, and Christian thinkers like Dean Mansel and D. Millman admit that the sect of the Essenes arose through the influence of the Buddhist missionaries who came from India" (*Complete Works of Swami Abhedananda*, vol.2, p.120).

Many incidents in Christ's life as well as the organization of the Catholic Church and its rituals suggest their Buddhistic and Hindu origin. The Gospel stories of the immaculate conception of a virgin mother, the miraculous birth, the story of slaughter of the infants by Herod, and the chief events of Christ's life seem like repetitions of what happened in the lives of Krishna and of Buddha. The idea of Incarnation is purely an Indian idea. It was not known among the Jews. The star over Buddha's birthplace and the prophecy of the old monk Asita are repeated in the Gospel story of Simeon. The temptation of Buddha by Mara, the evil spirit, the twelve disciples, with the beloved disciple Ananda, and the many miracles recall the stories in Christ's life.

Under cover of the legend of Barlaam and Josaphet, Buddha has found a place among the Catholic saints and has his saint-day in the calendar of the Greek and Roman churches.

The rosary, the veneration of relics, asceticism, baptism, confession, etc., are also of Indian origin. The name Josaphet is Bodhisattva in corrupt form.

There are innumerable similarities betweeen Hindu-Buddhist practices and doctrines and those of Christianity.

The Russian author, Notovitch, translated in 1894 a biography of Christ found in Nepal in a Buddhist monastery which said that Christ went there during the thirteen years of his life of which there is no record in the Gospels.

The French missionary travellers Hue and Gibet who visited Lhasa in 1842 wrote, "The crozier, the exorcism, the censer with the five chains, the blessings which the lamas impart by extending the right hand over the heads of the faithful, the rosary, the celibacy of the clergy, their separation from the world, the worship of saints, the fasts, processions, litanies, holy water — these are the points of contact the Buddhists have with us" (From *Legacy of India,* ed. by G.T. Garrat, Oxford University Press).

In an interview in Detroit in 1894, Vivekananda said, "Our religion is older than most religions and the Christian creeds came directly from the Hindoo religion. It is one of the great offshoots. The Catholic religion also takes all its forms from us, the confessional, the belief in saints and so on, and a Catholic priest who saw this absolute similarity and recognized the truth of the origin of the Catholic religion was dethroned from his position because he dared to publish a volume explaining all that he observed and was convinced of" [Swami's reference was no doubt to Bishop Brigandet's *Life of Buddha.*] (From *Swami Vivekananda, New Discoveries* by Marie Louise Burke, 2nd ed., p.208).

Introduction

The Catholic Church, however, developed with dualistic principles of God in heaven and creation below which have created an insoluble conflict between faith and reason. The conflict has reached its ultimate acuity in our day of scientific developments. Hindus believe that the non-dualistic teachings of Christ have not been generally understood in the West.

DIVINE INCARNATIONS. We find mention of prophets, messengers and messiahs in the different religions of the world. In Hinduism, Buddhism and Christianity we have the doctrine of Divine Incarnation.

The Christian religion as organized is dualistic. The Christians have a doctrine of incarnation fitting into their theology and their partial view of history and creation. They have only one incarnation.

According to the Eternal Religion (Sanatana Dharma) taught in the Gita, there are many divine incarnations. An incarnation is a special manifestation of the Divine in history. Such manifestations take place in response to special needs of the time, in the altered circumstances of life and history. They come in times of decline of civilizations due to materialism which causes disintegration of man and society.

Krishna in the Gita makes the classic declaration about incarnation. Buddhist tradition also makes mention of various incarnations of Buddha. So also do the Jains, another non-orthodox Indian religion.

The birth of an incarnation, like the birth of the universe, is a mystery. But the extraordinary phenomena and the saving power connected with the life of an incarnation and his own statement about his divine origin make those who have seen him, and who have felt his miraculous saving power, believe him. The extraordinary deeds and words of an incarnation about himself are the proof. They sometimes demonstrate their rulership over nature. They want the man who seeks freedom to believe in his own innate greatness by telling him that Truth is within him. A Sanskrit saying goes, "The sages hunt for Truth in their hearts." Great historical changes follow their teachings which confirm the reality of divine rulership.

The Bhagavad Gita

In Sanatana Dharma incarnation is periodic manifestation in time of the power of the Divine. It is a mystery, but the power play of the Divine in history is a fact of experience.

Krishna says in the Gita that incarnations start rolling anew the wheels of religion. Buddha also spoke of his movement as starting the wheel of religion. More about incarnations will be found in comments on certain verses in chapter 4.

INDIAN THOUGHT AND THE WEST. It is appropriate to say a few words here about the influence of Indian thought in the West. Orphic religion, Pythagorean philosophy, Neo-Platonism, Stoicism and several others not so well-known have been influenced by the Samkhya-Vedanta thought of India. In pre-Christian centuries Persia served as the middle ground between India and Greece. It is known that Indian archers with their long bows, one end of which was planted in the ground, fought in Darius's war against Greece. Brahmins and Buddhists were in Greece before Socrates. Later Alexandria became a great center of commerce and learning, where Buddhists and Brahmins congregated and where Neo-Platonism was born.

The essence of Socratic and Platonic philosophy has remained unintelligible in the West because of lack of insight into Indian thought. Plato's view of Reality is the same as that of the Upanishads. His method of attaining knowledge of the Good is that of Vedanta. In the *Phaedo,* Plato describes silent meditation as withdrawal of the senses from their objects and as stilling the processes of mind.

The Greek *theoria* of the Pythagoreans, of Socrates and Plato, from which the word 'theater' comes is the vision or *darshana* of the Upanishads.

Plato mentions that philosophic wisdom can only be communicated directly from teacher to disciple, like lighting one lamp by another. The *Timaeus* indicates after the manner of the Upanishads that the receiver of philosophic truth must be a fit person — fit by character and not by reason of intellect alone. Platonic thought is so un-Greek in the sense in which Greek thought is generally taken, namely, pure rationalism, that some philosophers, such as Nietzsche, have called it "un-Hellenic."

INTRODUCTION

Even Aristotle, the great rationalist and empiricist, upheld so strongly by teachers of philosophy in the West, is not fully understood. Aristotle speaks of intellect in the same sense as do the Upanishads — intellect which is not thinking logically but which grasps truth immediately. The Indian term for intellect is *buddhi,* the purest understanding.

Aristotle in his *Ethics* talks of God-like contemplation as the highest and happiest activity of man. His God is a self-contemplating intelligence. Many teachers in the West, limited by narrow naturalism and haunted by the dogmatic and dualistic tradition of Western religion, brush all this aside as a lingering Platonic fancy in Aristotle's mind.

The thought of Plotinus is Hindu. Eusebius in his biography of Socrates, relates an incident recorded in the fourth century B.C. in which Socrates met a Brahmin in the *agora* or the market place. The Brahmin asked Socrates what he was doing. Socrates replied that he was questioning people in order to understand man. At this, the Brahmin laughed and asked how one could understand man without knowing God.

The Socratic conception of freedom and virtue is that of the Upanishads. Socrates talked of the free man, the *autarch* — the man who is not just politically free, but who is self-ruled. The Upanishadic word for autarch is *swatantra,* self-governed.

Socrates defined virtue as knowledge. Virtue is character, the realization of the essence of man. This knowledge is the realization of the Apollonian dictum, *Know thyself,* which is exactly the same as the Upanishadic command, *Atmanam biddhi.* In the Gita, knowledge or wisdom is defined as character. Virtue is manliness — manifestation of the essence of man. Virtue comes from the Vedic word *vira* (hero, man).

Intellectuals in the West have long pondered over the Socratic definition of virtue as knowledge without being able to figure out precisely what it means.

Greek philosophy began in Asia Minor and Greek writers refer to the travels of Pythagoras, and others, to the East to gain wisdom. According to his biographer Iamblichus, "Pythagoras traveled widely, studying the esoteric teachings of the Egyptians, Assyrians, and even Brahmins." According to Gomperz, "It is not too much to assume that the curious Greek who was a contemporary of Buddha, and it may be of Zoroaster, too, would have acquired a more or less exact knowledge of the East, in that age of intellectual fermentation, through the medium of Persia. It must be remembered in this connection, that the Asiatic Greeks, at the time when Pythagoras still dwelt in his Ionian home, were under the single sway of Cyrus, the founder of the Persian Empire" (Gomperz, *Greek Thinkers*).

In a lecture on Samkhya philosophy in the nineties of the last century, Vivekananda said that Samkhya was the basis of the philosophy of the whole world. "There is no philosophy in the world that was not indebted to Kapila. (Kapila is the founder of the Samkhya philosophy. Krishna says in the Gita that, among the perfected sages, he is Kapila). Pythagoras came to India and studied this philosophy and that was the beginning of the philosophy of the Greeks. Later it formed the Alexandrian school, and still later the Gnostic" (*Complete works of Vivekananda*, 14th ed., vol. 2, p. 45).

I believe Vivekananda was correct because of the following historical reasons: it has already been mentioned that Gomperz links Pythagoras to Indian thought. At the time of Pythagoras, who was probably a contemporary of Buddha, the Persian Empire, extending over all of Asia minor, also included the Indus Valley. The Indian satrapy constituted the most populous one of the Persian Empire, and it paid a tribute proportionately larger than all the rest. In it lay Taxila (Takshashila) near the present district of Rawalpindi on the high road from Central Asia to the interior of India. Taxila was then a great center of commerce and learning. "Crowds of eager scholars flowed to it for instruction in the three Vedas and in the eighteen branches of knowledge. Tradition affirms that the great epic, the Mahabharata, was first recited in the city" (R.C. Majumdar, H.C. Raychandhuri and K. Datta, *An Advanced History of India*, 2nd ed., p. 64, Macmillan and Co.).

Buddha is reputed to have studied in Taxila. The above facts convincingly suggest that the Pythagorean and the subsequent Platonic philosophy owe their origin to earlier Indian thought and spirituality.

INTRODUCTION

It is believed that Dravidians from India went to Egypt and laid the foundation of its civilization there. The Egyptians themselves had the tradition that they originally came from the South, from a land called Punt which an historian of the West, Dr. H. R. Hall, thought referred to some part of India.

The Indus valley civilization is, according to Sir John Marshall who was in charge of the excavations, the oldest of all civilizations unearthed (c. 4000 B.C.). It is older than the Sumerian and it is believed by many that the latter was a branch of the former.

Some people called the Brahui who dwell in Baluchistan, which at present is a part of Pakistan, still speak the Dravidian language. It is likely that their ancestors were the people who sailed across the narrow waters at the entrance of the Persian Gulf to Oman and then to Aden along the southern littoral of Arabia, crossing over to Africa at the narrow strait of Bab-el-Mandeb, near Somaliland and proceeding north along the Nile Valley.

"We hear of Arabian trade with Egypt as far back as 2743 B.C. probably as ancient as was the trade with India" (Will Durant, *The Story of Civilization,* vol. 4, p. 157).

Both upon archaeological and historical grounds, India is mother of civilizations. Material skill and spiritual ideals spread from the Indus valley to Nineveh and Babylon, to the entire Middle East, to the Nile Valley and thence to Greece and Rome.

The heart of civilization is the aspiration after knowledge and freedom.

The subject of Indian influence on religion and philosophy in the West is too vast to dwell upon here, but we could not help mentioning it briefly in order to offer a perspective of religious and philosophical thought in the world.

EVOLUTION AND SAMKHYA-VEDANTA. The Gita mentions Samkhya philosophy, a rival school of Vedanta, in chapter 2. Though it rejects Samkhyan dualism, it accepts its analysis of nature and its scheme of emanations.

The Samkhyan philosophy or view of Reality is dualistic qualitatively; it accepts two principles as basic and independent of each other. They are the principle of consciousness (seer or spirit) and the principle of nature (*prakriti*) which includes both matter and mind. Quantitatively Samkhya is pluralistic because it admits of many spirits or selves though nature is one. In Vedanta Reality is non-dual. It is pure consciousness, nature being an integral part of it — the creative energy of spirit.

Nature is prakriti (procreatrix) and is constituted of three principles (*gunas*) which are always combined; namely, *sattva, rajas* and *tamas*. Sattva is the principle of balance and intelligence. Rajas is the principle of activity, while tamas is the principle of inertia. All the existents in nature are constituted of these three principles or elements in different degrees of combination.

Modern science has demonstrated that physical nature is a flow of energy and that this flow is not continuous or unbroken. Energy moves in quanta, in driblets or pulses of motion. There is always a break coexisting with its propagation. Rajas is the principle of motion, while tamas is that of resistance which breaks up the flow. Preponderance of tamas congests or glues energy, which becomes matter.

Sattva is the principle of balance. However in nature, in manifestation, there is no perfect balance. But in concentration when the mind is steady and in moments of calm serenity, there is reflection in it of the steady Spirit or Reality which is always the same — like the reflection of the blue sky in a calm lake.

The various parts of nature, mind and body, are constellations of these energies in different proportions or combinations. Mind has more of the sattvic element, it is superfine energy. The body has a preponderance of tamas. There are no real particles in nature, material or mental. The only persistent particle is the ego! It is, however, hard to smash the tough ego-particles. Truth alone dissolves the ego.

Beyond nature is Spirit which becomes self-manifest when its entanglement in nature ends through discrimination between Spirit and nature. This state of freedom of an individual is called *kaivalya* in Samkhya, which means 'aloneness' and which recalls the phrase of the Neo-Platonist Plotinus, "Flight of the alone to the alone." It was from Samkhya philosophy that the mystical tradition in philosophy, beginning with Pythagoras, entered Europe and assumed different names like Platonism, Gnosticism, Stoicism, etc.

INTRODUCTION

The Pythagorean theory that the world is made up of numbers is most likely derived from the Samkhya philosophy. Scholars in the West regard Pythagoras's numbers as ordinary numerals. It is very likely that this interpretation is not correct.

The Samkhya philosophy means literally the philosophy of numbers. This is because Kapila, the founder of the philosophy, analyzed Reality (spirit and nature) into twenty-five categories or principles. Sanskrit lexicographers are convinced that the enumeration of the principles gave the philosophy the name of Samkhya, the analytical philosophy or the philosophy of numerical analysis of spirit and nature, or simply the philosophy of numbers.

There is hardly any doubt that Pythagoras travelled east and got his religious philosophy from India. In ancient Greece, as in India, philosophy meant *theoria,* or vision, or darshan, i.e., perception of Reality. So the theory of numbers attributed to Pythagoras most probably refers to the twenty-five Samkhyan principles.

In that case we can avoid a seemingly incomprehensible theory unless we take into account the fine perceptions of modern science which resolve nature fundamentally into bits of motion interrupted by gaps of stillness or resistance. Such an explanation may not be altogether unlikely for philosophers who had the fine perception to discover the guna elements of nature.

Pythagoras also appears to have gotten his doctrine of transmigration of souls from India. Even the Western scholar Gomperz admits that the theory of Pythagoras was different from the Egyptian theory and was like the Indian theory.

Greece owes much to Egypt. The Egyptian civilization was younger than the Indus Valley civilization and its origin has been traced to India by several scholars of the West.

Vedanta rejects the fundamental dualism of the Samkhya system. Nature in Vedanta is the creative power of the Spirit.

On the other hand, Vedanta accepts the Samkhyan analysis of nature. The first manifestation or development of prakriti is called *Mahat* or the Great. It is called Mahat Brahma in the Gita in chapter 14. The sattva element is predominant in Mahat which is therefore intelligent. There are two parallel developments of Mahat. On one side, which is objective from the standpoint of the individual perceiver, Mahat develops into five infrasensible and sensible elements known technically as earth, water, fire, air and ether. These are not elements in the chemical sense, but the five different sensible qualities in nature, namely, color, taste, sound, touch and smell corresponding to the five organs of perception.

The Samkhyan elements are both fine and gross. The fine elements combine in different proportions to form the gross elements. The elements are conceived in their finest state as atomic. However these atoms are regarded as not real but only imaginary. I think it was Kant in the West who conceived the idea that atoms are a vortex of forces. We know today that electrons have a spin. Do they have bodies or are they just forces appearing to have impenetrable bodies which are matters of crude perception?

On the subjective side Mahat develops into the principles of intellect, ego, mind, and the organs of perception and action. Life force is included in mind. These elements plus the ten fine and gross sensible qualities constitute, with Spirit, the twenty-four principles of Vedanta and Samkhya. The twenty-three developments, plus the Unmanifest, are mentioned in verse 6 of chapter 13.

The subtle body is constituted of intellect, ego, mind and the ten organs. This corresponds to what in Christian philosophy is called the spiritual body of man.

Upon realization of Freedom or Self-knowledge, the whole of nature takes on the character of an insubstantial dream, as modern scientists are indicating in regard to physical nature when they compare it to an "Alice in wonderland" dream. One more point of distinction: upon returning from the experience of *Sat-Chit-Ananda* (Truth-Consciousness-Bliss) of Brahman, the wise man perceives nature as the play of conscious energy or as waves of bliss and not as unconscious nature. "After many births, the man of wisdom worships me saying all this is Krishna. Such a great soul is extremely rare" (*Gita,* 7:49).

MAYA, THE MYSTERY OF CREATION. The Gita mentions *maya* several times. Maya is a key concept of Vedanta. It is a statement of a mysterious fact; namely, a misperception which we regard as objective.

• 31 •

INTRODUCTION

The energy that makes the physical world is no substance. Egos are not substance, nor is there anything which is substantial in nature. Spirit alone is the substance.

The idea of reality is derived from within us from self-consciousness. Reality means substance, a datum which is the same under all circumstances though its qualities may change. There is no such thing in observed nature. Nature is quality (guna). The belief in the substantiality of nature is just a practical belief. It is derived from self-consciousness and is superimposed upon fleeting groups of changes or distinctions created by the senses.

It is only in *samadhi* or in superconscious experience that we are aware of what substance is; in ordinary experience the substance of pure consciousness is always mixed with and contaminated by changing thoughts, feelings and sensations. When consciousness is absolutely pure, call it pure thought or feeling, without any change obscuring or limiting its steadiness or unlimitedness, then we know what substance, reality of Self is.

All life, all activity is for the purpose of reaching this substance of which we speak but of which we have no experience. This is what we seek and search for vainly outside in the time-space universe of change. This is maya, the mystery of creation and our futile effort to find happiness in sensation.

The search for God and freedom and happiness is the search for substance. Worldliness is the abuse of substance. Ethics and religion are the right means for recovering from addiction to the pseudo-substance of the world. The real substance is within; it is the Reality, the Self and the purest delight without any reaction. Worldliness is seeking it outside in glamor and sensation. Drawn outside by the semblance of substance, we run into ruin, but the road to recovery and sanity is always open. The breeze of grace blows for all who have faith and who pray. When we seek substance outside and in sensation, love dies and the heart dries up.

It is not difficult to understand the fact of misperception in light of modern science, though it is no more than a hint. In a famous statement, Professor Alfred Whitehead said that we should thank ourselves for the beauty of nature, for the beautiful sunset and the sweet song of the nightingale; for out there nature is nothing but the hurrying and scurrying of material on the empty canvas of space-time. It is not difficult to see that we paint the universe of quality on the canvas of motion. But this is also a half-truth.

The ego itself is no more than an idea. We can never identify it as a substance through introspection; it is always a 'sense' (ego-sense) that attaches itself to varied feelings, ideas, etc. The ego changes as feelings change. It is elusive like the color we see or the sound we hear.

Knowledge is self-doubting, for it is never certain. If we analyze it we find it full of fictions. We have nouns and adjectives, substances and qualities, but where are they? Where is an entity in which quality inheres? Who moves? We know energy only during its state of manifestation or transfer. We have built up with our language a world of phantom realities and beliefs. This is not knowledge, but our conduct is based on this misperception.

Science is supposition. "The scientific world-view has ceased to be a scientific view in the true sense of the word" (Werner Heisenberg, *Uncertainty Principle*). Werner Heisenberg went later in life to Tagore's University in India, called *Shantiniketan* (Abode of Peace) in a rural and natural setting, evidently in search of what he missed in science, namely, the certain principle which is Reality or Truth but which is never known outside and therefore never spoken of but which is felt in the pure heart. It is the reflection of this which Heisenberg might have discerned in the spiritual writings of the poet.

In a lengthy conversation with Rabindranath Tagore in 1931 at Kapputh in Germany, Einstein said that there was an objective structure of the world and added as an illustration that the Pythagorean theorem would be true even if there were no human observers. Tagore pointed out that all scientific truths were human imagination; that they were relative to the human mind and that they had no meaning for a different kind of mind. Tagore mentioned that the world was maya, an appearance having no strict objectivity. Einstein concluded, saying that he could not prove that his contention was true but that he believed in it and was, therefore, more "religious" than Tagore. (The entire conversation is given in Tagore's book, *Religion of Man*, George Allen and Unwin Ltd., London.)

INTRODUCTION

Vedanta classifies perceptions into three categories, real, practical and illusory. Real perception is of Spirit, the only fact; illusory perception is private and peculiar fantasy; practical perception is perception of the common world of all observers. This is maya. All our troubles and dissatisfactions are due to this misperception. The Truth or Reality is dark as the night to the deluded (see end of chapter 2).

We wonder at the origin of this mystery. Modern science has come close to the view that there is no objective nature and that nature is like an "Alice in wonderland" dream. The ego and the world become insubstantial through analysis, but we cannot ignore them. This is practical truth, which is maya. But we want absolute truth, for the practical world does not give what we really seek.

When the ego and the universe are both seen as mysterious projections of the energy of the only substance, which is pure Truth-Consciousness-Bliss, the non-dual Reality, then the dreamer awakens from the dream. The mystery of creation or maya can only be hinted at. The knowledge of Truth can be had only by taking refuge in the Godhead, by surrendering or dissolving the ego.

Pure feeling, pure intellect or understanding (buddhi) and pure knowledge (jnana) are one and the same. Through love of God all the dualities of existence collapse into non-dual Reality, the blessedness of peace and freedom, from which we all have come and to which we all will return sooner or later.

Emanations from the Infinite are infinite. The division and dispersion of Reality in time are endless. Only mathematics can represent the infinity of creation in time. In that sense, the so-called Pythagorean dictum that the world is made up of numbers is true. Mathematics is the language of science.

Though mathematics (numbers) represents discrete energy movements, strict logic, in the sense of determinism or strict implication, does not apply to nature. Freedom or grace alters the course of life and physical events.

Mathematics stops when time stops; then numbers (Samkhya) dissolve into the non-numerical and non-dual existence of Vedanta. The world of mind and matter is a series (dynamic) of numbers or bits of energy or events upon which consciousness throws its shadow of personality and values.

LANGUAGE, SCIENCE AND TRUTH. It will be useful here to indicate further in the light of the language of today's science the spiritual and inexpressible nature of Reality.

Truth is both fact and the quality of a statement. The object of science is to find fact and express it in language for purposes of understanding and action. Communication of the truths of science is done through language which is an inadequate way of expressing the fact or happenings in nature which is basically a play of energy, i.e., motion. Only mathematics gives an adequate description of nature, for energy moves in definite and discrete quantities. So mathematics is the true language or expression of physical nature.

The mystery of creation can be graphically hinted at by mathematics. Creation begins with the division of the incomprehensible, timeless and motionless Real into the impersonal and personal aspects, represented in Indian mythology and iconography as an androgynous being where the male is inactive and impersonal and the female is dynamic and personal. Plato has a similar but simpler concept of androgynous origin of man and woman.

Nature is dynamic energy infinitely divided, giving the impression of endless bits of movement interrupted by gaps of motionlessness. In this sense, mathematics or number is the basic language or indicator of nature, the basic expression of science. The multiple universe is made up of definite quantities or units of energy in myriads of compositions. It is in this sense of the basic quantification of nature that the statement attributed to Pythagoras, who got his philosophy from India (Samkhya = number), namely, that the world was made of numbers, can be understood. In ancient India, *ganita* (number or mathematics) was regarded as the basic science or understanding of nature.

Upon being acquainted with the discoveries of modern physics, Tagore remarked that matter had vanished into mathematics. Sir Arthur Eddington called God a mathematician; Sir James Jeans, the astrophysicist, who prized moral values more, did not think it was a great compliment for God. Eddington's Deity is a remote being having no absolute intimacy with man and nature.

The math of the Infinite is given by the peace chant of the Upanishad — an infinite number of universes come out of the Infinite Spirit. Modern mathematics also envisages an infinite number of universes coming out of the timeless void before physical creation. Mathematics is the image of infinite Reality.

But even mathematics fails to indicate the logic of the basic chanciness of nature. Time is change. Mathematics represents physical change as a definite and discrete procession of energy units.

Mental happenings, which are non-spatial, cannot be represented by number because of association of thoughts and feelings. Chanciness of nature gives a hint of the psychic freedom that underlies physical nature. This is the realm of pure imagination.

Finally, the silent deep, the womb of time and change, cannot be expressed by numbers which can represent only a fractured existence or reality.

Mathematics gives the most adequate and universal description of physical nature as a procession of bits of energy. But nature is not logical in its conduct, for directions of energy are not always predictable and sometimes veer in an inexplicable manner.

Ramakrishna said about the nature of the world of maya or change, "There is much confusion in this world of His maya. One can by no means say that 'this will come after that' or 'this will produce that.'" His patron, Mathur Biswas, who revered him and called him Father, asked Ramakrishna once if God could break the laws of nature. Saying so, Mathur pointed to a white hibiscus plant and said, "Could this plant ever produce red flowers?" Ramakrishna replied that it could if God so willed. Next morning, Mathuranath was amazed and out of his wits to see that the same white hibiscus plant was sporting red flowers.

Truth which is not a report of the senses or an imagination is absolute and infinite, the womb of change and numbers.

Mathematics indicates that to know reality we have to go beyond numbers and thought to that which is inexpressible, namely, Pure Consciousness.

There are other interesting speculations in modern science which also throw light on the concept of maya.

Scientists speculate about many universes and about what is called the anthropic principle, according to which our particular universe, among all the possible universes indicated by mathematics, has been specially selected or designed for human beings like us; for it, only, seems to have the necessary conditions such as temperature, etc., for the origin and survival of life as we know it. It is similar to the story of "Goldilocks," who strayed into the bear-hut and found the chair, the soup-bowl and the bed made as if exactly for her. Fred Hoyle, however, speculates about other forms of life which may inhabit stellar gases, accommodating themselves to any temperature.

Other possible universes may not be empty or of this variety, and ideas of superspace point to subtler regions where subtle bodies may dwell. Ramakrishna once told a well-known social worker and philanthrophist, a convert to Christianity, who thought of doing good to the world, that there were innumerable universes in creation like the innumerable tiny crabs that appear on the banks of the Ganges. On another occasion he said, "I have seen all these truly...It has been shown to me that the ocean of consciousness is endless. From it all the creations arose and into it they dissolved again. Billions of universes arise from the space of consciousness and dissolve into it again."

Readers might have read in Joseph Campbell's well known writings on the "Hero" about the Purana story of the parade of limitless ants who were no other than Indra, King of Gods in aeons and aeons of cycles of creation. The mystery that surrounds our knowledge and universe is a slayer of the mind.

From the standpoint of science, a person is an organization, a constellation of forces (*samghata*) with a strange sense of selfhood or ownership as of a house, when in fact there are no such realities as body and ego. This is maya; this is illusion.

There is an exit in this maya; it is called *vidya maya,* the drive for freedom, while *avidya maya* is the appetite for selfish enjoyment. For the person whose vision is not obscured by the little 'I', for whom the third eye has opened, all is Brahman or God. This is the teaching of the Upanishads and the Gita. The Gita tells us to conduct ourselves remembering this and that one day the scales will fall from our eyes and the true picture will flash into view. Only, we have to listen humbly to the words of the Teacher who alone speaks with authority. We are saved from this dream and nightmare through knowledge of the Self which can be attained through devotion to the Personal God.

Reality is all that we want. Loving is the easiest way of ending our delusion. Life acquires meaning when it moves toward the Real. That's all religion is, and the Gita proclaims it in diverse ways. To quote Longfellow, "Tell me not in mournful numbers that life is but an empty dream," for this very life becomes real through loving service of the Divine in man and in creation.

MATTER AND SPIRIT. Earlier I mentioned Vivekananda's observation that science and religion would meet and shake hands and gave some instances of such meeting, recounting common conclusions about nature. Now I would like to discuss here the aptness of this profound remark in regard to another question which has engaged and defied the intelligence of philosophers since they started speculating about the origin of things.

Vivekananda himself gave a hint about it by mentioning that the question of intelligence coming out of dead matter and of matter coming out of intelligence (God or Consciousness) is like the proverbial chicken and egg question: which came first, the chicken or the egg?

The point is this: Reality is one, but people are divided about priorities: Which is first, matter or consciousness?

We, as individual observers in time and space, consider ourselves as spirits or conscious observers opposed to the observed nature which is matter. These are opposites and the gap between them is unbridgable. Logic cannot explain the origin of consciousness out of dead matter.

So also, we cannot logically explain matter coming out of pure consciousness or intelligence or God. This dualism is insurmountable in logic.

But there is a difference between the two points of view. Materialists have to be agnostic, i.e., non-knowers, while the enlightened saint who has reached the height of consciousness beyond speculative thought, by achieving singularity of mind through concentration and purity of heart, perceives after returning to the ordinary plane that the universe of time and space has arisen out of Pure Consciousness. The different objects are seen as forms of consciousness, like figures of wax. The sages of the Upanishads and the Gita declare that all is Brahman or Pure Consciousness, which is the substance, and all natural objects are constellations of Divine Energy.

The Divine Energy which creates the forms regarded as material is the will of a conscious personality.

Apart from the fact that materialism is unable to explain the emergence of life and personality out of the capriciousness of nature and offer justification of our ideals and dreams, we do not know what matter is. Materialists imagine that the expanding universe will one day wind up and disappear through 'singularity', into emptiness and non-existence from which it arose billions of years ago because of a mysterious explosion. Mathematicians further imagine the existence of limitless universes arising out of primitive emptiness, which sounds like Plato's 'ether', the mother of all creations.

Materialistic theories are ending in a kind of mysticism for not only do they fail to explain evolution of life and values, but also because there are no laws or causality in nature. At its heart nature is chaos. Nor do they know what matter is. It is also a mystery that, though being products of lawless nature, we presume to have certain knowledge.

Lawless nature is imagined to arise out of primitive emptiness. But is there any emptiness anywhere? Scientists are recognizing that there is no absolute vacuum anywhere. What is regarded as a perfect vacuum seems to be the reservoir of unknown energy.

Scientists also envisage the emergence of new universes out of this vacuum. Some, however, cannot imagine the origin of new universes without a tiny grain of so-called matter. Some have theorized that if someone "could compress ten kilograms of matter to occupy a space less than one-quadrillionth of that of an ordinary sub-nuclear particle, the result would be a seed that could trigger the birth of a new universe — one whose eventual inhabitants might see it in the same way we see our own universe." From an article by Malcolm Brown, *New York Times,* August 21, 1990.

It is no more than an idle dream.

Why do we need a tiny bit of matter for an explosion? Matter is energy. The beginning of creation is better conceived as the starting of a vibration in still Reality, like the sound of a gong or of *Om* — the out-breathing of Spirit as spiritual persons of India perceived long ago.

Space is nothing but energy in gross and fine forms. There are big stars and quasars as well as superfine radiations which are everywhere filling what we imagine to be a container, empty space, an idea derived from crude experience of sense. Space is energy in different forms.

The finer and subtler forms of energy are the space of mind, or *chitta.* Beyond mind there is no motion but the space of Pure Consciousness.

Physical energy has different basic forms. There are electromagnetic energy and other forces which tie together energy-bits and which repel them also, forming different kinds of bodies. Gravitation is the energy of total concentration, the wish of the universe to go to sleep.

The richness of Reality is not expressed by physical energy. Beauty and Love and Immortality which belong to Spirit are better reflected in finer forms of energy such as organized and purified minds.

To say Reality is Truth makes it non-emotional and abstract, but to say that it is Love makes it feeling and concrete.

The enlightened saint on the other hand perceives by turning his gaze within, through 'singularity' of mind, that the time-space universes of change arise from the space of Consciousness (*Chidakasha*), the so-called emptiness.

An invocation in the Upanishads gives the mathematics of the Infinite. It says, "The Infinite is above, the Infinite is below. (Spirit is Infinite, creation is Infinite.) Subtracting the Infinite from the Infinite, the Infinite remains." There are infinite manifestations of the timeless Infinite Consciousness.

Creation is still a mystery because we try to understand it as caused, though science tells us there is no cause in nature. However, creation is not seen as meaningless movement of dead energy, but as a game, a play where our profound aspirations and values are never denied as empty dreams.

Many years ago a friend asked me if Indians ever built philosophical systems like those of Descartes, Spinoza, Kant, Hegel and so on. Hegel belittled the Upanishads as poor thinking. I did not have a good answer then, but it is clear to me today that the big philosophical systems are all built upon the quicksand of unsystematic nature and uncertain knowledge.

Someone remarked apropos of the mountainous labors of the Western theoreticians of life and nature that philosophy is the finding of bad reasons for what one believes upon instinct. The various theoretical attempts of today to organize different systems out of man's ethical impulses, which have been spawned out of the line of thought called existentialism, are no more than materialism touched with sentimentality. It is a free-for-all time in philosophy. Mathew Arnold's famous definition of religion as ethics touched with emotion is applicable to philosophical thinking of today, with a slight twist: it is uncertain materialism touched with emotion.

Those who know better lead us to Truth and meaning in life through spiritual guidance.

The person of supreme realization sees in the words of the Gita, "All is Vasudeva, Krishna or Divinity... such a person is very rare."

This is the Truth the Gita teaches. It is going to be the ruling thought of the future. However, it is easy to say all is Brahman but difficult to realize it. "All excellent things are rare and difficult" (Spinoza).

Ramakrishna said, "It is easy to study and quote scriptures but difficult to realize their truth, just as it is easy to read music but difficult to play it." Great incarnations like Krishna teach us how to play the music of the Spirit.

Finally, there is this difference, ultimate and critical, between materialistic theories and guesses and spiritual knowledge or wisdom; namely, that while materialistic knowledge or science is uncertain, being always infected with doubt about the nature of Reality or Truth, wisdom is decisive and certain, "sun-

INTRODUCTION

dering all doubts," *(Katha Upanishad)*, just as the nature of a land-scape hidden in darkness at night is revealed clearly when the sun shines upon it. Knowers of Truth lead us to it and the real meaning in life through spiritual guidance.

SCIENTISTS AND RELIGION. Some great and renowned scientists have believed in God despite belief in determinism. Sir Isaac Newton, perhaps the greatest scientist of modern times, was a believer in God.

Sir Humphry Davy, the chemist and inventor of the first miner's lamp and the founder of the Royal Society of England, was a believer in God and also in divine incarnation. And Albert Einstein, second only to Newton according to the astrophysicist Chandrasekhar of the University of Chicago, believed in God and determinism. Sir Chandrasekhar was a student of Sir Arthur Eddington, F.R.S., who was also a believer in God.

All these great scientists were right in their belief in determinism if we understand nature in a larger sense than physicists do and as the Gita points out. Nature is both mental and physical. It is the play of a great Personality whose will is law. But this will is not bound by law. Its "freak is the greatest order" (Vivekananda). The free will of the Divine can change the course of nature. That Personality is the ruler of human destiny.

REALITY. Reality or objectivity cannot be predicated of the time-space universe of change *(desha-kala-nimilta)*, nor can the time-space universe be explained as something caused, for the very idea of cause begs the question. There is no explanation in science or philosophy for the time-space universe or our ideals.

Reality as assumed in common sense experience and science is relative. Absolute Reality, the ideal in science and philosophy, is never to be found in discourse or research. The ideal of Reality is the timeless duration of Self in us which we project in time, a moving shadow of Existence.

Reality is *Tao*, wisdom never spoken. But this hint of Reality is in all knowledge as existence. We cannot ever think of non-existence.

Knowledge of Reality is rare, but there is a hint of it in all knowledge as the ideals of Truth, Love and moral perfection of Purity.

We want activity and also peace which is not lack of activity. The peace that we seek is Reality beyond action and non-action.

DIFFERENT PATHS OR YOGAS. The Gita proclaims that there are many ways (*yogas*) of reaching the spiritual goal of life and that one should never disturb the faith of those whose understanding is poor. The wise should teach them by offering a helping hand.

All the different ways of knowing God have been classified into four broad paths; namely, 1.) *jnana yoga*, the way of wisdom, 2.) *bhakti yoga*, the way of love of God, 3.) *karma yoga*, the way of selfless action, 4.) *dhyana yoga*, the way of meditation. Though the Gita recognizes many ways of worshipping God, its emphasis is on the path of action based on devotion to God who is both Personal and Impersonal. "By my unmanifested form all the world is pervaded" (9:4).

The path of pure self-analysis and discrimination is too difficult for most and so is pure contemplation. The Gita emphasizes the path of action because religion is not only a personal venture, but a social obligation. Religious people should act for the good of the world (lokasamgraha). All life and all action can be turned into prayer and worship if duty is done as it should be done in the spirit of service to the Lord. One should also cultivate the background understanding that all is Divine.

Ramakrishna told his disciples to do whatever they like with the knowledge of *advaita* (non-dualism) in their pockets. Krishna made a similar statement at the end of the Gita when he told Arjuna:

> This is the wisdom which is more secret than the secret that has been spoken by me. Pondering over it thoroughly do as you like (18:63).

This advice is not a license for wild action, but for worship of the Divine present in everything.

RECOVERY OF HUMAN FREEDOM. Krishna declares that God dwelling in the hearts of all beings moves them to action. The question of human freedom arises when we do not see the fundamental truth.

INTRODUCTION

The ego is not real and its problems are not real. The problem is created by ignorance and leads to insoluble theological discussions.

There are no conclusive answers to ultimate questions such as human freedom and necessity. All our proofs and methods of proof, says Shankara, the eighth century paragon of Vedantists, in his introduction to the commentary on the *Vedanta Aphorisms*, rest upon a prior fact of ignorance, which is confusion of the pure Subject or Spirit with object or nature, which are as opposed to each other as light and darkness.

Even without the clear perception of the radical distinction between Self and nature which the enlightened have, we can still, with whatever practical information we have, see that our knowledge is uncertain for it rests upon many uncritical assumptions. Modern science is making this clearer by knocking out many of its previous presuppositions, and it now claims to be no more than a bunch of theories useful for practical purposes, but lacking the validity of fact.

When it comes to the question of individual freedom we come to this predicament. We do not know who is the individual in the body, nor how free is he. How much control does the individual have over the body he claims as his own? How many choices does he have? Are they his? Still we carry on with a cocksure belief in our own agency and we are held responsible for what we call our actions.

In addition, it is obvious that an individual is often able to reject many promptings from within and choose what he considers right. It is also clear that if he yields to temptations they finally get him. He has then no choice but only compulsions. This road of desire is one of very easy gradient; when you follow it for awhile, you hardly realize how far you have gone downhill, and one day, when you wake up, you discover that you are several thousand feet lower than when you began. It is a hard climb back. Freedom is recovered through faith.

Further, when a person uses his unspoiled sense of freedom to reject impulses, he discovers his freedom increases with the discipline of self-control, his taste changes and he appreciates ideas and ideals which now appear to be worth pursuing. An individual's capacity for intelligent choice is developed. Freedom expands with increasing self-control. One appreciates higher values and pursues them.

A person of unselfish motivation or a discoverer of the truths of science has greater influence on other minds, and through them on actions which are part of nature. Finally logic hints at the conclusion that only an universal mind has the complete freedom to do everything. Others who advance through control toward this larger existence, or the inner truth of Spirit, have an increasing feeling of freedom or sense of independence of nature.

Freedom is not slavery of body. Civilization is not a celebration of passion. The high qualities of love and charity, compassion and self-less action are its hallmarks. When a person works with self-less feeling he works like God. Perfect freedom is the Personality of God. God is Freedom. A little bit of It peeps through nature. This, the sages say, comes to us as our sense of Freedom. Religion is gaining back our freedom, lost in the fall from heaven (in the spirit's becoming enmeshed in maya).

No ultimate questions can be satisfactorily answered in the world of dualities. When one sees unity no answers are needed for there are no questions. Questions and answers, the sages hint, belong to schools of children. But then it is by asking questions that we reach the end of intellectual effort and plunge into what is called mysticism in order to find the lost pages of the book of the universe. Then there is no mystery anymore.

It is our dualistic world which is the great mystery, with its self-doubting knowledge and uncertainties everywhere, with its unrealizable hopes and dreams, with its attachments to objects which pass away and so on. Sir James Jeans entitled one of his popular books on science, *The Mysterious Universe*. We ourselves are ourselves the greatest mystery, to us and to our friends!

Determinism has disappeared from science, but nature is more than physical energy. Mind is part of nature. All nature is controlled by Divine will and its freedom is reflected in different degrees in the separate movements of nature in accordance with developments in evolution. Even in physical nature, in the behavior of particles, scientists today detect a kind of psychic quality, a grain of freedom. In man this freedom is enlarged and in the self-controlled person it is still more enlarged. Finally when a person becomes free he rises above nature; his spirit is no longer identified with mind or body. Freedom or Self is his nature; he is under no control. Ego's freedom is in obedience to God in selfless action. Then there is no longer the bondage of karma or action.

At the end, the Gita says surrender yourself completely to the Divine and the Divine will redeem you from sins. Ask no questions if you believe and dedicate yourself to God. Once you have decided to go after Freedom, too many questions will only impede progress as Buddha and Ramakrishna said. When you go to a doctor in an emergency, you don't insist on being satisfied about various theories concerning the cause of the trouble before treatment. Get treated and questions can wait. Complete surrender is the best way. It may or may not be easy. It is a matter of practice.

THE GITA AND VIOLENCE. Does the Gita advocate violence? This question comes up often among those who really have not thoroughly studied the work. Non-violence is the ideal for the individual, but society needs protection and cannot remain non-violent in the face of aggression. However, individuals who have attained perfection do not react with violence. The ideal is "resist not evil," which is the conduct of those who own nothing, who have no violence in them and who have good will toward all. The Gita mentions repeatedly that *ahimsa,* or non-violence, is the highest virtue (see comment in chapter 2).

THE GITA AND CONVERSION. Preaching is necessary for communication of Truth. True evangelism does not force dogma down the throats of reluctant listeners. There should be freedom to choose. Law and order in society are maintained by sanctions. Within them a person should be left free to choose his beliefs and express them. Idealism is rooted in love in the heart.

Fanaticism is born of ignorance and it is against spiritual truth. Besides idealism cannot be forced upon people.

Ramakrishna related the following story of a Hindu who was forcibly converted to Islam:

Once there lived a very pious Hindu who always worshipped the Divine Mother and chanted her name. When the Mussalmans conquered the country, they forced him to embrace Islam. They said to him, "You are a Mussalman. Say 'Allah.' From now on you must repeat only the name of 'Allah.'" With great difficulty he repeated the word Allah, but every now and then blurted out Jagadamba (Mother of the Universe). At that the Mussalmans were about to beat him. Thereupon he said to them, "I beseech you! Please do not kill me. I have been trying my utmost to repeat the name of Allah, but our Jagadamba has filled me up to the throat. She pushes out your Allah."

People stand at different levels of development and so grasp only what their heart and mind are capable of. The best preaching is by the example of character. Love, truth and simplicity are recognized without words.

A BEAUTIFUL CULTURE. It is proper to bring this introduction to a close by recounting a couple of stories from the Mahabharata which reflect the spirit of the beautiful culture which was born of the kind of teachings we find in the Gita, itself a part of the Mahabharata.

The first one is the story of a royal couple. I quote here from Vivekananda's narration of it in a lecture delivered at the Shakespeare Club, Pasadena, California, February 1, 1900:

There was a King Ashvapati. The King had a daughter, who was so good and beautiful that she was called Savitri, which is the name of a sacred prayer of the Hindus. When Savitri grew old enough, her father asked her to choose a husband for herself. These Indian princesses of ancient times were very independent, you see, and chose their own princely consorts.

Savitri consented and travelled to distant regions, mounted in a golden chariot, with her guards and aged courtiers to whom her father entrusted her, stopping at different courts, and seeing different princes, but not one of them could win the heart of Savitri. They came at last to a holy hermitage in one of those forests

INTRODUCTION

that in ancient India were reserved for animals, and where no animals were allowed to be killed. The animals lost the fear of man — even the fish in the lakes came and took food out of the hand. For thousands of years no one had killed anything therein. The sages and the aged went there to live among the deer and the birds. Even criminals were safe there. When a man got tired of life, he would go to the forest; and in the company of sages, talking of religion and meditating thereon, he passed the remainder of his life.

Now it happened that there was a king, Dyumatsena, who was defeated by his enemies and was deprived of his kingdom when he was struck with age and had lost his sight. This poor, old, blind king, with his queen and his son, took refuge in the forest and passed his life in rigid penance. His boy's name was Satyavan.

It came to pass that after having visited all the royal courts, Savitri at last came to this hermitage, or holy place. Not even the greatest king could pass by the hermitage, or *ashrama* as they were called, without going to pay homage to the sages, for such was the honor and respect felt for these holy men. The greatest emperor of India would be only too glad to trace his descent to some old sage who lived in a forest, subsisting on roots and fruits, and clad in rags. We are all children of sages. That is the respect that is paid to religion. So even kings, when they pass by the hermitages, feel honored to go in and pay their respects to the sages. If they approach on horseback, they descend and walk as they advance toward them. If they arrive in a chariot, chariot and armor must be left outside when they enter. No fighting man can enter unless he comes in the manner of a religious man, quiet and gentle.

So Savitri came to this hermitage and saw there Satyavan, the hermit's son, and her heart was conquered. She has escaped all the princes of the palaces and the courts, but here in the forest-refuge of King Dyumatsena, his son, Satyavan, stole her heart.

When Savitri returned to her father's house, he asked her, "Savitri, dear daughter, speak. Did you see anybody whom you would like to marry?" Then softly with blushes, said Savitri, "Yes, Father." "What is the name of the prince?" "He is no prince, but

• 48 •

the son of King Dyumatsena who has lost his kingdom — a prince without a patrimony, who lives a monastic life, the life of a *sannyasin* in a forest, collecting roots and herbs, helping and feeding his old father and mother, who live in a cottage."

On hearing this the father consulted the sage Narada who happened to be then present there, and he declared it was the most ill-omened choice that was ever made. The king then asked him to explain why it was so. And Narada said, "Within twelve months from this time the young man will die." Then the king started with terror, and spoke, "Savitri, this young man is going to die in twelve months, and you will become a widow; think of that! Desist from your choice, my child, you shall never be married to a short-lived and fated bridegroom." "Never mind, Father; do not ask me to marry another person and sacrifice my chastity, for I love and have accepted in my mind the good and brave Satyavan only as my husband. A maiden chooses only once, and she never departs from her troth." When the king found that Savitri was resolute in mind and heart, he complied. Then Savitri married Prince Satyavan, and she quietly went from the palace of her father into the forest, to live with her chosen husband and help her husband's parents.

Now, though Savitri knew the exact date when Satyavan was to die, she kept it hidden from him. Daily he went into the depths of the forest, collected fruits and flowers, gathered faggots, and then came back to the cottage, and she cooked the meals and helped the old people. Thus their lives went on until the fatal day came near, and three short days remained only. She took a severe vow of three nights' penance and holy fasts, and kept her hard vigils. Savitri spent sorrowful and sleepless nights with fervent prayers and unseen tears, till the dreaded morning dawned. That day Savitri could not bear him out of her sight, even for a moment. She begged permission from his parents to accompany her husband, when he went to gather the usual herbs and fuels and gaining their consent she went. Suddenly in faltering accents he complained to his wife of feeling faint, "My head is dizzy, and my senses reel, dear Savitri, I feel sleep stealing over me; let me rest beside thee for a while." In fear and trembling she replied, "Come lay your head upon my lap, my dearest lord." And he laid his burning head in the lap of his wife, and ere long sighed and expired. Clasping him to her, her eyes flowing with tears, there she sat in the lonesome forest, until the emmissaries of Death approached to take away the soul of Satyavan. But they could not come near to the place where Savitri sat with the dead body of her husband, his head resting in her lap. There was a zone of fire surrounding her, and not one of the emissaries of Death could come within it. They all fled back from it, returned to King Yama, the God of Death, and told him why they could not obtain the soul of this man.

Then came Yama, the God of Death, the Judge of the dead. He was the first man that died — the presiding deity over all those that die. He judges whether after a man has died, he is to be punished or rewarded. So he came himself. Of course he could go inside the charmed circle, as he was a god. When he came to Savitri he said, "Daughter, give up this dead body, for know death is the fate of mortals, and I am the first of mortals who died. Since then, every one has had to die. Death is the fate of man."

Thus told, Savitri walked off and Yama drew the soul out. Yama having possessed himself of the soul of the young man proceeded on his way. Before he had gone far, he heard footfalls upon the dry leaves. He turned back, "Savitri daughter, why are you following me? This is the fate of all mortals." "I am not following thee, Father," replied Savitri, "but this is also the fate of woman, she follows where her love takes her, and the Eternal Law separates not loving man and faithful wife." Then said the God of Death, "Ask for any boon except the life of your husband." "If thou art pleased to grant a boon, O Lord of Death, I ask that my father-in-law may be cured of his blindness and made happy." "Let thy pious wish be granted, duteous daughter." And then the King of Death travelled on with the soul of Satyavan. Again the same footfall was heard from behind. He looked round, "Savitri, my daughter, you are still following me?" "Yes, my Father; I cannot help doing so; I am trying all the time to go back, but the mind goes after my husband and the body follows. The soul has already gone, for in that soul is also mine; and when you take the soul, the body follows, does it not?" "Pleased am I with your words, fair

Savitri. Ask yet another boon of me, but it must not be the life of your husband." "Let my father-in-law regain his lost wealth and kingdom, Father, if thou art pleased to grant another supplication." "Loving daughter," Yama answered, "this boon I now bestow; but return home, for living mortals cannot go with King Yama." And then Yama pursued his way. But Savitri, meek and faithful, still followed her departed husband. Yama again turned back. "Noble Savitri, follow not in hopeless woe." "I cannot choose but follow where thou takest my beloved one." "Then suppose, Savitri, that your husband was a sinner and has to go to hell. In that case goes Savitri with the one she loves?" "Glad am I to follow where he goes, be it life or death, heaven or hell," said the loving wife. "Blessed are your words, my child, pleased am I with you. Ask yet another boon, but the dead come not to life again." "Since you so permit me, then let the imperial line of my father-in-law be not destroyed; let his kingdom descend to Satyavan's sons." And then the God of Death smiled, "My daughter, thou shalt have thy desire now. Here is the soul of thy husband; he shall live again. He shall live to be a father and thy children also shall reign in due course. Return home. Love has conquered Death! Women never loved like thee, and thou art the proof that even I, the God of Death, am powerless against the power of true love that abideth."

Vivekananda continued, "This is the story of Savitri, and every girl in India must aspire to be like Savitri, whose love could not be conquered by death..."

The Mahabharata is full of hundreds of beautiful episodes like this. Another memorable story from the Mahabharata is given below, again in the words of Vivekananda from his book entitled *Karma Yoga:*

A young sannyasin (monk) went to a forest; there he meditated, worshipped and practiced yoga for a long time. After years of hard work and practice, he was one day sitting under a tree, when some dry leaves fell upon his head. He looked up and saw a crow and a crane fighting on the top of the tree, which made him very angry. He said, "What! Dare you throw these dry leaves upon my head!"

As with these words he angrily glanced at them, a flash of fire went out of his head — such was the yogi's power — and burnt the birds to ashes. He was very glad, almost overjoyed at the development of power — he could burn the crow and the crane by a look.

After a time he had to go to the town to beg his bread. He went, stood at a door and said, "Mother, give me food." A voice came from inside the house, "Wait a little, my son." The young man thought, "You wretched woman, how dare you make me wait! You do not know my power yet." While he was thinking thus the voice came again, "Boy, don't be thinking too much of yourself. Here is neither crow nor crane." He was astonished; still he had to wait.

At last the woman came, and he fell at her feet and said, "Mother, how did you know that?" She said, "My boy, I do not know yoga or your practices, I am a common everyday woman. I made you wait because my husband is ill, and I was nursing him. All my life I have struggled to do my duty. When I was unmarried, I did my duty to my parents; now that I am married, I do my duty to my husband; that is all the yoga I practice. But by doing my duty I have become illumined; thus I could read your thoughts and know what you had done in the forest. If you want to know something higher than this, go to the market of such and such a town where you will find a *Vyadha* (a hunter and a butcher, regarded as of very low caste by caste-ridden people), who will tell you something that you will be very glad to learn." The sannyasin thought, "Why should I go to that town and to a Vyadha?" But after what he had seen, his mind opened a little, so he went. When he came near the town, he found the market and there saw, at a distance, a big fat Vyadha cutting meat with big knives, talking and bargaining with different people. The young man said, "Lord help me! Is this the man from whom I am going to learn? He is the incarnation of a demon, if he is anything." In the meantime this man looked up and said, "O Swami, did that lady send you here? Take a seat until I have done my business."

The sannyasin thought, "What comes to me here?" He took his seat; the man went on with his work, and after he had finished he took his money and said to the sannyasin, "Come sir, come to my home." On reaching home the Vyadha gave him a seat, saying, "Wait here," and went into the house. He then washed his old father and mother, fed them, and did all he could to please them, after which he came to the sannyasin and said, "Now sir, you have come here to see me. What can I do for you?" The sannyasin asked him a few questions about soul and about God, and the Vyadha gave him a lecture which forms a part of the Mahabharata, called the *Vyadha Gita* (The Hunter's Song). It contains one of the highest flights of Vedanta.

When the Vyadha finished his teaching the sannyasin felt astonished. He said, "Why are you in that body? With such knowledge as yours why are you in a Vyadha's body, and doing such filthy, ugly work?" "My son," replied the Vyadha, "no duty is ugly, no duty is impure. My birth placed me in these circumstances and environment. In my boyhood I learnt the trade; I am unattached, and I try to do my duty well. I try to do my duty as a householder, and I try to do all I can to make my father and mother happy. I neither know your yoga, nor have I become a sannyasin, nor did I go out of the world into a forest; nevertheless, all that you have heard and seen has come to me through the unattached doing of the duty which belongs to my position."

The truth of the Gita continues to find expression in the art and literature of modern India. Poet Tagore depicts in the poem below the feeling of the cultivated at the sight of a common scene.

> With a glance of your eyes you could plunder
>   all the wealth of songs struck from poets'
>   harps, fair woman!
> But for their praises you have no ear,
>   therefore I come to praise you.
> You could humble at your feet the proudest
>   heads in the world.
> But it is your loved ones, unknown to fame,
>   whom you choose to worship,
>   therefore I worship you.

INTRODUCTION

> The perfection of your arms would add glory
> to kingly splendor with their touch.
> But you use them to sweep away the dust,
> and to make clean your humble home,
> therefore I am filled with awe.
> > *(Collected Poems and Plays,*
> > Macmillan and Co.)

Perception of the truth of personality, integrity and love humbles our ego and inspires the feeling of awe.

The Gita's message of Freedom is both to man's head and heart. It is clear today in the light of modern science what the ancient sages of India declared thousands of years ago that Reality, the hidden truth of creation, the Spirit, is never attained by intellectual effort. This secret is never grasped by intellect however sharp and clever it may be. Also no great work can be accomplished by cleverness.

The deep truths of life and creation are hidden away in the hearts of men. Our heart knows what our intellect cannot fathom. Without moral growth and genuine longing in the heart, the deep truths of existence remain obscure.

But it is also true that intellect cannot be ignored, for it cannot accept as truth what goes against reason. The truth that the Gita proclaims is not only an answer to our heart's longing, a fulfillment of our idealistic dreams and aspirations, but is also the goal of reason. It is the truth which is certain and which makes sense of man's striving for peace and happiness in the otherwise uncertain world of commerce, of gain and loss, of pleasure and pain, of success and failure and of fear and anxiety. The only thing beyond doubt in this uncertain and unpredictable world is the living Lord in our heart. And Truth is simple, much more simple and elegant than the equations of science and mathematics, for Truth is simplicity itself.

In this so-called age of science and reason and of calamitous events in individual and collective life — the brutality and violence, the fear and anxiety, the general uncertainty which grips masses of people and the lack of intelligent guidance — the paramount need is for recovery of faith in the Truth of man not to be found in the market-place of the world. The Gita's lasting appeal is due to its ability to communicate this in an intelligible, up-to-date manner.

It has been my endeavor to communicate the message of the Gita in the light of experience and teachings, especially of those who in our time have embodied and reflected it in their lives, and also in view of the special circumstances of today's world when diverse peoples and cultures have come into intimate contact with one another and when science, psychology and dogmas of sectarian religions have not only proved themselves inadequate to comprehend the fundamental truths of cosmos and life, but also have been unable to throw light on man's ideal conduct and life's meaning.

CHAPTER ONE

The Yoga of Arjuna's Despondency

P RELUDE: The Gita, the Sermon on the Battlefield, was delivered by the Divine Teacher Krishna to Arjuna, a royal hero and disciple, on the eve of a great battle between two sets of cousins, one led by Arjuna and the other by Duryodhana.

Sanjaya, a minister, related the battle to Dhritarashtra the blind king and father of Duryodhana. Sanjaya was given special power of vision (television) to see the battle scene from a distance in order that he might report the happenings to the king who could not see.

The teacher of Duryodhana, who is mentioned in the beginning, is Drona, while Bhishma, the common grandsire of the contestants was the general on the side of Duryodhana.

The Gita begins with the question of Dhritarashtra to Sanjaya, the narrator.

DHRITARASHTRA SAID:

1. O Sanjaya! What did the warriors do, ours and those of the Pandavas, who had assembled in the sacred field of the Kurus?

THE YOGA OF ARJUNA'S DESPONDENCY

2. Seeing the army of the Pandavas deployed in battle array, King Duryodhana went to the teacher (Drona) and said:

3. O Teacher! Look at the great army of the sons of Pandu which has been drawn up by your talented disciple, the son of Drupada.

4-6. Here are heroes, great archers who are equals of Bhima and Arjuna in battle — Yuyudhana (Satyaki), Virata, Drupada, the great warrior, Dhrishtaketu, Chekitana, the heroic King of Kashi, Purujit, Kuntibhoja, Shaivya, the chief among men, the mighty Yudhamanyu, the manly Uttamauja, the sons of Subhadra and Draupadi: all of them are great warriors.

7. Know also, O Best among the Twiceborn! the most distinguished generals on our side. I am recounting their names for your information.

8. Yourself (Drona), Bhishma, Karna, Kripa, the victor in battles, Ashwathama, Vikarna, the son of Somadatta and King Jayadratha.

9. There are many other heroes who are ready to lay down their lives for my sake. They are all equipped with various weapons and skilled in war.

10. The strength of our army led by Bhishma is without limit while theirs led by Bhima is limited.

11. Now let all of you post yourselves at the head of the formations according to your assignments and support Bhishma.

SANJAYA CONTINUED:

12. Letting out a mighty roar like a lion, the aged and valiant grandsire of the Kurus (Bhishma) blew the conch, filling Duryodhana's heart with delight.

13. Then all at once conches, drums, kettledrums, gongs and horns sounded and the noise was tremendous.

14. Then Krishna (Madhava) and Arjuna, who were seated in a great chariot drawn by white horses, blew their heavenly conches.

15. Krishna blew his conch Panchajanya, Arjuna his Devadatta and Bhima of frightful deeds and of wolfish appetite blew his mighty conch Paundra.

16. Prince Yudhishthira, the son of Kunti, blew his conch Anantavijaya, while Nakula and Sahadeva blew their Sughosha and Manipushpaka.

17-18. And the King of Kashi, the supreme archer Shikhandi, the great warrior Dhrishtadyumna, and Virata and the invincible Satyaki, Drupada and the sons of Draupadi, O Lord of Earth (Dhritarashtra)! and the strong-armed sons of Subhadra, all blew their conches separately.

19. That terrific din rent the hearts of Dhritarashtra's sons and resounded through earth and sky.

20. Then, O Lord of Earth (Dhritarashtra)! seeing the sons of Dhritarashtra drawn up in battle array, Arjuna seated in the chariot flying the banner bearing the crest of the monkey-god took up the bow as the time approached for the missiles to be thrown and spoke to Hrishikesha (Krishna).

ARJUNA SAID:

21-23. O Achyuta (Krishna)! Draw up my chariot between the two armies so I can review those who are there ready for war with whom I have to fight in the ensuing battle. I want to see those well-wishers of ill-advised Duryodhana who have assembled here for war.

THE YOGA OF ARJUNA'S DESPONDENCY

SANJAYA SAID TO DHRITARASHTRA:

24-25. Thus addressed by Arjuna (Gurakesha), Krishna (Hrishikesha) stationed the great chariot between the two armies, facing Bhishma, Drona and all the other kings and said to Arjuna: Look at the descendants of Kuru assembled here.

26. There Arjuna saw among the two armies uncles, grandfathers, teachers, maternal uncles, brothers, sons, grandsons, fathers-in-law and friends.

27. Having seen all the friends stationed there, Arjuna was overwhelmed with great pity and sorrow.

ARJUNA SAID:

28-29. O Krishna! Seeing my own people assembled here to fight, my limbs are weary and my mouth is drying up. My body trembles and my hairs are standing on end. The bow Gandiva is slipping from my hand and my skin is burning.

30. O Keshava (Krishna)! I am unable to remain steady and my mind is wandering — and I see evil omens.

31. O Krishna! I do not see any good in killing my own people in war; I do not desire victory, nor kingdom, nor pleasures.

32-33. O Govinda (Krishna)! Of what use to us are kingdom and pleasures and life, when those for whose sake we desire kingdom, pleasures and happiness — the teachers, fathers, sons, grandparents, uncles, fathers-in-law and other relatives — stand here for battle, giving up hope of life and fortune.

34. These, O Madhusudana (Krishna)! I do not want to kill even for the sake of sovereignty over the three worlds, not to speak of this earth alone.

35. What pleasures can be ours, O Krishna! by killing the sons of Dhritarashtra? Sin alone will possess us by killing these opponents.

36-38. Therefore it is not right for us to kill the sons of Dhritarashtra and their friends. How can we be happy, O Krishna (Madhava)! by killing our own people? Even if they, overcome by the greed for kingdom, do not see the evil of destroying one's kin and the sin of enmity toward friends, why should not we, O Janardana (Krishna)! have the sense to turn away from it when we see clearly the sin of destroying one's kin?

39. With the destruction of the family, its age-old laws perish. When the laws perish, the whole family is overcome by lawlessness.

40. When lawlessness prevails, the women of the family become dissolute, and when they become dissolute, confusion of orders takes place.

41. Confusion of orders causes the destroyers of families to go to hell, and their forefathers, too, descend to hell, being deprived of offerings of rice and water.

42. The misdeeds of those who cause mixture of orders destroy the immemorial laws of caste and family.

43. O Janardana (Krishna)! We have heard that the persons of families whose laws have been destroyed live eternally in hell.

44. Alas, what a great sin we have set ourselves to commit as we have become ready to kill our own people out of greed for the pleasure of the kingdom.

45. It will be better for me if the armed sons of Dhritarashtra kill me unresisting and unarmed.

SANJAYA SAID:

46. So saying, Arjuna, with mind laden with grief, sank down to his seat in the chariot, relinquishing his bow and arrow.

Colophons similar to the example below appear in the Sanskrit text at the end of each chapter. They mention its topic, setting and also define the nature of its teaching.

The Gita or the Divine Song is an Upanishad containing the discourse between Krishna and Arjuna, which forms part of the Chapter on Bhishma in the great epic, the Mahabharata of a hundred thousand verses which was composed by Vyasa. It is the scripture of the yoga of action based on the knowledge of Brahman.

A scripture has two goals: first, revelation of spiritual truth and second, prescription of means for its realization.

Thus the colophon sets the tone of the Gita's teaching.

CHAPTER TWO

The Yoga
of Wisdom
(Samkhya)

SANJAYA SAID:

Krishna (Madhusudana) spoke thus to sorrowful Arjuna who was overwhelmed with pity and whose eyes were full of tears.

1.

THE BLESSED LORD SAID:

2. Whence has this delusion come over you, O Arjuna! at the moment of crisis? This is unworthy of a nobleman (Aryan); it does not lead to heaven and is disgraceful.

3. Do not give way to unmanliness, O Partha (Arjuna)! It does not befit you. Discard this petty weakness of heart and arise, O Destroyer of Enemies!

ARJUNA SAID:

4. How can I, O Slayer of Foes (Krishna)! fight Bhishma and Drona with arrows in this war? They are worthy of my worship.

5. It is better to live in the world by begging than to slay these venerable teachers. By slaying them I will only taste pleasures and wealth stained with blood.

6. Nor do we know which is better — whether we conquer them or they conquer us. The sons of Dhritarashtra, after slaying whom we would not care to live, are confronting us here.

7. With my nature corrupted by pity and mind deluded about duty I ask you: Please tell me for certain what is good. I am your disciple; teach me who has taken refuge in you.

8. I do not perceive anything which will allay this sense of withering grief even if I obtain dominion over earth without an enemy or even sovereignty over gods in heaven.

SANJAYA SAID:

9. Having thus spoken to Hrishikesha (Krishna), Gurakesha (Arjuna), the Tormentor of Enemies, declared to Govinda (Krishna): I will not fight, and became silent.

10. O Bharata (Dhritarashtra)! To him who thus stood grieving between the two armies, Hrishikesha (Krishna), smiling as it were, spoke these words.

THE BLESSED LORD SAID:

11. You are lamenting for those for whom there should not be any lament; yet you speak words of wisdom. The wise do not grieve for the dead or the living.

12. Never was a time when you or I or these kings did not exist; nor will any of us cease to exist afterwards.

13. As childhood, youth and old age are to the indwelling spirit in the body, so also is its migration to another body. The wise have no delusions about it.

14. O Son of Kunti (Arjuna)! Sense-contacts give rise to feelings of heat and cold, pleasure and pain; they come and go and do not last forever; endure them.

15. O Best among Men! He who is unaffected by these dualities and who is the same in pleasure and pain deserves eternal life.

16. The unreal has no existence; there is no nonexistence for the Real. This final truth about them both has been seen by the seers.

Existence of individual objects in time is the shadow of the true existence of the timeless Real. Existence in time is splintered existence. The Gita teaches the essential non-duality of the Real.

17. Know that which pervades all this is indestructible. No one can bring about the destruction of the Eternal Spirit.

Man is spirit. Bodies originate and decompose in time. Spirit is above time. It has no origin and no destruction.

18. These bodies of the incarnated Spirit, which is eternal, indestructible and imperceptible, have been declared to be perishable. Therefore, O Descendant of Bharata (Arjuna)! fight.

19. He who considers it to be a slayer and he who thinks it is slain — both of them do not know; for it neither slays nor is slain.

20. It is never born, nor does it ever die; after coming to be, it does not cease to be; it is without birth, eternal, imperishable and timeless; it is not destroyed with the destruction of the body.

21. How can he, O Partha (Arjuna)! who knows this to be imperishable, eternal, birthless and changeless, slay anyone or cause anyone to slay?

22. As a man puts on new clothes after discarding the old ones, so also does the embodied spirit enter into new bodies after giving up the old ones.

23. Weapons cannot sunder it, nor fire burn it. Water cannot wet it, nor the wind dry it.

24. The Eternal Spirit cannot be sundered; it cannot be burnt or made wet or dried; it is eternal, all-pervasive, changeless and immovable.

25. It is said to be unmanifest, unimaginable, unchangeable; therefore knowing it to be so you should not grieve.

26. And even if you think, O Mighty-armed One! that it is born every time and dies every time with the body, you should not grieve over it.

27. Death is certain for one who is born and certain also is the birth of one who is dead. Therefore you should not grieve over what is inevitable.

As the Gita points out later, non-violence or "resist not evil" is the highest virtue. It is practiced by individuals who renounce the pleasures and powers of the world for the sake of eternal life.

Violence is never an ideal in a civilized society, but it cannot be avoided. Rulers of societies (the Kshatriyas, or the guardians of Plato) have to employ it for their preservation. Even this terrible action can be performed as selfless service when lawless societies prey upon others out of greed.

Non-violent resistance is the most civilized method of facing evil. Only the very brave, developed individuals can practice it and inspire others to do so.

Non-violence in thought, word and deed is the ideal of the yogi, as the Gita points out toward the end.

There is no birth or death or change for the Real, the essential man, but in the relative world of maya, the world of egos and their objects, there is transmigration of the subtle body composed of fine organs, mind, intellect and ego-sense as long as there is desire for experience. The subtle body transmigrates and is drawn by its desires to an appropriate gross body (the physical body as we know it — the vesture of the soul).

CHAPTER TWO

An individual is a gross physical body (the vesture) plus the subtle body of fine organs, mind, intellect and the ego-sense, which are portions of the process called nature and which reflect and individualize the pure unitary Existence or the Real (*Sat-Chit-Ananda*).

Earlier in the chapter Krishna talks of the real Self (*Paramatman*), which is never born and which never dies. Later he talks of the transmigrating self (*jivatman*) in the universal process of maya. This is called the empirical self. It lasts as long as the individual has desires.

There are two innate tendencies in an individual: one is the desire for experience (pleasure and power); the other is the desire for freedom. There comes a time in the life and history of an individual when the desire for freedom from the bondage of nature (limitation of consciousness) becomes manifest in the moral and aesthetic ideals of man and in his quest for Truth and Immortality. We dream of these in time, but dreams of the timeless Absolute can never be realized in time.

Mathematics cannot explain history and man's ideals. Maya or the universe is not logical. Mathematics is a development of logic. Logic is an invention of the practical mind of man for practical ends. And as we know, it does not apply to life and history.

Mathematics can calculate energy movements by equations, but as quantum physics demonstrates, the direction of energy is not strictly determined or predictable. Randomness prevails in history and evolution. Logic does not explain evolution of life and mind from matter because it divides nature artificially into matter and mind. Logic and mathematics are practical tools for managing life in the world.

The human heart is not satisfied with the practical. Demands of love outstrip the practical needs of the individual, his or her hunger and passion. Our dreams and ideals beckon us to Truth that is beyond time and the merely practical.

The practical world of competing individuals is a jungle where egos clash and which is somewhat relieved by conscience and aesthetic dreams. This is how Vivekananda described the nature of the practical world in reply to a friend who had written to him to be cautious in his criticism of false accusations made by Christian missionaries. Vivekananda wrote, "I hate the world, this dream, this horrible nightmare with its books and blackguardism, with its churches and chicaneries, with its fair faces and false hearts, with its howling righteousness on the surface and utter hollowness beneath, and above all its sanctified shopkeeping" (*Letters of Swami Vivekananda*, 3rd ed., p.212).

Practice of love takes us toward Reality. Love has therefore been described in the Upanishads, of which the Gita is the essence, as the origin of creation and as also the summit of consciousness (the Bliss of Brahman or the Bliss that is Brahman).

> 28. Beings are unmanifest in the beginning, they are manifest in the middle, they are unmanifest again after destruction. So, O Descendant of Bharata, (Arjuna)! what is there to lament about?
>
> 29. One looks upon it as a wonder, another speaks of it as a marvel, and another hears about it as a wonder, while some do not even understand it after hearing.
>
> 30. The Spirit which dwells in all bodies is eternal and can never be slain. O Descendant of Bharata (Arjuna)! You should not therefore grieve for anyone.
>
> 31. Even considering your vocation, you should not waver, for there is no higher good for a Kshatriya than a righteous war.
>
> 32. Only lucky Kshatriyas, O Partha (Arjuna)! come by without effort a war like this, which is like an open door to heaven.
>
> 33. Now if you do not fight this righteous war, you will incur sin for relinquishing your duty and honor.
>
> 34. Besides, people will dwell on your infamy forever. The disgrace of a person of honor is more painful than death.
>
> 35. The great warriors will assume that you have withdrawn from battle out of fear, and you will be poor in the estimation of those who thought much of you once.

36. Your enemies will also say many unspeakable words ridiculing your prowess. What can be more painful than that?

37. If you are slain in battle you will go to heaven, and if you win you will enjoy sovereignty. Therefore, O Son of Kunti (Arjuna)! arise, resolved to fight.

38. Treating alike pleasure and pain, gain and loss, victory and defeat, get ready for battle. Acting thus you will not incur sin.

39. This is the wisdom of Samkhya which has been imparted to you, O Partha (Arjuna)! Now listen to the understanding according to yoga, equipped with which you will cut the bondage of karma.

Buddhi or understanding or intellect is a key word in the spiritual philosophy of India. It is the faculty of knowledge. Pure understanding is intellect in the sense Plato and the ancients used it. Spinoza also hinted at it. It is intellect which is not discursive reasoning but which grasps the object immediately. The most immediate or purest understanding is Self-knowledge in which there is no distinction between the knower and the known. It is in this sense that Ramakrishna said that the pure buddhi or pure intellect was the same as the pure Self. Pure knowledge, the purest awareness, is pure Self in which the knower and the known are one.

It is in the above sense that buddhi or understanding has been called one or integral in the following verses. The yoga (integral) understanding is the understanding of one who engages in action with conviction that nature alone is acting, while the Self is above action. Man's true Self is above nature and its three gunas.

A higher perception is that all things, all distinctions are forms of consciousness.

The Samkhya understanding is the understanding of contemplatives who avoid action.

Samkhya here means Vedanta which briefly means that Reality is Brahman (Sat-Chit-Ananda, or Existence-Consciousness-Bliss), and that all creation is the active energy of that Reality.

THE YOGA OF WISDOM (SAMKHYA)

Yoga, literally meaning union or method of union with Reality, here means action, karma, as a means of knowing Reality. This is the dominant theme of the Gita; namely, how a life of action in the world can be a means for attaining wisdom without retiring from the world. Yoga in the traditional sense of pure contemplation is described in the sixth chapter.

There are, as Ramakrishna says, infinite ways to the Infinite. But broadly these ways have been classified into karma (action), bhakti (devotion), jnana (knowledge) and yoga (contemplation). These distinctions are not absolute; in practice they are combined in different degrees by the spiritual aspirant. For example, it is not possible to practice karma yoga or yoga of action without discrimination or devotion.

40. In this path no effort is lost and no fault is committed. Even a little of this practice saves one from great fear.

41. In this path understanding, O Descendant of the Kurus! is unvarying, while the understanding of unsteady persons is many-branched and endless.

Understanding is what is called intellect in Western philosophy.

42-43. Persons without discrimination are occupied with the ritualistic injunctions of the Vedas and deny all else. They are full of desires and eager to go to heaven. They say flowery words of praise about the complicated rituals which result in rebirth and which are the means of securing enjoyment and power.

44. Unwavering understanding does not come to those who are attached to enjoyment and power, whose mind has been stolen by them.

45. The ritualistic Vedas belong to the world of nature (the three gunas). Rise above nature and its dualities, be always steady and self-possessed, free from any desire for acquisition and preservation of gain.

In the verses above Veda stands for the ritualistic portion (*Karma Kanda*) of the vast literature called the Vedas. There is another portion of this literature called the *Jnana Kanda* (the portion on wisdom). The Gita is the essence of the Upanishads which are part of the portion on wisdom.

The three gunas are the three constituent principles of nature (prakriti). They are sattva, rajas and tamas. Sattva is the principle in nature which reveals the existence of objects. Perceptibility of things is due to sattva. Rajas is the principle of activity; tamas the principle of inertia or resistance which obscures.

The three principles always co-exist in different proportions in nature. Sattva, duration, is serenity which reflects pure existence of Spirit. Rajas clouds it by change, while tamas darkens it by dullness.

The element of sattva is dominant in mind, the element of rajas is dominant in life, while the element of tamas dominates in minerals and vegetation.

The gunas co-exist. There is no activity without resistance, no uninterrupted flow of energy in nature (cf., quanta, waves, photons); there is always a break. Matter is 'congealed' energy, though not absolutely congealed, for in that case nothing could exist (see Introduction).

46. For the wise Brahmin, all the Vedas are of as much use as a small reservoir when there is a flood everywhere.

Ritualistic actions are for persons who have cravings; to the seekers of Freedom they are of no use.

47. You have the right to action alone, never to its results. Do not desire results of action nor be attached to non-action.

A karma yogi acts in the world with the idea of service and not with the desire for personal gain. He is neither elated nor disheartened by results. Work is done in the spirit of worship. Such work purifies the mind; Truth is reflected in the purified mind. As the Gita points out in the next chapter, none can remain absolutely inactive.

The Yoga of Wisdom (Samkhya)

48. Being established in yoga and being the same in success and failure, work without attachment for evenness of mind is called yoga.

Man's ideal of action, which is the ideal of living, is given in the above verses.

Man's ideal is freedom from bondage, or the human condition of anxiety, fear and pain, of which the existentialists speak. The existentialists of our time, who trace their origin to Kierkegaard who used the word 'existence' to indicate the nature of the philosophical problem of man, point out the failure of centuries of philosophical thought in the West to give clear answers to civilized man's most pressing problems, which are moral — the values and directions of life; in short what a man should do and how he should live; has he a goal and so on.

This kind of thinking is not new, for philosophy began with these questions among thoughtful and successful men in India and also in Greece. For Socrates the important problem was the moral problem, for the solution of which one has to look into one's self ; know thyself (*atmanam biddhi; Gk., gnothi se auton*).

In the West science has dealt a mortal blow in our time to philosophical speculations about Truth and Reality and Value.

It is interesting to consider in this connection the opinion and observations of Einstein who started life with hope of devoting himself to religion but discarded it when he found the religion around him to be so unreal.

However he did not lose sight of his moral values and desire to know Reality. He admitted later that science was not enough for man and that he needed revelation for moral values.

Einstein was a kind of Brahmin in his moral character. He loved truth and simplicity; he was not attracted by success or other fleeting glamorous things of life. He admired Gandhi and had his picture in his study in Princeton with two others of important scientists.

Besides, Einstein was on the brink of discovering Reality. He was on the right track when he said that pure thought could reveal Reality.

He also had a kind of mystical experience and thought much of contemplation, though he never went beyond his belief in a deterministic universe. He had, despite his belief in dualism and determinism, glimpses of the ultimate Vedantic experience as will be seen from the following excerpts from his letters to Queen Elisabeth of Belgium at the beginning of the Nazi rampage in Germany.

"Still there are moments when one feels free from one's identification with human limitations and inadequacies. At such moments one imagines that one stands on some spot of a small planet, gazing in amazement at the cold yet profoundly moving beauty of the eternal, the unfathomable; life and death flow into one, and there is neither evolution nor destiny, only being."

And again: "Except for the newspapers and the countless letters, I would hardly be aware that I live in a time when human inadequacy and cruelty are achieving frightful proportions. Perhaps some day solitude will come to be properly recognized and appreciated as the teacher of personality. The Orientals have long known this. The individual who has experienced solitude will not easily become a victim of man's suggestions" (Jeremy Bernstein, *Life of Einstein*).

It is to the credit of existentialists that they have identified the true philosophical question. Some existentialists lacking intellectual guidance take a leap in the dark and embrace religion like Kierkegaard and Martin Buber; others, like Sartre and Jaspers, choose secular and moral goals. Anyway they have made it clear that life's important things are beyond intellectual discovery.

The ideal of karma yoga is based on the perception of Reality, the goal of man.

Action with selfish desire perpetuates the miserable condition of bondage. There are few morsels of pleasure in the world and much misery and our heart remains empty. We have to turn inward to find fulfillment, the ultimate togetherness that all of us seek.

The road is long but we have to begin. It is not easy but it may be so for some, for no law rules the Law-giver. In the world of commerce and selfish aims, people live like thieves being chased by policemen, as Vivekananda once said.

There is a way out for all. One does not have to retire from the world for salvation. One can erode the little self which obscures the Supreme Self or Reality by doing the kind of work one is doing but in a different spirit. That is why Krishna says karma yoga is skill in action.

Tolstoy came upon the secret of karma yoga because of his love of truth and compassion. He wrote, "The work you do out of love without a thought of reward is the work of God."

Later in the Gita, Krishna urges Arjuna to work like him; that is, like God, without a selfish motive and for the good of all.

There is some love everywhere, love that is disinterested. A mother works for love of the child. When one works with the idea of service in the spirit of worship without asking any reward, one works like God. True, only a free man can work in that spirit, but a spiritual seeker must begin. In time, the ideas of me and mine, the cause of bondage, vanish and the Truth manifests itself. Karma yoga begins at home. "Charity begins at home."

Karma yoga teaches how all work can be turned into an act of worship. It is said that French Premier Clemenceau (World War I) declared that had he known the secret of work taught in the Gita, his life of action would have been transformed into a life of worship.

49. Action with desire, O Dhananjaya (Arjuna)! is far inferior to action with understanding. Take refuge in understanding. Those who desire fruits of action are pitiful.

50. A person of understanding becomes free from good and evil even in this life. So practice yoga; yoga is skill in action.

Spinoza speaks of spiritual life as improvement of understanding.

51. Renouncing the results of action, wise persons of understanding become free from the bondage of rebirth and gain the untroubled state.

52. When your understanding overcomes your turbid delusion, then you will be indifferent to what has been heard and what is to be heard .

"What has been heard" refers to ritualistic religion in the mantra part of the Vedas.

53. When your understanding, distracted by the Vedic (ceremonial) texts, dwells firm and unwavering in the Self, then you will have wisdom.

ARJUNA SAID:

54. O Keshava (Krishna)! What are the marks of a person of steady wisdom who is established in superconsciousness? How does a person of steady understanding speak? How does he dwell, and how does he conduct himself?

THE BLESSED LORD SPOKE:

55. When, O Arjuna! a person gives up all the desires of mind and finds pleasure in the Self by the Self, he is said to be steady in wisdom.

56. One who is unworried amid sorrows, desireless amid pleasures and is without attachment, fear or anger is said to be a person of stable understanding.

57. He who is without attachment everywhere and who does not welcome or hate whether he experiences good or evil is a person of steady wisdom.

58. When a person withdraws the senses altogether from their objects just as a tortoise draws its limbs inward, then his wisdom is steady.

59. Objects recede from an individual who starves the senses even though there is no loss of craving for them, but even the craving is lost when the Supreme is seen.

60. O Son of Kunti (Arjuna)! Even the mind of a discerning and striving individual is forcibly stolen away by the turbulent senses.

61. Restraining them all the yogi should remain devoted to me; he whose senses are under control is a person of steady wisdom.

62-63. Dwelling on sense-objects a person becomes attached to them; from attachment comes desire, from desire anger, from anger delusion, from delusion loss of remembrance, from loss of remembrance loss of understanding, and from loss of understanding he perishes.

64. But a disciplined individual whose senses roam under control among the objects of sense, free from both attachment or aversion, attains peace of mind.

65. All his sorrows end upon attaining peace of mind, for the understanding of a peaceful mind becomes steady quickly.

66. A person without concentration has no understanding, nor does he have contemplation. How can he who is not peaceful be happy?

67. Among the roving senses, the one which the mind follows steals away the understanding of a person just as the wind sets a boat adrift in water.

68. Therefore, O Mighty-armed One! he whose senses have recoiled in every way from their objects is a person of steady wisdom.

69. That which is night to all beings — in that, the sage of vision is awake. That in which all beings are awake is night for the sage.

The enlightened sage, one who is liberated from egoistic consciousness, perceives Reality (Truth-Consciousness -Bliss) beyond maya, the relative, temporal world of egos and their objects; while the unenlightened person considers maya, or the universe of change and plurality, as real and objective. The enlightened person perceives the temporal existence as the moving image of eternity (Plato). Brahman, Paramatman and indivisible Truth-Consciousness-Bliss are terms which indicate the untrammelled Existence, the 'Emptiness' of the Buddha, the still waters of creation (karana salila), the source of limitless universes, like the innumerable waves in the ocean, which are all ideas or imaginations of the Cosmic Mind (cf. Plato).

The many universes of which modern mathematicians and cosmologists speculate, and of which the ancient Hindu scriptures speak, are the freaks of the creative energy of the Real conceived as Mother of the Universes (*Magna Mater*) or Time (*Kali*). Matter, life and mind are all gross and subtle aspects of this conscious and living Power.

There is only one body, one life, one mind and one personality. All individuals are parts of that personality, the *Mahamaya*, the Great Enchantress, Mother of Universes, gross and subtle. Creation is her game. The human condition of pain and suffering is due to ignorance. Freedom and bliss and eternal life belong to all essentially. Spiritual practices are for breaking a bad dream.

According to the view current in the West, nature is the play of physical energy. But nature is much more than the vibrations of physics. Life and mind are in nature. Nature is the active power of Spirit (*Mahakala*). We are all parts of that Personality. "We live and move and have our being in God" (from the speech of St. Paul at Areopagus in Athens, quoting the belief of Stoics and Cynics that all was God).

> 70. Just as the ocean stands still like a rock though waters flow into it, even so the person in whom all desires are lost attains peace, but not so the desirer of desires.
>
> 71. Giving up all desires, the person who lives without craving and without a sense of me and mine attains eternal peace.
>
> 72. This, O Arjuna! is called the poise of Brahman; no one who gains this is ever deluded. Even if one attains this understanding at death, he merges in Brahman (eternal life).

The Yoga of Action (Karma Yoga)

ARJUNA SAID:

1. **O Janardana (Krishna)! If you consider wisdom superior to work, then why do you commit me to this terrible action?**

Earlier in the second chapter Krishna spoke highly of action, while later at the end he extolled the unwavering poise in Brahman which is commonly supposed to be attained by contemplation alone. Arjuna sees a difficulty, which is the common misperception that action is opposed to contemplation.

2. You seem to confuse my understanding with words of mixed intent. Tell me decisively that alone by which I can attain the highest (shreyas).

There are two broad, basic human goals: *preyas* and *shreyas* (the pleasant and the good, cf. Socrates). This good is the Supreme Good and not the relative good of the world, which is pleasant. The highest good, the *summum bonum*, is called shreyas in Sanskrit.

3. O Blessed One (Arjuna)! In days of yore I spoke of two ways of devotion in the world: the path of knowledge for men of contemplation and the yoga of action for men of action.

Contemplatives who meditate discriminate between the eternal and the transient (the real and the unreal), while those who are active perform duty without a selfish motive. The goal is the same. The distinctive paths are a matter of emphasis due to differences in human nature. The two paths join in the end.

4. A person does not gain freedom from action merely by refraining from action, nor does one attain perfection through mere renunciation of action.

The Self that is beyond all action is not realized by mere outward renunciation of action. Action as such does not produce Self-knowledge; action with detachment purifies the mind, which reflects Truth.

5. No one can stay even for a moment without action. All are driven to work helplessly by the forces of nature.

There is no freedom as long as a person thinks he *has* to act.

6. The fool who restrains the organs of action but keeps dwelling in his mind on sense-objects is called a hypocrite.

7. But, O Arjuna! he who controls his senses by the mind and engages in the yoga of action with the organs of action only and without attachment is superior.

8. Perform works that have been enjoined (by the scriptures); action is superior to non-action. Even your physical life cannot be maintained without work.

THE YOGA OF ACTION (KARMA YOGA)

9. Except for work done as a sacrifice, action in this world creates bondage. Therefore, O Son of Kunti (Arjuna)! act without attachment in the spirit of sacrifice.

10. At creation, Brahma (the creator), having created the living beings along with sacrifice, said: May you grow by this (sacrifice); let this be like the cow which yields the milk of your desires.

The Gita gives a wider meaning to the idea of sacrifice than that which is enjoined in the work-portion of the Vedas as a means of gaining many kinds of desired results.

To the karma yogi, whose goal is freedom of self from the bondage of nature, all action is worship and is not for gain in the world or beyond. Life's ideal is continuous sacrifice of the little self of desires.

11. Propitiate the gods with this sacrifice, and let the gods foster you. Serving one another in this manner you will attain the Supreme Good.

12. Propitiated by your sacrifice the gods will give you the enjoyments you desire. Truly he is a thief who enjoys the gifts of gods without returning them to the gods.

13. The good people who eat food that was offered as sacrifice become free from all sins, but those evil people who cook only for themselves eat sin.

14. Living beings have their origin in food; food comes from rain; rain originates in sacrifice; and sacrifice originates from action.

15. Action originates from nature (Brahma); nature originates from the Imperishable Spirit; therefore, the all-pervading Spirit is ever present in sacrifice.

Brahman means both *Saguna* (with gunas) and *Nirguna* (without gunas) Brahman. Saguna Brahman is the conscious creative

Chapter Three

energy manifesting this universe and countless others. It is nature (prakriti) in the comprehensive sense of a Personality producing the grades of being which are distinguished as matter, life and mind. The emergence of distinctions out of Nirguna Brahman (pure Spirit) is a mystery for intellect, a created thing. Tagore, the renowned Bengali poet, wrote, "Creation is a mystery; it is dark like the night; delusions of knowledge are like fog in the morning." It is inscrutable magic.

Pure Spirit is Nirguna Brahman, the Reality which can only be hinted at as something beyond the duality of ego and its objects, but it can never be grasped by reason or indicated by language for they belong in the world of creation, the world of dualities. One can say facetiously, but not truly, that Reality or Nirguna Brahman is the "emptiness" on the other side of the "Big Bang!"

Creation is a process in time. The experience of change co-exists with ideas of dimensions and ideas of cause and effect. There cannot be any time or space without motion. The past is a memory, the future an anticipation of events. The past and the future have no other location except in the mind. Time (change) is the dream of the Great Dreamer.

The idea of space is derived from experience of motion, an event in time. Without experience of change there cannot be any idea of space. When mind stops, time and space and the entire universe relapse into Reality. Outwardly this is imagined as the collapse of the universe of time and space and change into some kind of "singularity" which is the imagination of mathematicians and which is nothing but some idea of emptiness or incomprehensible existence where the universe of motion retires into some kind of sleep.

In Samkhya and Vedanta philosophy, time and space are called *vikalpas* i.e., concepts which are empty but useful for structuring experience. Just as we use a piece of string to tie together a bundle of loose papers, so also we use in language concepts which are empty but which are needed to put together bits of perception for purposes of communication. Space and time are such ideal concepts without an objective basis; they are not percepts or sense impressions. We cannot understand motion without a container. Similarly, there are verbs which are vikalpas which we use not to denote action but stasis, e.g., we say a chair is standing there, or a book is sitting on the table and so on, where no action is meant on the part of the chair or the book.

All that we regard as the history of an individual and of the cosmos is a process in the universal mind. Matter, life and mind are sort of different grades of processes, subtle and gross vibrations which obscure and diversify the one Spirit, the Essence, the Reality of all.

The best way to indicate the indescribable mystery of creation is to say that as the Spirit opens its eyes to look outside, the universes jump into view, and as it closes its eyes, they dissolve into emptiness or nothing.

The universe, history and time and individuals are all in the imagination of the cosmic mind or its dreams. When the dream breaks, the ego disappears with its problems and the mortal man becomes immortal, awakening to his innate Freedom and Eternity — the ideals which we vainly pursue in time. In modern physics the subjective element or consciousness is intruding more and more into the region which was not so long ago regarded as objective. That is why scientists are saying that consciousness is fundamental, that it is original (Max Planck). Some are also saying that there is no objective reality, that nature is like an "Alice in wonderland" dream, a figment of the imagination. Many years ago Vivekananda in his lectures on Vedanta compared the universe with the dream of Alice in order to convey to the audience the theory of maya.

In Reality, there is no process and no evolution. The height of religion is to attain this perception.

The Personal God, the object of love and devotion, does not disappear from our world of relationships. Vedanta proclaims He or She is the only Person. His or Her will governs all that is, and He or She can grant us freedom by His or Her Grace. Vedanta does not do away with devotional worship.

The best way to conceive Reality and manifestation is to imagine it as a vast ocean on the surface of which waves play. Water is both still and active in the ocean (Ramakrishna). Correct imagination is the door to realization (Vivekananda).

CHAPTER THREE

Pure Spirit as mentioned earlier is pure Love-Existence-Truth (*Sachchidananda*). God is the essence of ineffable love. We become God-like as our love becomes deeper and broader. This is spiritual progress, realization of the innate drive in us for freedom and bliss.

We work in the world for gain. But if work corrupts our spirit and brings no love or joy or feeling of freedom in our heart and does not allay our fears, what good is work? True, material possessions and sense-pleasures are tempting, but if they are gained at the cost of integrity, they may inflate the ego and give one a sense of power; however, they do not cure us of our anxieties and fears. An individual who loves money and power sells his soul for a mess of pottage.

Sir Sarvepalli Radhakrishnan was appointed India's ambassador to Moscow by Pandit Jawaharlal Nehru, free India's first prime minister. Stalin was at the time head of the Communist party and the Soviet government. Stalin believed in power and relied on it. On one occasion Stalin told Radhakrishnan that India should strive hard to gain power quickly. To this Radhakrishnan replied quoting the Bible, "For what doth it profit a man, if he gain the whole world, and suffer the loss of his own soul?" (Matt. 16:26). Stalin did not reply and remained silent. Stalin surely recalled the words of Christ, for as a young man he had been a student in a seminary in Georgia. (I heard this story from Swami Ranganathananda of the Ramakrishna Mission to whom Radhakrishnan had related it. The Swami had been in Moscow to lecture on Vedanta.)

Hardly anybody knew what went through Stalin's mind. But his daughter Svetlana became deeply interested in Indian spirituality early in life. In a letter which she wrote to me she said that she became "acquainted with Indian thought" when she was a school girl of seventeen. She later became interested in Ramakrishna and Vivekananda and was influenced enough to write the following at the end of her letter, "I still believe as I have already said here, that 'all religions are true'. I believe people should not try to oppose one form of religion to another one. The main thing is not that. The main thing is to find the best way for oneself to behave in this difficult and controversial life. And finding this way

— or these ways — the Hindoo philosophy has done a lot of good to me. And this is the origin which can never exhaust."

Karma yoga is the right spirit of work. It cannot be practiced without a deep understanding of human nature and its goal, and without purification of mind through spiritual striving. The ultimate human search is the search within.

> 16. The person, O Partha (Arjuna)! who does not follow this ordained wheel of action is sinful and addicted to sense-pleasures. He lives in vain.
>
> 17. But for the person who delights in the Self alone, who is happy with the Self and satisfied with it, there remains nothing to be done.
>
> 18. There is no reason at all for him in this world to engage in action or to refrain from it. Nor does he depend in the least on anyone for any reason.
>
> 19. Therefore perform duty always without attachment. Doing work without attachment, a person attains the Supreme Goal.
>
> 20. King Janaka and others gained perfection through work alone. You should engage in action considering also the good of humanity.

Religion is thought by many to be a selfish preoccupation with one's salvation and not only an asocial but also an irrational preoccupation.

This superstition was propagated by so-called rationalists like Freud and Marx in modern times in the West.

Many in the West believed that Freud and Marx with their beliefs in the dogmas of the nineteenth century science cornered the market on the understanding of man and civilization. The evil consequences of such belief are apparent in the collapse of order in individual and social life, in increasing violence, neurosis and drug habits.

The modern age of Europe ushered in by intellectual and scientific developments and prosperity due to conquest and exploitation of colonies in the East is characterized by disbelief in the stories of the *Old Testament* and in religion in general. Secular thinkers in the West, led by England, have since then tried to build ethical theories on the basis of social need and self-interest. This trend continues into today and we have theories of conduct based on selfishness, social need and biological determination. This is secular or relativistic ethics.

These theories do not explain the ethical impulse of man. It is obvious to a perceptive person that kindness and love are products neither of cold calculation nor of individual or group interest.

In the last century Thomas Huxley, a Darwinian, sought to justify ethics on grounds of social need. There has not been any more advance on that argument since then.

Tolstoy wrote a devastating reply to Mr. Huxley's position, which will always be a good one to secular theorists of morals and humanism. It is also a comment on how far a modern man is from realization of a truly ethical society. I quote from his essay on *Religion and Morality:*

Whence this ethical process came Mr. Huxley does not explain, but in Note 19 he says that the basis of this process consists in the fact that men, as well as animals, prefer on the one hand, to live in a society, and therefore smother within themselves such propensities as are pernicious to societies, and, on the other hand the members of societies crush by force such actions as are prejudicial to the welfare of society. Mr. Huxley thinks that this process, which compels men to control their passions for the preservation of that association to which they belong, and the fear of punishment should they break the rules of that association, composes that very ethical law which it behoves him to prove.

It evidently appears to Mr. Huxley, in the innocence of his mind, that in English society of our time, with its Irish destitution, its insane luxury of the rich, its trade in opium and spirits, its executions, its sanguinary wars, its extermination of entire nations for the sake of commerce and policy, its secret vice and hypocrisy — it appears to him that a man who does not overstep police regulations is a moral man, and that such a man is guided

The Yoga of Action (Karma Yoga)

by an ethical process. Mr. Huxley seems to forget that those personal qualities which may be needful to prevent the destruction of that society in which its member lives, may be of service to the society itself, and that personal qualities of the members of a band of brigands are also useful to the band; as also, in our society, we find a use for hangmen, jailers, judges, soldiers, false-pastors, etc., but that the qualities of these men have nothing in common with morality.

Some have also thought that the heart of religion is its ethical practice. Such people, rejecting what they thought was purely a dream, namely religion, originated ethical societies and raised slogans of moral rearmament. They are to be commended for what they do. But in this relativistic world of science and values they fail to provide an ideal that is absolute. Without faith in an ideal and without practice based on an ideal, so-called rationalistic, relativistic ethics do not carry a person very far toward improvement of personal conduct or society or betterment of international relations.

Brotherhood of man and oneness of creation are not empty slogans, but truths based upon spiritual perception.

Ethical action arises from largeness or purity of heart. When the heart becomes free of the desires of the little self, it reflects Reality. The *Bible* says, "Blessed are the pure in heart for they shall see God." We all want God whether or not we are able to grasp the idea. The truth of the goal dwells in the heart. That goal, the ethical ideal or the spiritual goal, cannot be attained without faith and without effort based on it.

It is true that eager spiritual seekers often live away from society and family to be intensely active in realizing Truth, just as artists, scholars and scientists sometimes shun people to remain absorbed in their work. Christ withdrew from the world for thirteen years. Buddha left home and family and the world for years before he started the first missionary activity in the world. So did Muhammad. But they all came back to society from the seclusion of contemplation and started movements that created great civilizations by bringing people together in the pursuit of a common faith, a common ideal for the community.

◆ 86 ◆

The idea of service goes with the practice of religion. Christian missionaries often ridiculed Hinduism as devoid of social content. They did not understand the true spirit of religion, nor were they acquainted with India's history and also they saw in the dark days of India a caricature of religion in many places. Further, a sense of superiority made them think that they were better than the natives, though their lips preached the fatherhood of God and equality of men.

Karma yoga is the ideal of service. It is much more than what is commonly understood in the West as ethical action. Ultimately and in the absolute sense, as Plato also pointed out, Truth, Goodness, and Beauty are all one. This is the Greek version of Sat-Chit-Ananda. The moral, rational and aesthetic ideals are one in the end.

This verse also indicates that practical Vedanta originated in ancient India with philosopher-kings like Janaka.

21. In a society, whatever the best does, the others follow; whatever he sets up as the standard, the people imitate.

We learn by imitation. We imitate what we love. Thomas a Kempis, author of *Imitation of Christ* became a saint by imitating his Master.

22. O Partha (Arjuna)! In the three worlds there is nothing I have to do, nothing that I may seek, nothing that I do not have, yet I am engaged in action.

The ideal of life in the world is God-like action — action with freedom. The three worlds are the higher, the middle and the lower worlds of existence.

Ideal activity is the creative activity of the artist who creates out of delight and love of the Beautiful. It is like the dancing of a person out of sheer delight, the pure joy of existence. God, the Creator, is called Kavi (the poet or artist) in the Vedas. Creation is the dance of Shiva (creator) out of pure delight.

This is the ideal of the karma yogi who serves out of love without a thought of reward. One thus realizes one's divinity and freedom.

The Yoga of Action (Karma Yoga)

23. If I, O Partha! did not remain engaged in action untiringly, then men would follow my example in every way.

People do not attain perfection or peace of mind by mere outward renunciation of action or by so-called retirement at any time.

24. All the worlds will cease to exist if I do not act. I will be the cause of confusion of order and of the destruction of all beings.

The universe of change is the activity of the living God in perfect freedom. This activity, which is play, does not limit God's freedom. Activity does not necessarily create bondage.

25. The wise person, O Descendant of Bharata (Arjuna)! who desires the welfare of the world should act without attachment, even as the unwise act with attachment.

The wise person is free from the bondage of nature. He acts freely, without compulsion, out of love for all. When he acts, he sees God acting through him. The unwise thinks mistakenly, due to ego-sense, that he acts and is therefore subject to results of actions.

The wise, the liberated person, who has gained everything, the summum bonum, has no need for action. But Krishna, the Divine Ruler of the universe, says that higher still is the ideal of Divine Action. Ramakrishna said the same thing to Vivekananda who wanted to remain absorbed in Divine Bliss. He told him that there was a higher state than that. That is what Vivekananda came to follow —imitation of God.

26. The wise should not unsettle the minds of the ignorant who are attached to action, but should engage them in action by performing all action well, with detachment.

The enlightened individual who instructs the unenlightened aspirants by word of mouth alone may not be understood by those who have not secured a firm hold on the spirit of karma yoga. It is easy to slip from the path without guidance.

Also some ignorant persons may think that by refraining from action as the wise do they may attain perfection and peace. This is what the Gita means by unsettling the understanding of the unwise — by mere instruction without an example. People may easily slip from the right spirit of work consonant with civilized life without a leader who inspires by both word and action (cf. Gandhi).

The work-ethic of America to which politicians sometimes allude is somewhat akin in spirit to karma yoga. But even here it is easy to slip from that idea when there are no longer good practitioners of work-ethic, as in the earlier days of belief and dedicated individuals.

27. A person deluded by egoism thinks he is the actor when all actions are performed by the gunas of prakriti (constituents of nature).

Body, life, mind, ego, all belong to nature. Pure Spirit is opposed to it. As Shankara says in his introduction to the Vedanta sutras, "Spirit and nature are opposed to each other like light and darkness."

The goal of man is to realize his true Self which is beyond time and change. One has to remember constantly in reading the Gita that nature (prakriti) is not just physical motion but the play of the Supreme Personality of which the gross, the thickest part, is physical nature. All changes are the actions of an active personality. The ego which reflects this truth feels itself to be an instrument. It becomes the servant ego and reflects the Spirit beyond nature.

Prakriti in Sanskrit is the same word as procreatrix in Latin from which the word creation is derived. Nature is all that has life, body and mind.

It is necessary to remember at the beginning, though the Gita will come to it later, that the Personal God is the highest truth in maya. Personal God is the Inner Ruler, the guide and friend through whose worship and grace the individual in bondage realizes his freedom.

28. But the person, O Great Warrior! who knows the truth about the distinction between Self and the gunas does not become attached, thinking that the gunas (sense-organs) are occupied with the gunas (sense-objects).

The idea is that in all action some elements of nature are occupied with other elements. In action, mind and sense-organs are occupied with sense-objects, that is the gunas are occupied with gunas. The enlightened person knows that the Self is not acting, while the deluded one thinks that he is acting.

29. Persons deluded by the gunas (elements) of nature (prakriti) become attached to the sense-organs and their objects. The all-knowing wise man should not unsettle the minds of those who are poor of understanding and who know little.

It is the 'I' sense, the sense of me and mine, which is the cause of bondage. It is a mysterious appearance and eludes all search. To get rid of it is, as Vivekananda said, like lifting oneself with one's bootstraps, or like jumping out of one's skin. Therefore, those who have become free say that it is through the grace of the Guru, the Teacher, that one becomes free.

The Upanishads also declare that the one whom the Self chooses becomes free. But, "Grace is like the wind that blows for all, always," as Ramakrishna said. We have only to unfurl the sail to catch the wind.

It is the grace of the Supreme Personality, the creator of all, the Father, or better yet the Great Mother (Magna Mater), who has produced all the creatures, has built into them tendencies, one outward for enjoyment of objects, another the drive upward for freedom. Sooner or later the drive for freedom gains momentum as worldly experiences fail to satisfy the senseless, unlimited demands of the ego as it is buffeted endlessly by pain and sorrow due to disease, old age, death, bereavements and failures of all kinds.

Our spiritual effort in the beginning is a slow inching forward toward death of the ego and also occasionally falling backward.

CHAPTER THREE

When, however, dissatisfaction with the dreadful unreality of the world becomes intense as in the case of heroic seekers, the race is swift and freedom is at hand.

As Vyasa says in his commentary on the *Yoga Aphorisms of Patanjali*, freedom is at hand for those who have the swiftest momentum. But everyone, says the Vedantin, will attain freedom one day. "None will remain hungry," says Ramakrishna, "everyone will be fed, but some will have to wait till evening." No one need despair, for the sage in the Upanishads declares that all are children of the Immortal Bliss. Freedom is the divine right of man.

The Gita teaches in endless ways how to approach the Supreme Truth in thought and deed. Finally when realization comes, the ego vanishes with all its problems.

To get rid of the illusion of the ego is the goal of religion. This is the meaning of the saying that those who long for eternal life have to die to this life. Religion can be defined in innumerable ways. Essentially it is love of death — death of the little self or ego. Here I want to record a memorable event which occurred in 1951.

Swami Nikhilananda of the Ramakrishna Order had invited Count Armand de Richelieu, who was descended from the line of the famous Cardinal Richelieu, known as the Grey Eminence of France, to the Ramakrishna-Vivekananda Center in New York City for lunch. I was there along with others.

The Count, who was nearly eighty years old, came with his fourth wife, an American, who was many years younger. The Count said that when Vivekananda was in Paris he used to attend his classes regularly. But the Count always sat in the last row for he did not want to be noticed. One day, after several sessions, when the class ended, the Count was leaving quietly by the door when Vivekananda suddenly appeared in front of him, and holding him by the hand said, "Young man, I have noticed that you have been attending my talks regularly. I can give you something, if you want it."

"What is it Swami?" the Count said. "I can give you love of death," Vivekananda replied. "Love of death!" said the Count surprised, "What shall I do with love of death?" The Count continued, "I have youth, I have health and I have wealth. I want to enjoy life. What do I do with love of death?"

The Yoga of Action (Karma Yoga)

The Swami, the Count recalled, did not press him further, but only said, "You will one day know what I mean and will want it."

The Count then told us that after long years (he had met the Swami in the late nineties of the last century), he had understood what the Swami meant, but alas, he was gone and the opportunity lost!

Love of death is the death wish of the ego, the spiritual goal. Religion is the call to eternity. Even a distant glimpse of it, as the Gita says, saves one from great fear.

> **30. Ascribing all work to me, with the mind dwelling on the Self, fight without desire, without a sense of me and mine, and without sorrow.**

Krishna, the Divine Incarnation, asks Arjuna to ascribe all work to him, the Personal God of creation, and fix his mind on the impersonal Self.

> **31. Those men of faith who follow this doctrine of mine always and without demur also become free from the bondage of works.**
>
> **32. But know those who decry this and who do not follow my word to be devoid of all understanding, lost and mindless.**
>
> **33. Even an enlightened individual works according to his nature. Beings follow their nature; what can repression accomplish?**

Nature here means the inherited tendencies of the past which become manifest in the present life of an individual. They run their course, but the person who becomes free is not affected by them.

"Repression" in the verse above means the forcible suppression of all the activities of the sense-organs. Physical hunger and thirst belong to the body and continue as long as the present body lasts, but they do not bind the enlightened. It is the cravings in the mind and identification of Self with them which is the cause of bondage. The following verse makes it clear.

34. Feelings of love and hate reside in the sense-organs in regard to their objects. Do not come under their power, for they are enemies of the aspirant after Freedom.

Knowledge or Enlightenment comes from drawing the mind away from the roving senses and turning it toward the conscious spirit, the Self which is within. When the mind ceases running outward and stops altogether without being agitated by outward desires, the pure Spirit, the Real Man becomes self-revealed, free and blissful.

35. Better is one's vocation though faulty than another's well-performed. It is better to die following one's vocation. The vocation of another is fraught with danger.

As human society develops there is division of labor. People are born with different aptitudes and talents, and they serve best when they follow their natural bent. This idea crystallized in early Indian society when the members of the community became divided into four broad classes according to their natural talents and abilities: the Brahmins (priests), the Kshatriyas (warriors), the Vaishyas (tradesmen) and the Shudras (menials).

One performs best when one follows one's nature. And no matter what one's profession is one can, by doing one's duty honestly, advance spiritually and gain freedom. Each is great in his own place; that is, one who performs his duty, defined by his station in life, in the right spirit is able to reach the ultimate goal of freedom. All work no matter how low it may look in the estimation of the ignorant can be a means of spiritual development.

In his later years Tolstoy wrote some fables which expressed this deep truth. One of these great short stories portrays the life of a shoe-maker who was honest and not greedy and who turned out beautiful shoes with complete devotion to work to the best of his ability.

In his writing on karma yoga Vivekananda mentions that a dutiful shoe-maker who turns out a fine pair of shoes with complete devotion to work alone is as great as a dutiful king on the throne. It is honest work which builds character. The aim of spiritual discipline is to build character. A man of character does not sell himself for a mess of pottage.

Arjuna was a warrior by vocation. He was urged to respond to his terrible duty without personal feelings.

ARJUNA SAID:

36. How then, O Varshneya (Krishna)! does a person commit sin as if driven forcibly to it even against his will?

THE BLESSED LORD SAID:

37. It is desire, it is anger born of the passionate element in nature, insatiable and fierce. Know this to be the enemy here (in the world).

38. As fire is enveloped by smoke, as a mirror is covered by dust, and as an embryo is covered by the womb, in the same manner discrimination is obscured by passion.

39. O Son of Kunti (Arjuna)! Wisdom is enveloped by this insatiable desire, the constant foe of the wise.

40. The sense-organs, the mind and the intellect are said to be its seat. Through these, desire deludes the embodied spirit and obscures wisdom.

41. Therefore, O Best among the Bharatas (Arjuna)! restraining the sense-organs first, slay this sinful destroyer of wisdom and discrimination.

42. The sense-organs, they say, are superior (to their objects). Mind is superior to the sense-organs. Intellect is higher than mind, while the Self is superior to intellect.

43. Thus knowing, O Mighty-armed One! the One beyond the intellect and restraining the self by the Self, slay the redoubtable enemy in the form of desire.

CHAPTER THREE

In the above verses an analysis of the embodied self is given following the description in the *Katha Upanishad*. An individual is analyzed into body, sense-organs (both of action and perception), mind, intellect and Spirit. The body is like a chariot, the horses are the sense-organs, the reins are the mind and the intellect is the charioteer, while the rider is the Self. Plato analyzes the individual similarly, but not so elaborately.

Passion belongs to nature and is born of rajas, the active element in it. As the serene or calm element (sattva) comes to dominate the mind, the awareness that Self is separate from the body-mind complex develops and the power of control increases. It is by looking up or deep inside that the power of control increases. This is prayer, development of the power inherent in us by appealing to God within. This is activity too. But this activity, or rajas, is the activity counter to the activity of desire for objects outside.

Vedanta proclaims that every man has infinite power within him which is manifested through faith and practice. Civilized societies assume that the power to reform belongs to all or almost all who break the law. That is why punishment is called correction. But what is called correction is mostly suppression; the aggressive and predatory instincts lurk in the psyche. True, it is believed that harmful tendencies can be given a positive direction, but there is in general no philosophy to inspire the gradual eradication of the pleasure principle of greed and lust, which is the root of all troubles.

To some, suppression of the pleasure principle which is inherent in an individual is at the root of the "discontents of civilization" (Freud). They mention love, but it is not selfless, nor does it appear to be very different from a nervous condition such as obsession.

Vedanta asserts that all self-regarding tendencies derive from the superstition that the individual is an ultimate fact. The desire for pleasure covers the truth of man. At one end, love is almost entirely physical and the unity transient. At the other, it is pure and spiritual and permanent. At one end, it is narrow and it creates bondage. At the other, when it is free from passion, it is freedom and liberation. At one end, the togetherness is transient and goes with fear, anxiety, jealousy, hope, etc. At the other, it is free, clean, pure and whole.

The institution of marriage and family life in civilized societies is a step toward the goal of freeing love from its impurities, pure feeling from turgid passion, and gold from alloy.

CHAPTER FOUR

The Yoga
of Knowledge
(Jnana Yoga)

THE BLESSED LORD SAID:

 I announced this imperishable yoga to Vivas-van; Vivasvan spoke it to Manu and Manu to Ikshvaku.

Imperishable yoga here means the path of action combined with wisdom. The teaching was handed down in different ages by a line of teachers, royal sages or philosopher kings.

2. The royal sages, O Tormentor of Enemies! knew this yoga which was handed down from one to another. It was lost in the vast expanse of time.

3. You are my devotee and friend, so I will communicate this yoga, the supreme secret, to you today.

The Hindus call their religion Sanatana Dharma or Eternal Religion. Hinduism was a name given to the religious beliefs and practices of the Indian people by foreigners.

There is only one religion of man which may be called man's return journey to Reality or Truth. The so-called different religions or opinions or creeds are different ways of reaching the one goal.

THE YOGA OF KNOWLEDGE (JNANA YOGA)

The creeds are not the Truth, but different paths leading to the same and one goal. There are infinite ways of reaching the same goal (Ramakrishna).

There are cycles of creation and of civilization. The Teacher (Krishna in the case of the Gita) comes again and again in each cycle.

ARJUNA SAID:

4. Your birth is later; Vivasvan was born earlier. How can I understand that you spoke this yoga to Vivasvan (the Sun God) in the beginning (of creation)?

In the following four verses (5-8), Krishna propounds the philosophy of history and the fact of Divine Power stepping down onto the stage of human civilization when it falters in its ascent toward its moral goal.

There are two broad movements in nature (dualities called *dvanda* in Sanskrit, *yin* and *yang* in Chinese), one progressive, another atavistic. Science helps man to gain practical ends but does not illuminate human life. For this reason, Einstein said that science is not enough; we need revelation. Revelation can only mean revelation of some moral truth or the spiritual goal of man.

The goal of evolution is to manifest the truth of man in history. Evolutionists tell us that evolution is a random process — a sudden inexplicable emergence of new qualities and powers in life. But we can see a 'method' in this randomness. There are in time higher and higher manifestations of life and intelligence out of dormant, inconscient, sleeping existence. Evolutionists do not know the origin nor the mechanism nor the goal of evolution. It is, according to yoga and Vedanta, the progressive manifestation of spirit in history. Its goal is the enlightened individual, the philosopher (in the Platonic sense), the saint, the free person.

Civilizations which cease to progress by manifesting the higher moral truths die, and the torch is carried on by another which incorporates in its society the higher values. Higher civilizations are those which express in their constitutions and social life the deeper truths of man. "Thy kingdom come, Thy will be done, here on earth as it is in heaven" (Luke 11, 2) is the aspiration of a spiritual person, the aspiration to reflect the spiritual truth of unity in the world of human relationships — spiritual togetherness of man. Some large-hearted political leaders are inspired by the ideal of humanity, a reflection in time of the spiritual truth of man.

But time tarnishes everything. As society becomes complex and love of pleasure and money becomes dominant, people are diverted from the original inspiring truths. It is on such occasions that the Ruler of the human mind, the Power that governs history, steps down on its stage to redeem humanity. The redeeming Power manifests itself in human form as the Guru, the Teacher, who collects round him a band of disciples to turn again the wheel of righteousness. It is this creative minority which sets the standards of life which become incorporated into the constitutions of societies according to the capabilities of their members.

Krishna points out, as did the Buddha and other incarnations of divine power, that they appear in times when civilizations are in crisis. Incarnations put derailed civilizations back on the track.

Incarnations also come specially to redeem those who yearn for Truth amid encircling falsehoods.

Krishna says that God also destroys. The world is a mixture of good and evil. The changing world never becomes perfect. Perfection is beyond time, beyond good and evil. Vedanta says that Perfection is already in man. The dualities of good and evil are in maya. There is no perfection in history till it winds up.

We are often worried by the presence of evil in a world governed by God. But one cannot have a world without good and evil. You cannot have a good story or creation without a villain in it. And sometimes God sends someone to punish evildoers, said Ramakrishna, just as a landowner sometimes sends a tough superintendent to bring order to his domain ravaged by evil tenants.

THE BLESSED LORD SAID:

5. O Arjuna, the Tormentor of Enemies! Many lives of mine as well as of yours have gone by. I know them all, but you do not.

The Yoga of Knowledge (Jnana Yoga)

6. Though I am birthless and the Lord of creatures and my Self never changes, yet controlling my own nature I incarnate myself by my power.

Divine Incarnation is a mystery. The Power, the Personality that governs the universe, the Power that is All in All, reveals itself in the created world of maya, the region of "the many and the variable," in human form. The limited form is in maya and obeys the laws of maya ostensibly, but within it there is consciousness of the Supreme Personality who can bestow freedom on others by a glance, by a touch, by its will.

Such a Personality appears in the world through immaculate conception like Krishna, Buddha, Christ and Ramakrishna. Behind the appearance of the limited human being there is consciousness of the unlimited knowledge and power of the Supreme Personality.

Incarnations of God come with awareness of their historic mission. They make it known in many ways. They come to set in motion again the wheel of spiritual evolution in the new situation of history. Some of their intimate disciples become aware of it, and they dedicate their life for the master's work.

It is a fact of history that despite scriptures and writs, priests and temples, religion gets tarnished and materialism rears its head, now and then relying on the half-truths of cock-sure practical science and being lured to hedonism by a false sense of security. Good and idealistic people in such a society long for help. It is for their sake, as well as for history, that the Divine becomes manifest in time.

Language cannot explain creation or Divine Incarnation or prove God, for all proof and methods of proof beg a world of multiplicity or duality. But it is a fact that Divine Power manifests itself in history and shapes it. There comes in history in a time of crisis in civilization a great leader with a band of followers to turn mankind away from destruction, sorrow and suffering, and from relapsing back into chaos. He lays down moral laws for man's ascent to freedom. These laws are more or less expressed in social and political institutions, in taboos and constitutions.

Why this game? No logic can explain what is beyond duality and logic. But it is a 'fact' that we tire of the game of the world and want to go home. We aspire after an ideal, after freedom and love and eternal life, which are not to be found here on earth. Vedanta says the realization of freedom is a matter of knowledge, a matter of discarding the illusion of our limitedness. The desire for freedom is built into the constitution of man. We know this. Life is a mystery which can never be solved except by superior knowledge or revelation.

We find ourselves in bondage. We want help. Help comes to those who have faith, who believe in God. Those who do not believe remain long in the game till they get thoroughly tired and want to go home. Then the Power appears in human form as the Guru, the Teacher, to lead them beyond the delusion of ignorance, to where there is no difference between the Guru and the disciple.

As long as one is in the world of maya, one maintains an attitude of devotion, for it is easy to fool oneself with the belief in one's perfection. This is the meaning of humility or effacement of the little self before the Teacher of all.

There is need for authority in every department of life. Management and managers who have the expertise are essential in running the various businesses of society. But the most important business of all is the business of living. We need authoritative utterance from one through whom Truth shines in its utter simplicity and purity.

Ramakrishna gave a graphic example: suppose you are enclosed in a small place with walls all around. You see only what is inside. But if there is a hole in the wall, you will catch a glimpse of the infinite world beyond. A Divine Incarnation is like that hole through which one catches a glimpse of infinity.

7. O Descendant of Bharata! Whenever religion becomes tarnished and irreligion prevails, I create myself.

When faith declines people lose their ideals and pursue pleasure and power as the primary goals of life. Materialism leads to strife and agony and the collapse of order and civilization.

Krishna came at the beginning of the Kali Yuga, the Dark Age.

The Yoga of Knowledge (Jnana Yoga)

"According to the *Vishnu Purana* (4:24), the syndrome of the Kali Yuga is recognized by the fact that during the epoch property alone confers social rank, wealth becomes the sole criterion of virtue, passion and lewdness the sole bonds between mates, falsehood the sole criterion of success in life, sexuality the sole means of enjoyment and an outward, purely ritualistic religion is confounded with spirituality" (Mircea Eliade, *Man and Time*, Bollingen Series XXX.3, Pantheon Books).

History has a moral or spiritual aim. It is the ascent of man from primitive existence to freedom of spirit, from ignorance to knowledge.

Some philosophers and historians in the West have seen a moral purpose in history. Aristotle said that the Divine is drawing the world to it like a magnet. Some modern Western philosophers have echoed the idea, saying that the world is heading toward Deity. Arnold Toynbee believed in the religious mission of history. He mentions with commendation the medieval Arab historian, Ibn Khaldun, who thought justice to be the goal of civilization.

But there is no perfection in time, only ups and downs. However, we see that in time new situations develop in man's history, which call for a fresh understanding of the ancient truths couched in a language suited to remove the perplexities of the period. *Zeitgeist*, spirit of the time, demands a new statement.

New developments call also for a fresh statement of the eternal truth. This restatement is called, or named, the Yuga Dharma which is, speaking broadly, the Religion of the Age.

It will be apt here to call attention to the great historical facts of our time. First of all, this is the age of science which has knit the world together into a small neighborhood. Science has also shown the futility of philosophical speculations, the attempt of reason to grasp Reality by formula. Science is pointing to the fact that consciousness is fundamental in our experience and nature is assuming more and more the character of the dream of "Alice in wonderland."

Science has also made education widespread and is thus removing the superstitions of people everywhere. All this will be of help to men around the globe to recover their lost faith in human destiny by having a larger concept of religion through the ageless authoritative utterance of Vedanta in the Gita.

The new world needs a broader basis for the world civilization of the future than economic and political arrangements. The United Nations is a political dream; it is a necessary institution. But the new world order of peace and common human interest will rest on an understanding of the essential Truth of man which is Vedanta. Divinity is the basis of true humanity.

Arnold Toynbee who, as mentioned earlier, had a religious view of history remarked in his *Study of History,* "…it seems unlikely that the vaster structure of world-order, which it is our task to build today, can ever be securely based upon the rubble foundation of mere economic interests."

Some in the West believe that democracy and free market are the last word in history and human evolution. Men need gold and enjoyment, but if they make them the primary goals of life they cannot avoid catastrophes. Political democracy and economic affluence need to be guided and controlled by a spiritual vision, recognition of the Truth of man.

In the absence of philosopher-kings like Janaka, society needs to be guided by the counsel of mature men of renunciation; otherwise, democracy may be too much for humanity. Thucydides, the historian of the Peloponnesian War, wrote in his famous book that in Periclean Athens there was so much democracy that even an ass brayed along with the air of a free citizen!

Shankara (eighth century A.D.) says in the introduction to his commentary on the Gita that Krishna came down on earth to protect the sage and the hero, for only if they are protected, will the world be protected. The recognition that the saint is more important for civilization than the hero is not altogether lost upon members of aristocracy and persons of wealth. The Countess Pourtales of France, daughter of the Duke of Talleyrand, was interested in Indian thought and yoga. Once during a conversation I mentioned that General de Gaulle was a great man, a hero. The Countess quickly rejoined saying, "But your Gandhi was greater, he was 'le sage, le sage'".

Gandhi was much more than a politician. He was like the saint Dadhichi of the Mahabharata who gave his bones for fashioning the weapon for the destruction of a great demon.

The world, civilization, is preserved by power guided by spiritual vision, by aristocrats piloted by philosophers (Plato).

8. I incarnate myself in every age for saving the good, for the destruction of the wicked and for the establishment of religion.

God sometimes comes as thunder and lightening for the wicked.

9. He who knows truly this miraculous birth and work of mine is not reborn again after death but comes to me.

10. Many who are without desire, fear and anger, who are devoted to me and have taken refuge in me, have been purified by such austere practices of wisdom; and they have become united with my essence (Brahman, the Self).

Constant denial of the little self of selfish desires and assertion of the freedom of the higher self in thought, word and deed are difficult and austere practices. Suffering all injury without a thought of reacting is said to be one of the qualifications required of those who are aspirants after freedom, walking the path of knowledge.

11. In whatever way people worship me I favor them in the same manner. Men follow my path (come to me) in diverse ways.

History is moving toward Deity. Knowingly or unknowingly, men are moving toward Reality. There is some kind of faith everywhere, more or less intelligent.

Even a psychologist like Jung, who started as a Freudian, was led by his investigations to an enlarged view of the unconscious and to the discernment of the religious need of an individual as the ultimate need, overriding his narrow personal desires. Failure to come to terms with this need is the basic psychological problem, without recognition of which an individual can never be whole and healthy. It is to Jung's credit that he perceived this general need, though, lacking personal experience, he could not speak with authority as to the precise nature of the goal of human drive. Perfect togetherness or integration is the good ego's feeling of its being close to Reality or God.

Jung felt the truth of religious need deeply and honestly; that is why he visited the monastery of the Ramakrishna Mission in India about the time when the big temple of Ramakrishna was being dedicated. I was present then in the year 1938.

Psychologists talk about integration or wholeness of individuals which they call individuation. There are, however, no individuals or integrated persons in society. There are only divided minds or beings or '-dividuals', if one may use the outrageous expression.

Only the enlightened who have seen the Reality behind the ambivalent mind are the truly integrated individuals — those whose egos have become diluted in the waters of Reality and who are one with Truth. The rest are floundering; they cannot be saved or healed without faith. Small peccadillos can be smoothed over by friendly counsel, but grave breaches of moral law are not healed without reformation through faith.

"The patterns of the Infinite are infinite," said Ramakrishna. All societies from the most primitive to the very advanced have faith in a Power that is above the constraints of nature. What is called animism is a witness to this belief, which has truth in it though mixed up with a lot of irrational crudity.

From shamans to the most enlightened gurus (spiritual teachers), belief in human destiny, in freedom of spirit, is expressed in uncouth or in sophisticated fashion. Even today, many who are religious fail to recognize the higher truth of what they believe in.

Religion is return to Reality. There are many ways for reaching the goal. An old Sanskrit hymn to Shiva (the beneficent Deity) declares, "People take to different ways, straight or crooked, as their tastes dictate, yet you are the one goal of all as the ocean is of rivers."

Ramakrishna declared that God had made different religions for different people. The various religions are different ways of reaching the one common goal and are suited to the developments of worshippers of different kinds. A mother, he indicated, makes strained spinach for her baby, but she cooks rare steak for the grown-ups. The different religions are different creeds or ways, suiting the needs of different worshippers.

God answers the prayers of believers. The best prayer is for enlightenment. Love God and don't ask for anything else. God takes care of all the needs of a devotee who relies on Him. "Everything will be added unto you" (Christ). Spinoza also said, "Love God without any thought of return."

12. People worship gods desiring results of sacrifices, for the fruits of action are quickly gained on earth.

Worldly gains are achieved quickly in time; whereas, Freedom is not easy to attain, as the Buddha said.

13. I have originated the four orders according to division of temperament and work. Though I am their creator, know me to be changeless and without action.

The four orders of Brahmins, Kshatriyas, Vaishyas and Shudras to which Krishna refers are divisions of members of a society according to their character and ability. These were not castes in their original sense. The four orders mentioned here are like the orders mentioned in Plato's *Republic:* philosopher-kings, guardians, tradesmen and those who perform menial services (slaves).

The Mahabharata of which the Gita is a tiny section mentions that in the beginning there was only one class of men in the world and that the four orders evolved on the basis of differences in vocations. It also says that character is the factor which determines caste.

The modern caste system of India, which is a travesty of truth, is not what the Gita had in view.

14. Actions do not touch me, nor do I desire their results. He who knows me thus is not affected by action.

One knows God when one knows he is Spirit. Spirit is above nature. When we play just for fun, the results of the game do not affect us. The free person knows it is God who is playing, that nature is his game and there is no motive for the play. It is an expression of the delight of Pure Existence.

15. So knowing, the past seekers after freedom engaged in action; therefore, perform action alone as the ancients did in the past.

"So knowing" means knowing the free, detached activity of the Lord. The ancients are the royal sages like Janaka mentioned earlier.

16. Even the wise are confounded about what is action and what is inaction. Therefore I will tell you what is action, knowing which you will be free from evil.

17. One has to understand what is action (enjoined by the scriptures), and what is non-action, for the meaning of action is inscrutable.

Why and how we should act, or the conduct of life, is difficult to ascertain without guidance. We are dealing here with the philosophy of work in general.

18. He who sees inaction in action, and action in inaction, is intelligent among men.

The wise man knows that Spirit, or Self, is above nature and that God alone acts. He is aware that the action does not belong to him, even though he acts with love or in the spirit of service. The non-action of a fool, or dullard, who should act out of a sense of duty but refrains, because of fear or some other reason, only creates further bondage. As another scripture on the highest wisdom (*Ashtavakra Samhita*) points out, non-action on the part of a fool is action; that is, activity which creates bondage.

THE YOGA OF KNOWLEDGE (JNANA YOGA)

The fool who desists from action out of a sense of fear when his parents are being insulted or abused performs a bad action, which adds one more rivet in his chain of bondage.

Practice of the idea of 'non-agency' develops the feeling of detachment in the heart, which gradually erases the ego which hides Pure Consciousness or True Being.

19. He whose undertakings are all free from resolutions prompted by desire and whose sense of agency has been burnt by the fire of knowledge is said to be wise by the learned.

A wise man's action is originated by God, the Inner Controller.

20. Giving up attachment to the results of action, being always content, and having no recourse, he does not do anything at all though he becomes engaged in action.

21. He who is without desire, whose mind and senses are under control and who has renounced all objects of enjoyment does not reap any harm.

The desireless yogi does only what is necessary for maintaining the body; he incurs neither virtue nor sin by such action.

22. He who is satisfied with whatever comes by chance, who is unaffected by the dualities of sense contacts, who is without enmity and the same in success or failure does not become bound though he engages in action.

23. All work done as sacrifice by the person who is without attachment, who is without egotism, whose mind is established in Self, becomes entirely dissolved.

The work done by the wise man has no binding effect on the doer. The wise person, the enlightened knower of Brahman, who performs sacrifices for the good of the people (who works for the general good) is not bound by the results of action. The following verse which many orders of monks in India recite before they eat is the height of spiritual realization — that whatever exists is all

Brahman or the Godhead (the sacrifice, the oblation, the instrument and the sacrificer).

24. The act of offering is Brahman, the oblation is Brahman. Brahman has offered the oblation in the fire that is Brahman. He who has the understanding that all actions, objects and instruments of action are Brahman, realizes Brahman.

The Upanishads, of which the Gita is the essence, teach that all is Brahman. Brahman, the ineffable Reality, has become the universe without in any way being diminished by the expression, as in this world material is transformed into other material and disappears into it. An Upanishadic invocation says, "Subtracting the Full from the Full, the Full remains." The universe of change or maya does not diminish or exhaust in the slightest the fullness of Reality beyond time. The change is from Brahman without diminishing anything of Brahman.

Imagination is the door to realization. As our imagination gets more and more comprehensive, it approaches Reality. Finally imagination vanishes, the mind stops and Reality becomes self-manifest.

Because of our identification with a portion of nature, we do not see the great Self. To see the great Self everywhere is the final goal of all spiritual practices. Vivekananda gave a wonderful hint. Just as in a jigsaw puzzle we do not see the figure at first glance, but after repeated trials, the picture flashes into view; so also, by trying to see God within and outside, the Truth reveals itself in time. This attempt naturally goes with purification of mind and the attempt to see God first within oneself through reflection and meditation.

The following verses about sacrifice point to a basic institution in civilization as well as in the spiritual life of an individual.

Life is not a position, it is a movement. Life progresses by discarding what is narrow and small and by grasping what is broader and bigger. Progress, individual and social, is built on sacrifice. All societies and civilizations have the institution of sacrifice to gods or God. Mankind advances on sacrifice.

The Yoga of Knowledge (Jnana Yoga)

In life, people sacrifice a lot of things for material success and passing pleasure. And if they have no spiritual outlook, they sacrifice their soul and conscience for these things and end up in trouble, in jail or in a psychiatrist's hands.

There are noble sacrifices, too. But the highest sacrifice is the sacrifice of the little self for the highest gain, "gaining which a person does not consider any other gain superior to it" (chapter 6). Religion is a continuous sacrifice until the illusion of the little ego vanishes and the eternity of life and bliss becomes manifest.

It is not difficult to see that social progress and spiritual gain are achieved on the basis of sacrifice. All foundations, charities and endowments derive from the idea or principle of sacrifice. The institution of sacrifice begins crudely in primitive societies with sacrifices of animals and even men. The idea gets clearer and culminates in the ideal of sacrifice of the ego, its surrender to Reality.

In the age of the Gita, ritualistic sacrifice was widespread. The Vedas record many and great sacrifices. That was the common religion and one may say it was rampant. Great spiritual teachers and philosophers revolted against it and taught the purer religion of self-sacrifice for the everlasting gain of spiritual freedom and fearlessness. Buddha was in that line; he was a Vedantist.

Sacrifice can have many forms and objects. Some of them are given below.

25. Some yogis (followers of the path of action) offer sacrifice in the form of worship of gods; others offer sacrifice itself by sacrificing it into the fire of Brahman.

Some sacrifice is of material offering to gods; while those who seek freedom offer the little self into the fire of Brahman by renouncing the act of sacrifice itself.

26. Some offer their senses such as hearing and the rest as oblation in the fire of control. Still others offer sound and other sense-objects as oblation in the fire of the senses.

27. Others offer all actions of the senses and of the life forces into the fire of the yoga of self-control, lighted by knowledge.

28. Others offer goods as sacrifice; some their austerities, some their yoga practices, while some others of firm vows, their scriptural studies and their wisdom.

29. Others who practice breath-control sacrifice the incoming breath into the outgoing, the outgoing into the incoming, after restraining them both.

These are breath-control practices called *pranayama,* which is ultimately the control of nerve-forces or life forces.

30-31. Some others who control their diet sacrifice life-breaths into life-breaths. All these who practice sacrifice and those whose blemishes have been removed by sacrifice and who partake of the sacred food left after sacrifice attain to the eternal Brahman. When there is no success in this world for him who does not sacrifice, O Best among the Kurus! how can it be in the other?

32. Many sacrifices of this kind have been expounded in the Vedas. Know them all to be born of action. Knowing thus you will be free.

The Self is without action. When one has the knowledge that all these actions do not belong to Self which is above them, one is liberated from the world of good and evil.

33. O Tormentor of Enemies! Sacrifice of knowledge (wisdom that liberates) is superior to sacrifice with materials, because, O Partha! all actions find their completion in wisdom.

Life's goal is wisdom. The goal of activity is serenity, which is attained through sacrifice of the feeling of agency into the fire of wisdom or knowledge

THE YOGA OF KNOWLEDGE (JNANA YOGA)

34. Know that through humble submission, repeated inquiry and service, the wise knowers of Truth will instruct you on wisdom.

Only the wise can instruct others in wisdom. Plato wrote to friends of the tyrant Dionysius of Syracuse that true philosophy is communicated directly from teacher to pupil like lighting one lamp with another.

Instruction becomes effective when it is communicated by a real person who has experienced its truth in life. Lip service to it does not influence listeners. The Katha Upanishad asserts that one should approach the best, the enlightened, to understand.

In the course of history as the teaching spreads it also becomes thin. People in time become suffocated by pollution, physical and psychological. And the Lord comes to purify the atmosphere. Those who are lucky become immediate followers. Others who long for fresh air are inspired by them. Gradually like a leaven it spreads through society and elevates it to a higher level.

It is also true that false prophets appear like artificial products when the demand is for the real bread of life.

Humility, non-assertion of the ego, is essential for learning. Obstinate and arrogant persons do not learn, nor those whose nature has been corrupted by love of money and pleasure. They say in India that a rogue never pays heed to tales of virtue.

It is also necessary to have intelligence. This intelligence is not necessarily intellectual. It is the capacity for grasping the subtle truths of life. Just as prudence does not necessarily imply the possession of a high degree from a university.

In life's spiritual journey doubts are inevitable, repeated questionings necessary, and in the absence of the human teacher, the mind of the true aspirant, says Ramakrishna, becomes the teacher. One has to be truly humble and hold on doggedly to the instruction of the teacher.

Sometimes intellectual brilliance stands in the way of spiritual growth; it hardens the ego instead of eroding it.

The ego is softened and eliminated through service of the teacher. One spiritual teacher told an inquirer that the aspirant after Freedom should stay like a devoted dog at the teacher's door. Doggedness is essential for spiritual realization as it is necessary also in achievements in the world.

35. O Son of Pandu (Arjuna)! Knowing this you will never again succumb to delusion and by this you will see all beings without exception in the Self and in me.

The enlightened individual perceives that all creation is projection of the Spirit, i.e., all change (time-space-causation) is like the "outbreathing" of Spirit, as the Veda declares.

There is an ancient Sanskrit hymn in praise of the teacher which begins as follows, "My salutation is to Dakshinamurti who appears in the form of the teacher, who sees the universe within himself like a city reflected in a mirror but appearing to be outside, by maya, as in the dream, and who when the dream breaks knows only himself (the Self-alone) as the non-dual Reality."

To our great surprise, a priest-physicist recited in Sanskrit the above verse in a program on the universe on television in the spring of 1991.

Vivekananda composed a song in Bengali in which are related the stages of the inward, philosophic search for and realization of the Truth of the universe. An English translation is given below:

> There is neither the sun, nor the lovely moon,
>   nor a star.
> In the infinite space floats shadow-like
>   the image universe.
> In the primeval, undivided mind the world
>   process floats;
> It floats and sinks and rises again in the ceaseless
>   stream of 'I'.
> Slowly the throng of shadows depart and merge
>   in the aboriginal abode.
> Now flows unbroken the feeling of pure 'I' and 'I'
>   alone.
> That flow also ceases, void merges in the Void,
> Beyond the reach of speech and mind,
> He knows whose heart knows.

36. Even if you are the worst sinner amongst all the sinners, you will cross over this ocean by the boat of wisdom alone.

When wisdom dawns, the entire history of an individual, all his experiences, takes on the character of dreams. The little self with its fears, anxieties, wishes, experiences, pain and sorrow, and all time and existence become reduced to phantoms of imagination. This is the meaning of redemption. It is becoming one with Reality which is all love and pure existence, from which myriads and myriads of universes are projected into existence as the scriptures tell us.

37. As lighted fire turns wood to ashes, so also the fire of wisdom reduces all actions to ashes.

38. There is nothing as pure here on earth as wisdom. The one perfected by the yoga of action (karma yoga) knows it in himself in the course of time.

39. The person of faith, who is devoted to Truth and who has conquered his senses, gains wisdom; and gaining it, he finds eternal peace without delay.

Faith is essential in spiritual life. Awakening of faith is essential for spiritual progress. The name of one of the chief sermons of Buddha is *Awakening of Faith (Shraddhotpadana Sutra)*. Faith is awakened by contact with holy men who feel the presence of God.

40. The ignorant, the person without faith, and the doubter perish. The doubter has neither this world, nor the other, and never any happiness.

A person without faith and confidence is dull and inactive. There is no gain in life, spiritual or earthly, for the indolent and passive.

There is doubt because the worldly tendencies of our mind drag us to pursuits of power and enjoyment and cloud the vision of Reality or Truth or God within us. It is easy to be convinced of the reality of desires and of stone and dirt and to remain suspicious about the meaning of idealistic promptings of the heart as indicating anything beyond admirable sentiments or feelings or pointing to any super-personal Truth. Philanderers are never 'misled' by the deep meaning of love.

Science has today dispelled the belief in an objective reality. But doubts about God and Spirit persist. The one way to dispel such doubts is for a thinker to look within to find out the doubter. If the search can be carried to its final end, the doubter will vanish with his doubts and Reality would stand self-revealed. It is not easy. It is a challenge to those intellectuals who have doubts about Truth and God.

It is also a challenge to persons seeking the meaning of art. Art is revelation of Spirit in figures and forms of nature. Art-experience in its highest is love of an object without an 'itch'; for the object gives a glimpse of the deep Beauty and Truth within us all—the Truth and Beauty in the heart of creation.

41. O Dhananjaya (Arjuna)! Actions do not create bondage for one who has renounced action through yoga (of detachment), whose doubts have been sundered by wisdom and who is established in the Self.

The free man sees that all agency belongs to God and that the Great Mother pulls the strings of the ego.

42. So, O Descendant of Bharata (Arjuna)! cut asunder this doubt in your heart born of ignorance with the sword of wisdom. Have faith in yoga and arise.

The venture in spiritual life, the journey, begins with faith. All doubts and vacillations which accompany a spiritual traveller diminish with progress, and the unreality, the dream-like quality of the world of time, flashes into view as faith becomes wisdom, the ultimate perception.

CHAPTER FIVE

The Yoga
of Renunciation
# of Action

ARJUNA SAID:

1. **O Krishna! You commend renunciation of action and again praise yoga. Please tell me unmistakably which is better of the two.**

Arjuna's doubts are not dispelled. It is common to see an opposition between the life of action in the world and the life of contemplation away from the world.

Arjuna was a hero; he had the duty to defend king and country. He was no paid mercenary, and he had a spiritual ideal. The unpleasant and terrible duty of fighting his kin appalled him. He was shrinking from duty from personal considerations.

There are persons in the world who long for peace and who feel a conflict between their urge for a quiet and contemplative life and the work they are obliged to do. They would run away but cannot.

Krishna pointed out that the conflict between work in society and contemplation is not insurmountable. A life of action can also be a life of worship. Krishna, the Divine Worker, asks Arjuna to follow his example and perform his duty without a selfish motive, out of love for the ideal. That way work will be transformed into worship and the ego which is a bar to the realization of Self will become eroded and Truth will become self-manifest.

The ideal of general welfare or service to humanity (lokasamgraha) is the dominant theme in the Gita.

God works in the world and wants his devotee also to work. Vivekananda told an American audience: "God says, 'love me and love my dog.'" That is a higher ideal than the pursuit of personal salvation.

There are many misconceptions about spiritual life and religion. Even a profound scholar like Professor Alfred Whitehead said, "Religion is what a man does with his solitariness."

Religion is the highest love. It is ultimately the love of all, for all is God. This is the ideal of man.

THE BLESSED LORD SAID:

2. Renunciation and the yoga of action both lead to the Supreme Good (summum bonum). But of the two, the yoga of action is superior to renunciation of action.

Renunciation is technically the giving up of active life in the world. Yoga means both union of the individual self with the Supreme Self and also the method of union. The yoga of action or karma yoga is the method of achieving enlightenment through performance of action as service without attachment to results, or duty for duty's sake.

3. Know him to be a man of renunciation always who neither hates nor desires. Free from these dualities he, O Mighty-armed one! escapes bondage.

A man of renunciation (sannyasi) is one who has left the world for a life of contemplation. But one who pursues the path of disinterested action is also called by Krishna a man of renunciation.

4. Ignorant people declare the path of knowledge (Samkhya) and the path of action (yoga) to be different, but not the learned. The results of both are reaped by complete devotion to either one.

THE YOGA OF RENUNCIATION OF ACTION

The path of knowledge entails constant discrimination between the Real (Pure Self) and the unreal (nature or body-mind complex) and assertion of one's identity with Pure Consciousness.

> **5. The same place that one reaches by the path of knowledge is also arrived at by the path of action. He who perceives them (Samkhya and yoga) to be one perceives truly.**

> **6. But O Mighty-armed One! renunciation is difficult to achieve without recourse to the yoga of action. The sage who is established in karma yoga realizes Brahman soon.**

True renunciation is rejection of me and mine and cannot be achieved without unselfish performance of duty. Self-less service leads to clarity of understanding and finally to the realization that Self is above action and free.

Brahman is Reality or Sat-Chit-Ananda; i.e., Existence-Consciousness-Bliss, pure heart or pure feeling and existence.

> **7. He who has achieved union with Spirit, whose mind is pure, who has conquered the body and the senses, and whose Self is the Self of all the beings is not tainted though he works.**

The knower or the wise man is the pure observer, the indwelling Spirit in all beings. Action apparently also belongs to the wise man, but God acts through him.

> **8-9. The man who is united with the Divine knows, that in seeing, hearing, touching, smelling, eating, going, sleeping, breathing, speaking, emitting, grasping, and opening and closing eyes, it is his senses which are occupied with their own sensations. He knows that he is doing nothing.**

All activity belongs to nature. The ego mistakenly thinks it is acting.

10. Attributing all action to the Divine, he who works without attachment is not touched by sin, even as a lotus leaf is untouched by water.

Imagination is the door to realization. We have to think away the superstitions which are upon us, due to ignorance, by thoughts which are contrary and which reflect Truth. When an idea comes down from head to heart, from imagination to feeling, it becomes real. Reality or Truth is in the hearts of all, beyond all dualities.

11. Giving up attachment to results, the yogis perform actions with body, mind and intellect and sense-organs only for self-purification.

According to Samkhya psychology, which Vedanta accepts, mind is the faculty which receives, compares, contrasts, remembers, and stores within impressions received through the senses, while intellect stands for the faculty which decides and identifies the precise nature of a sensation or perception. We can hear a sound but fail to identify it immediately. The faculty which compares and contrasts the presentation with similar impressions filed in the mind and determines the precise nature of it is buddhi or intellect.

12. The yogi renouncing the results of action attains supreme peace. The non-yogi being attached to results because of desire becomes bound.

13. Renouncing all actions by the mind, the person of self-control dwells happily in the nine-gated city without doing or causing anything to be done.

The nine gates are the eyes, the ears, the nostrils, the mouth and the organs of excretion and generation.

14. The Lord creates neither the agency, nor the actions; nor does he join results to actions of the people. It is nature which acts.

The Lord is the Self, above nature, which is the real Self of man also.

15. The all-pervading Spirit accepts neither the sin nor the merit of any one. Knowledge is covered by ignorance; creatures are deluded by it.

What science calls the physical universe is the gross portion of dynamic energy, the subtler parts of which include mind and ego-sense. These are all tiny sparks of one Personality. Beyond It is the Impersonal, the Energy which is asleep as it were (Shiva). One who realizes his true identity with the Impersonal Self is untouched by sin or virtue, which belong to action.

16. But the sun-like knowledge of those whose ignorance has been dispelled by wisdom reveals the supreme Brahman in all things.

When the sun rises, the darkness that covers the landscape is removed; so also when the knowledge of Reality dawns, it reveals the unity underlying the superficial distinctions of maya which cover it.

17. Those who have this understanding, whose Self is the Reality, who are devoted to it and whose blemishes have all been washed away by wisdom are not born again.

The wise man is forever released from the human condition.

18. The man of wisdom is same-sighted toward a learned and humble Brahmin, toward a cow, toward an elephant, toward a dog and also toward an outcast.

Brahman or Sat-Chit-Ananda (Existence-Knowledge-Bliss) is the Reality, the substance of all that exists.

Vivekananda wrote to a friend in America:

Gold and silver, my dear Mary, have I none, but what I have I give to thee freely, and that is the knowledge that the goldness of gold, the silverness of silver, the manhood of man, the womanhood of woman, the reality of everything is the Lord — and that this Lord we are trying to realize from time without beginning in the objective, and in the attempt throwing up such 'queer' creatures of our fancy as man, woman, child, body, mind, the earth, sun, moon, stars, the world, love, hate, property, wealth, etc.; also ghosts, devils, angels and gods, God, etc.

The fact being that the Lord is in us, we are He, the eternal subject, the real ego never to be objectified, and that all this objectifying process is mere waste of time and talent. When the soul becomes aware of this, it gives up objectifying and falls back more and more upon the subjective. This is the evolution, less and less in the body and more and more in the mind —*man* the highest form, meaning in Sanskrit, *manas,* thought — the animal that thinks and not the animal that 'senses' only. This is what in theology is called 'renunciation'. The formation of society, the institution of marriage, the love for children, our works, morality, and ethics are all different forms of renunciation. All our lives in every society are the subjection of the will, the thirst, the desire. This surrender of the will or the fictitious self — or the desire to jump out of ourselves, as it were — the struggle still to objectify the subject — is the one phenomenon in the world of which all societies and social forms are various modes and stages. Love is the easiest and smoothest way toward the self-surrender or subjection of the will and hatred, the opposite.

People have been cajoled through various stories or superstitions of heavens and hells and rulers above the sky, toward this one end of self-surrender. The philosopher does the same knowingly without superstition by giving up desire... (*Letters of Swami Vivekananda,* 3rd ed., p. 315).

The way of wisdom is looking directly into one's Self.

19. Even here they conquer rebirth whose minds are established in sameness, for Brahman (Reality) is flawless and the same, and for this reason they are established in Brahman.

Reality is the peace that passeth all understanding, the sweetness in the heart of creation. That is the goal which is nearest of the near and farthest of the far.

20. One should not be elated by getting the pleasant nor be worried at obtaining the unpleasant. He who has this steady wisdom and who is without delusion is the knower of Brahman and established in it.

21. He whose mind is not attached to outside contacts of the senses and who feels happiness in the Self is united with Brahman and enjoys everlasting happiness.

22. The pleasures which come from sense-contacts are but sources of pain. They have a beginning and an end. The wise do not delight in them.

23. He who can even here, before he gives up the body, contain the impulses of desire and anger is a yogi and is happy.

24. The yogi who is happy within, who takes delight in himself and who has the inner-light attains nirvana and mergence in Brahman by becoming one with it.

The Gita uses several times the word *nirvana* which Buddha used and which is generally almost exclusively identified as a Buddhist term for enlightenment. It means extinction of the 'I' sense, of the fire of desire, the cause of ignorance and relative existence. The word is to be found extensively in pre-Buddhistic Sanskrit literature. Vedantists use in general the positive term of Self-knowledge.

Buddha also used the positive word *bodhi* which means wisdom. The word Buddha means the enlightened. The family name of Buddha was Siddhartha.

25. The sages whose stains have been removed, whose doubts have been dispelled, who are self-controlled and engaged in doing good to all beings attain nirvana in Brahman.

There is a higher aim in life than the goal of personal escape from trouble and bondage. The height of spiritual realization is the experience of unity of existence. It is the experience of the *Buddhahridaya,* the heart of the Buddha or the Enlightened. It is the experience of all-embracing love. As mentioned in an earlier comment, God, in an early Sanskrit book of aphorisms on devotion, is defined as the essence of ineffable love. This large-heartedness, manifest in the lives of special messengers of the Divine, is the source of moral principles and philanthropy in society.

Krishna in the Gita emphasizes the ideal of lokasamgraha, the ideal of service to society.

Vivekananda said, "The only God to worship is the human soul in the human body. Of course all animals are temples, too, but man is the Taj Mahal of temples. If I cannot worship in that, no other temple will be of any advantage."

Swami Shivananda, a disciple of Ramakrishna, wrote in a letter, "What work in a person's life can be higher than the service of man? What other broad means are there for cleansing the mind except this? God is easily revealed in the heart through self-less service of others."

Birth of the new, independent India is due to this inspiration. Almost single-handed Vivekananda, who did not live to be forty, lifted up India with both hands from self-doubt and lethargy. His life exemplifies the religion of the Gita.

Gandhi, who was called Father of the Nation and who regarded the Gita as a mother-like source of inspiration, said his love for India increased a thousand fold after reading Vivekananda. Nehru called Vivekananda a pillar of modern day India.

26. Unity with Brahman (Brahma-nirvan) exists on either side for sages who are without desire and anger, who are self-controlled and who are the knowers of Self.

The wise are free both before and after the dissolution of the body; i.e., on either side of death, before and after.

27-28. Removing contact with sense-objects outside, fixing the sight between the eyebrows, making even the incoming and outgoing breath through the

nostrils, the sage who has the senses, the mind and the understanding under control, who is without desire, fear or anger, and who is striving after emancipation is always free.

The above is a prelude to the next chapter in which the traditional yoga method of concentration is recounted.

29. Realizing me as the enjoyer (goal) of sacrifice and austerities, as the great Lord of all the worlds and as the friend of all beings, he (the yogi) attains peace.

The Lord is the friend who dwells always in the hearts of all beings, as the benefactor who seeks no return. The only image which reflects the unconditional love of God and enlightened souls in the world is the selfless love of a selfless mother uncorrupted by views of modern society.

CHAPTER SIX

The Yoga
of Meditation
(Dhyana Yoga)

RELUDE: The word "yoga" needs some explanation for readers who are not familiar with Sanskrit and Indian terms.

Yoga originally meant yoking or joining, both the words originating from a common Indo-European root. In spiritual philosophy, yoga came to mean both union with the spiritual ideal and the method of such union.

The Eternal Religion (Sanatana Dharma), or the so-called Hindu religion maintains that there are myriad roads for realizing the spiritual goal or the Reality which is the source and support of all existence. As the saying goes, there are more ways than one to skin a cat. All the many and different approaches to the Divine, the one and common goal of all, have been classified into four broad methods; namely, jnana yoga (the way of wisdom), bhakti yoga (the way of devotion), karma yoga (the way of action) and dhyana yoga (the way of meditation or concentration).

THE YOGA OF MEDITATION (DHYANA YOGA)

These methods are logically separate but in actual practice they are combined, and spiritual seekers choose one or the other as their main method of advance. They all lead to the same goal, as the Gita proclaims.

The Gita refers to all the diverse paths though its dominant theme is the yoga of action combined with wisdom and devotion. Some chapters of the Gita, such as this one, deal mainly with one or the other of the different yogas.

The Gita is practical instruction for seekers of Truth. Religion or God is not the conclusion of indecisive rational thinking or what is known as philosophy. To twist a phrase of the existentialist philosophers, the Real is prior to appearance, subject is prior to object.

In this chapter, the method of meditation is emphasized, and the two chief methods of arresting the activities of the mind (the practices of concentration and renunciation) are mentioned.

THE BLESSED LORD SAID:

1. He who performs works which have been enjoined by scriptures, without seeking their results, is a person of renunciation and also a yogi, not so one who does not light the fire or who gives up work.

The reference is to sacrificial rites, which were considered at the time duties and which the men of renunciation who retired from the world gave up. But even those who do not leave the world and perform ceremonial duties without desire for results are also men of renunciation, the Gita proclaims.

2. O Son of Pandu (Arjuna)! What is called renunciation, know that to be yoga. For without renunciation of desire (for results), none can be a yogi.

The word "yogi" means both a karma yogi (one who pursues the path of action with detachment) and also a dhyana yogi (one who follows the path of contemplation).

3. For the sage who wants to be stable on the path of contemplation, work is said to be the means. For the very same one who has become stable on the path of contemplation, renunciation of all works becomes the means.

Here, the Gita extols the path of action and holds that God-like action by men of wisdom is superior to the life of complete renunciation of action. But it also recognizes that there are spiritual aspirants who choose the path of pure contemplation alone.

In the time of Buddha, and long before that, yoga was known as the path of pure contemplation. Buddha practiced it.

Withdrawal from the world and exclusive devotion to contemplation are sometimes essential for those who do higher work for humanity. Withdrawal from society and return to it after enlightenment are features in the lives of gigantic movers of world history. It is big ideas which pull civilizations forward.

Also, as Ramakrishna said, God relieves the seeker of his duties as he approaches realization of wisdom, just as a mother-in-law (in an Indian home) relieves the pregnant daughter-in-law of her chores progressively as the time for delivery approaches.

4. When a person renounces all desires and is not attached to sense objects, he is said to be settled in yoga.

Yoga here means dhyana yoga, or the path of contemplation.

5. Save the self by the self, do not depress the self, the self itself is the self's friend as also its enemy.

In this instance, self (*atma*) is used in the sense of mind, and mind, as in the following verse, can be substituted for self. Vyasa, commentator on the *Yoga-Sutras*, says that mind is ambivalent. The river of mind flows both ways, toward evil and toward good. The upward tendency of mind is released and strengthened through detachment and practice. A clean mind has better taste. Our taste becomes simpler and purer through idealism and practice.

6. The mind is a friend of him who has conquered the mind by the mind. The mind itself acts like an enemy for him whose mind has not been subdued.

The divided mind is unified through practice of detachment and selflessness and made to flow toward the good.

7. The self of one who has conquered himself and has attained peace is the same in heat and cold, pain and pleasure, honor and dishonor.

This is the state of the person who is free while still living (jivanmukta).

8. The yogi who is satisfied with wisdom and knowledge, who has conquered his senses, who has reached the highest and looks upon a clod, a stone or gold in the same way, is said to be established in yoga.

Wisdom here means knowledge of Self and knowledge refers to the Samkhyan principles, the grades of evolution of nature (see Introduction).

9. He who is samesighted toward friends, companions, enemies, neutrals, the odious, consorts, saints and sinners is outstanding.

This is a continuation of the characteristics of one established in wisdom.

10. The yogi should always practice concentration of mind alone in a quiet spot, restraining body and mind without desire and without possessions.

The above verse and the following ones describe the practice of pure contemplation which is yoga in the technical and traditional sense. This is the idea behind Christian practices of communion and the Quakers' observance of silence.

CHAPTER SIX

The goal of yoga concentration is to attain a state of perfect stillness of mind when the Self of man becomes self-revealed. Then an individual knows his true identity and nevermore confuses his Self with passing thoughts, emotions and drives, identification with which produces the limited ego-sense.

Practice of quietness naturally requires a quiet place. An awakened person enjoys quietness and non-action in the midst of the noise and bustle of action. One who treads the path of karma yoga practices this inwardness amid the turmoil of everyday life. But such a karma yogi, too, sometimes retires into solitude for meditation in order to develop the power of detachment needed to work in the din of the world.

The absorption into the Impersonal Absolute is often confused with some kind of nihilism. However, as mentioned several times earlier, the Self is not only the source of all life and existence in time, but also the unalloyed, boundless ocean of bliss and freedom.

11. One who wants to practice meditation should place his seat firmly on a clean spot, neither too high nor too low, and cover it with tender grass, deer skin and cloth, one above the other in that order.

12. Taking his seat there and making the mind one-pointed by restraining its activities and those of the senses, he should practice yoga for self-purification.

13-14. Holding the spine, the neck and the head steadily in a line and gazing at the tip of the nose without looking in any direction and without movement, the yogi of peaceful mind, fearless and established in the vow of celibacy, should sit absorbed in me by controlling his mind.

There should not be any trace of physical love in the mind of one who wants to have the knowledge of Reality. All the great religions have emphasized this and enjoined vows of celibacy for those who aspire after the highest. Plato also mentions pure love as the Reality in his dialogues, the *Phaedo* and the *Symposium*.

The Yoga of Meditation (Dhyana Yoga)

Persons who have had sex but have eschewed it afterwards have also been able to taste the purest love.

Ramakrishna said, as all past great teachers from time immemorial have said, that God cannot be realized unless the heart is free from the least trace of desire. He said that sex is the root, and desires are its branches. It is the pleasure of life which draws the mind away from Reality. Without total conquest of it, none see God. "Blessed are the pure in heart for they shall see God" (Matt. 5:8).

True marriage, with or without papers, is a step toward purity and a necessity for the vast numbers of spiritual aspirants.

It is hard to get away from the fascination of sex in a culture dominated by the pleasure principle. Sex and violence go together. They are wild in their primitive state. Civilization begins with their control and disciplined use. Pure love and non-violence go together.

It is not possible to achieve purity without grace, but the wind of grace is always blowing, as Ramakrishna said. No ego can conquer desires, for the ego itself is the offspring of desire. The Gita teaches for this reason perfect humility and self-surrender (ego-surrender) to the Divine. No one knows, no one can tell who may or may not have grace. But the great yearning, like that of St. Augustine who struggled for chasity for thirteen years is "like the dawn before sunrise" (Ramakrishna). Gandhi, like St. Augustine, struggled for chastity for years before he succeeded. Buddha was married and had a child before he renounced the world.

The *Yoga Sutras of Patanjali* assert that non-violence (love), truthfulness, non-stealing, continence and non-acceptance of gifts are the virtues to be practiced by a yogi.

15. Thus joining the mind constantly, the self-controlled yogi attains the supreme peace of freedom (nirvana) which is my nature.

Again the Gita uses the word "nirvana" in the sense of extinction of desire. In a positive sense, it is the realization of unalloyed Bliss.

16. O Arjuna! Meditation (yoga) is not for him who eats too much, nor also for one who hardly eats, nor for one who sleeps too much or is awake too much.

Buddha also discarded the severe ascetic practices which made his belly shrink so much that it touched his spine. Buddha taught the middle way.

17. Meditation (yoga) removes the sorrow of the yogi who is moderate in eating and recreation, moderate in his efforts and moderate in sleep and wakefulness.

It is possible to indulge in extreme asceticism without spiritual gain, if there is no clear understanding of the goal. This form of asceticism is called demoniac in chapter 16 of the Gita.

The middle and rational way is the best, though toward the end aspirants are carried away almost helplessly to extreme effort.

Yoga "removes sorrow" means that enlightenment removes the pain that is in the heart of nature and confers on the yogi the eternal bliss of Brahman.

Yoga and Buddhism point to the fact that it is insatiable want and the everlasting pain of natural life which drives people on the quest for truth and freedom. A Samkhya-yoga aphorism asserts that philosophical inquiry begins under the impact of threefold pain; namely, physical pain, mental pain, and suffering caused by natural disasters.

The *Yoga Aphorisms of Patanjali,* as well as Buddha, base the spiritual quest of man upon the fourfold truths of pain, its cause, its cure and the method of curing it. Existentialism in the West began with a recognition of this truth.

There are only two incontestable facts in our world of uncertainties: bondage which is common, and freedom which is rare. Both are facts of experience. However, the drive toward freedom is built into the constitution of man. The ascent of man is toward the ideals of Truth-Beauty-Goodness, Sat-Chit-Ananda, which is the trinity of Vedanta.

18. When the controlled mind dwells only on the Self without desire for anything, then the yogi is said to be united (with Truth).

Yoga is joining or uniting the mind with Truth; that is, dissolving the mind in steady Reality.

19. A lamp in a windless place does not flicker. Know this to be the example of the concentrated mind of the yogi.

20. That where the mind stilled by the practice of yoga rests, where the self seeing the Self delights in the Self;

21. Where the yogi experiences the supreme happiness beyond the reach of the senses, but perceived by the pure intellect alone, and established wherein he never swerves from the Truth;

22. And gaining which he does not consider any other gain superior, and established in which he is not shaken by the severest of pain;

23. Know that to be yoga (samadhi, or complete absorption of mind in Spirit) which is complete cessation of painful contacts. This yoga (samadhi) should be practiced with fortitude and a mind free from attachment.

Verses 20 to 23 make one sentence and describe the nature of the yoga of pure meditation as described in the classic textbook on yoga by Pantanjali.

24-25. Giving up all desires born of allurement and withdrawing all the senses from everywhere (from all their objects) by the mind, one should gradually retire the mind with the help of unwavering intellect, and settling it on the Self, should not think of anything at all.

Intellect (buddhi) is reason or understanding, the faculty which determines the precise nature of the object of perception.

We make a distinction between science and the common sense view of things. Both are knowledge; one is closer to reality, the other is remote.

It is intellect which knows. When intellect is very pure (cf. 'pure thought' of Einstein), then it knows or determines that all is Knowledge (Reality).

The purest intellect or buddhi has been declared to be the same as Atman or Spirit (Ramakrishna). This Knowledge is also bliss or the highest good, happiness and existence.

> **26. Drawing the restless and wandering mind away from wherever it turns to, the yogi should bring it under the control of Self.**
>
> **27. Supreme happiness comes to this yogi whose mind is peaceful, who is without distractions, who is stainless and who has become one with the Godhead (Brahman).**
>
> **28. Joining the mind thus with the Self always, the yogi, free from all stain, enjoys supreme happiness born of contact with Brahman.**

The two verses above picture nirvana (extinction of the flame of the ego) in a positive manner as Supreme Happiness. The fictitious ego is drowned in the Ocean of Bliss. This is Self-realization or becoming one with the Godhead.

> **29. He who has achieved the union of yoga is same-sighted everywhere and sees the Self in all the beings and all the beings in the Self.**

One sees the Divinity within oneself first, before seeing it in all beings. Practice in karma yoga begins with the idea of service to God in every being and finally matures into realization of the Self everywhere. An idea becomes real when it becomes a feeling in the heart.

The Yoga of Meditation (Dhyana Yoga)

The ethical ideal or the source of ethics is in the unity of existence. Spirit is most manifest in human beings; therefore man is the best temple for worship.

30. I am never lost to him who sees me everywhere and all in me; nor is he lost to me.

Once one realizes the unity of existence, one is nevermore deceived by the appearance of many. This is Krishna as the Godhead speaking.

31. He who being established in unity worships me, who is in all beings, dwells in me in whatever state he may be in.

External conditions do not affect the poise of the wise who have achieved unity with the Godhead.

32. O Arjuna! He who sees with an equal eye the pleasure and pain of all, as he sees his own, is regarded as the best yogi.

Shankara, the great commentator, comments that a yogi never acts against the welfare of any being and is non-violent.

Arjuna said:

33. O Madhusudana (Krishna)! I see no steady pursuit of the yoga of same-sightedness that you have just spoken because of restlessness of mind.

34. The mind, O Krishna! is restless, turbulent, strong and obstinate. I consider its control to be as difficult as that of the wind.

The Blessed Lord said:

35. Doubtless, O Mighty-armed One (Arjuna)! the mind is restless and difficult to control, but it can be restrained, O Son of Kunti (Arjuna)! through practice of meditation and renunciation of desires.

CHAPTER SIX

Practice and renunciation are key words in spiritual practice for gaining wisdom or knowing God. Practice means repeated and unrelenting effort, doggedness in the pursuit of the spiritual goal. Persistence is the general requirement for success though no one can lay down any rule for the Divine who is self-governed.

> **36. Union with Self (yoga) is difficult to achieve, I agree, by one who is not self-controlled, but it is possible for one with self-control through proper means.**

Proper means are persistent efforts at practice of concentration and of detachment.

ARJUNA SAID:

> **37. O Krishna! What road does a person of faith but of no application travel when his mind slips from the path of yoga without achieving perfection in it?**

> **38. O Mighty-armed One (Krishna)! Does the yogi who has slipped from both the paths, failing to be stable in the path of Brahman because of delusion, perish like a piece of torn cloud?**

What happens to those who leave the world but fail in their spiritual quest? Is their life an utter loss?

> **39. This doubt of mine, O Krishna! you have to dispel entirely; for none else but you is capable of removing it.**

In this universe of chance and uncertainties, only the Divine in our heart or the Divine Incarnation can speak with authority. All human knowledge is infected with doubt.

THE BLESSED LORD SAID:

> **40. O Partha (Arjuna)! Such a person is never lost here or hereafter. My Friend! No doer of good ever comes to grief.**

> **41. Gaining the worlds where the righteous go and dwelling there for many years, the person who has**

slipped from the path of yoga is born in the house of
the pure and the affluent.

42. Or he is born in the family of learned yogis. Such
a birth in the world is rarer.

43. There he, O Scion of the Kurus (Arjuna)! recol-
lects the last life's understanding of the spiritual aim
and struggles evermore for perfection.

44. Because of past habit, he is drawn helplessly, as
it were, toward Perfection. Even an inquirer after
yoga reaches beyond Vedic ritualism.

There are two kinds of religion: one, ritualistic religion practiced
with desire for material gain; the other, pure spirituality for gaining Freedom. Both of these are to be found in the Vedas, as mentioned earlier. Even one who inquires after the higher religion has
better taste than those whose religion is ritualistic and petitionary.

45. Striving harder than before and becoming free
from stain, he achieves perfection after many births
and realizes the supreme end.

46. The yogi is higher than the ascetic, higher than
the learned scholar, higher than the worker. Therefore, O Arjuna! become a yogi.

47. Among all the yogis, one who worships me with
faith and with his heart devoted to me is the best in
my opinion.

After giving an account of the path of strict contemplation,
Krishna concludes with an eulogy of the yogi who combines yoga
with personal devotion to the Lord. Here again, the Gita emphasizes karma yoga, the yoga of action for the good of humanity,
combined with the paths of wisdom and devotion. Worship of
Divinity with detachment from the fruits of action is common
practice among seekers of enlightenment and freedom. The
essence of spiritual practice is to get rid of the feelings of me and
mine which stand in the way of realization of Truth.

The Yoga
of Spirit and Nature

THE BLESSED LORD SAID:

1. **O Partha (Arjuna)! Listen now how by practicing yoga with your mind devoted to me and with me as your refuge you will know me fully and without doubt.**

It is clear from the above verse that the yoga of action (action with detachment) which Krishna has expounded in the earlier chapters is meant to be combined with devotion to the Lord. This is also indicated later in chapters 12 and 18.

2. I will tell you in full about this wisdom with its manifestations, knowing which there remains nothing more to be known here in this world.

The words in the text are *jnana* which is wisdom, or knowledge of Spirit, and *vijnana*, which means knowledge of the principles of nature; in other words, Pure Consciousness and the basic emanations.

The Gita is the essence of the Upanishads where it is asserted that Pure Consciousness is the Reality and nature its manifestation, and that knowing Brahman or Reality, one knows everything. "All this is Brahman," says the Upanishad.

3. Among thousands of men scarcely one strives for perfection, and among those who strive for it only a rare one knows me truly.

There are not many who strive after the Good, and even among those who strive after it, only a very rare person reaches the heights.

4. Earth, water, fire, air, space (ether), mind, intellect and ego are the eight divisions of my nature.

The above is the Samkhyan analysis of nature on the objective and subjective sides. Earth, etc., are the five subtle elements on the objective side corresponding to the five classes of sense-objects of perception. Space here means the medium of sound vibrations. They are not elements in the chemical sense. Mind, intellect and ego are developments on the subjective side. There are further developments on the objective and subjective sides into gross objects and the sense-organs of perception and action respectively.

The above are developments of the Power of Spirit, which is known as maya, the Divine fireworks. For a fuller account of the evolution of nature see the Introduction.

5. This is inferior nature, O Mighty-armed One! Know my other nature, which is higher and which is Spirit upholding the world.

The individual spirit and the elements of nature on the subjective and objective sides (mind, intellect, ego and organs as opposed to the objects of perception and action) are called the two natures of the Supreme Spirit. The individual spirit is a limitation of the Supreme Spirit — the conscious agency of an individual.

The Upanishads declare, like the Gita, that everything originates from Brahman. The *Mundaka Upanishad* declares, "From the Supreme Person originate life, mind, all the organs, space (ether), air, fire, water and the earth, the upholder of all" (2:1.3).

·6. Know these to be the source of all beings. I am the origin and end of the entire universe.

7. O Winner of Fortune! There exists nothing whatever higher than me. All this (the visible universe) is strung on me like gems on a string.

8. I am the taste in water, the light in the moon and the sun, Om in all the Vedas, sound in space and manliness in men.

Om is the sacred mono-syllable, the indicator of Reality, appearing first in the Upanishads, which may be uttered on various sacred occasions.

9. I am the pure fragrance in earth, the brightness in flames, the life of all beings and the austerity of ascetics.

10. O Partha (Arjuna)! Know me to be the eternal seed of all beings. I am the intelligence of the intelligent, the spirit of the spirited.

11. I am the strength of the strong, bereft of desire and passion. Among beings, O Best of the Descendants of Bharata! I am desire that is not opposed to law (dharma).

The word *dharma,* which is usually translated as religion, stands for a variety of things. It means among others, the properties of a substance such as a mineral or a plant. It also means the rules that govern a society, the principles that are proper for the conduct of business or any profession. In short, dharma means the characteristic features and principles which hold a thing or an organization together. The many departments of life have their particular dharmas for attaining their goals. These are matters of conduct, rules and regulations.

A civilized man of awakened consciousness seeks the goal of freedom and perfection of life. That goal is beyond society and history. This is the true meaning of the dharma of man or religion. It is only through proper conduct of life that man attains the Supreme Good. Such conduct or obedience to a higher law is also religion. This is the meaning of Sanatana Dharma or Eternal Religion.

The Gita points out that this supreme end of man can be attained through worship or *upasana*. This means approaching the Ideal through work, devotion, wisdom and contemplation, which are different ways or paths to one common goal. The essence of this practice is desirelessness or love of God. Through such practice, the real goal which is within us is revealed to the seeker, and the mortal man becomes immortal.

Life, however, is never lived without some kind of desire. As long as there is the ego-sense, there is desire. Also there are people at different levels of evolution whose desires and appetites vary. Civilized societies whose leaders are enlightened lay down different rules for the spiritual advance of members according to their development. Their desires, regulated by law, are not seen as irreligious.

A good society keeps alive through its various institutions the ideal that the goal of life is not money or pleasure or power, but freedom from all want by conquering nature without and within. Life lived with this understanding is driven by its inherent potential toward wisdom. Life is awakened and inspired by the teaching and company of the good.

12. Whatever be the modes, serene, active or dull, know them all to be born of me alone. They are in me, but I am not in them.

The Gita maintains non-dualism; the world of change flows from the changeless Spirit without diminishing it.

13. Deluded by the moods born of the three modes (gunas of nature), the whole world does not know me, the Imperishable One beyond them.

The Eternal Reality, the Self of all remains hidden behind the changing forms of nature.

The *Katha Upanishad* says, "The Self-existent one made the senses outgoing; therefore they see that which is outside and not the Self within; but some rare sage desirous of immortality saw the Inner Self by turning his gaze within" (2:1).

14. This divine maya of mine, made up of the modes, is extremely difficult to overcome. But those who take refuge in me alone cross over it.

The modes are the three gunas. It is only through Divine grace that maya, the delusion that the material universe of space-time is substantial, is overcome. The *Katha Upanishad* declares that the road to Truth is difficult to traverse for it is narrow as the sharp edge of a razor and that the Divine reveals Itself to him alone whom it chooses.

It is by turning our gaze and by surrendering the ego to the Great Self within that one crosses beyond the delusion of bondage.

15. Those evil-doers who are deluded and the dregs of society, whose understanding has been stolen away by maya and who are demoniac in nature, do not worship me.

The world is the see-saw of forces, good and evil. The delusive imagination of self-centered individuals is the evil aspect of maya, while faith, charity, philanthrophy, etc., are good maya which leads one to the gates of Freedom.

16. O Arjuna! Best of the Descendants of Bharata! Four classes of virtuous persons worship me: the afflicted, the inquiring, the solicitors of wealth and the wise.

The wise do not ask for anything. God takes care of them. They are free and without desire. The others, who ask for rewards, are also good, and their faith leads them, if it is unwavering, to freedom from desire.

17. Among these, the wise person who is always united with me, and whose devotion is to me alone is the best. I am very dear to him, and he is also dear to me.

The free man's worship is the best, it is love for love's sake. This is not the so-called free man's worship in Bertrand Russell's famous essay where man, free from religious dogmas, surveys an inhospitable universe, cold to the fragile plant of life.

In Russell's essay, *Free Man's Worship,* the free man is one who has rejected the dogmas of religion but is idealistic enough to pursue the goals of love, beauty and truth. The essay is a good summons to man's spirit and it is possible for such a worshipper to reach what Vedanta says is the Truth which is the goal of true religion. However, man is not born free, nor does he become free by rejecting religious dogmas. Man with selfish desires is never free. To be free he has to reject all dogmas including those of science, for belief in the reality of sense-perceptions on which science rests is only another dogma.

Russell's summons to courage sounds like a man whistling in the dark. The free man of the Gita is above nature and united with Divinity. Man, says Vedanta, is born in chains but struggles for freedom beyond.

18. All these are good, but the wise person, in my opinion, is my very Self. For being united with me, he dwells in me alone, the Supreme Goal.

Those who believe and pray advance toward Truth even if they pray for material goods and power. Through prayer mind becomes purer and begins to realize that the best prayer is not a selfish petition, but the longing for manliness, the strength to overcome all weakness and dependence. The goal of life is Truth which we do not seek outside. Through prayer the veils are removed, through dependence on God the ego becomes more and more diluted and finally it becomes completely diluted in the still waters of Reality. The wise person is one with God and sees that God is pulling all the strings of the puppet ego.

19. After many births, the man of wisdom worships me, realizing that I am all that is. Such a great soul is very rare.

CHAPTER SEVEN

The height of wisdom, say the Upanishads, is the knowledge that all is Brahman (God). Truth or Godhead is that in which all differences melt into the unity of Sat-Chit-Ananda. Such realization takes a long time. But no law rules God. Ramakrishna said God is like a child and sometimes gives knowledge, it seems, capriciously. There are persons who become illumined suddenly.

There are few seekers of Truth. Most people desire enjoyment and power.

"I am all that is" means that all is Brahman. The seer sees the manifold universe as a world of forms of the same substance to which we give different names. The multiple universe is one of name and form. Ramakrishna said he saw the world and its many objects as wax figures of different shapes. It is a rare experience.

One can imagine that if one had superfine microscopic vision he might see the material universe as constellations of white light.

It is a rare thing to experience the unity of existence, the Divine Presence everywhere, through the veil of the manifold. Incarnations sometimes give a hint of this truth to the special bearers of their message by a touch or by a word.

Not long ago Ramakrishna manifested this power to prove this truth of Vedanta, as related by Swami Saradananda in *Sri Ramakrishna, the Great Master:*

Narendra, who was later to adopt the monastic name of Vivekananda, came to Ramakrishna while he was a college student. At the time he was a member of the Brahmo Samaj, a theistic society modelled on the Christian church, based on dualistic principles, but deriving inspiration from the Upanishads.

One day while he was visiting, Ramakrishna told him about the non-dual Reality of Brahman, unity of all existence. Narendra could not understand it and went to Hazra, a devotee who lived at the temple garden and who used to have his seat near Ramakrishna's room, and said, "Can it be ever possible that the water-pot is God, the cup is God, whatever we see and all of us God?" Hazra and Narendra both burst into laughter ridiculing the idea.

Hearing Narendra laugh Ramakrishna came out of his room like a boy with his cloth in his arm-pit and coming to them smiling said affectionately, "What are you both talking about?" He then touched Narendra and went into ecstasy.

Narendra said to us afterwards, "There was a complete revolution in the state of my mind in a moment at the wonderful touch of the Master. I was aghast to see actually that there was nothing in the whole universe except God. But I remained silent in spite of seeing it, wondering how long the state would last. But that inebriation did not at all diminish that day. I returned home; it was all the same there; it seemed to me that all that I saw was He. I sat for my meal when I saw that all — food, plate, the one who was serving as well as myself — were nothing but He. I took a mouthful or two and sat quiet. My mother's affectionate words —'Why do you sit quiet; why don't you eat?' — brought me to consciousness and I began eating again. Thus I had that experience at the time of eating or drinking, sitting or lying, going to the college or taking a stroll. I was always overwhelmed with a sort of indescribable intoxication. When I walked along the streets and saw a carriage coming along before me, I did not feel inclined, as at other times, to move away lest it should collide with me. For I thought, I am also that and nothing but that. My hands and feet always remained insensible at that time. I felt no satisfaction whatever when I took my food. It seemed to me as if someone else was eating the meal. Sometimes I lay down while eating and got up in a short time to continue eating. On some days I thus ate much more than the usual quantity of food. But that did not bring about any disease. My mother was afraid and said, 'You, I find, are internally suffering from a terrible disease.' Again she sometimes said, 'He will live no more.' When that overwhelming intoxication diminished a little, the world appeared to me like a dream. Going for a walk on the bank of the Hedua tank, I knocked my head against the iron railings round it to see whether what I saw were dream-rails or actual ones. On account of the insensibility of my hands and feet I was afraid that I might be going to have paralysis. I could not escape that terrible intoxicating mood and overwhelming condition for some time. When I came to the normal state, I thought that that was the indication of non-dual knowledge. So what is written in the scriptures about it is by no means untrue. Since then I could never doubt the truth of non-duality."

CHAPTER SEVEN

The experience that Vivekananda (Narendra) had was like the experience of St. Paul on his way to Damascus, which converted him.

"All see the Eternal One, but only the devotee in his solitude recognizes Him" (Kabir, medieval Hindu saint).

20. Persons whose sense of discrimination has been stolen away by many desires are constrained by their nature to worship other gods by following different rites.

Such worship is comparable to prayers to saints and angels for particular benefit.

21. I give to the devotees unshakable devotion to the forms they want to worship faithfully.

22. Equipped with that faith, the devotee engages in worship of his favorite god and receives therefrom the desired rewards ordained by me alone.

23. But the fruit which the people of poor understanding receive is perishable. The worshippers of gods go to them, but my devotees come to me.

There have been worshippers of gods, angels, spirits, saints all over the world from prehistoric times. Krishna declares that all powers come from Him. Gods and saints and angels are not independent. They are like everything else in nature, creations of the Lord.

The result of worship of gods, etc., is small and transient. The intelligent ones see that it is impossible to ford the interminable sea of desires and troubles, and therefore seek the Supreme Good.

24. Men devoid of understanding, without knowledge of my supreme, imperishable and changeless nature, think that I, the Unmanifest, have become manifest.

Krishna here clarifies the concept of maya. Maya, or the magic universe, is not a real transformation of the Absolute or Brahman.

The universe is not a substance. It is the imagination, a mysterious projection, of the Power of the Absolute. The Absolute is not diminished or exhausted by this projection, as in this world a piece of material disappears into a transformed object. The Absolute remains the same Absolute, inexhaustible and unimaginable, after creation. The process that is nature or universe is the magic of God and not his substance.

The peace chant at the beginning of the *Brihadaranyaka Upanishad* gives the mathematics of the infinite, which can be understood in the light of today's science. The chant says, "This (Brahman) is infinite, that (creation) is infinite. Subtracting the infinite from the infinite the infinite remains."

The numberless universes that modern mathematicians imagine coming out of the timeless and motionless void do not diminish the void. This, however, is imagination about the origin of material universes and not knowledge, but a hint.

According to Vedanta endless universes of conscious and unconscious beings arise from timeless Consciousness without diminishing its fullness. Ramakrishna told a philanthropist who believed in doing good to the world that there were numberless universes like crabs on the banks of the Ganges.

Mathematics (number) is the image of the Infinite in time. As the universe contracts to disappear, time contracts and the speed is infinitesimal.

Emanations of the Infinite are infinite in time. Endless universes come out of eternity, the Infinite beyond time. There is no end to numbers and their fractions in time. When the collapsing universe disappears into nothingness, numbers vanish into zero. Reality is imaged by mathematics but never grasped by it. Reality is zero (*shunya* of the Buddhists). It is Absolute Silence, Pure Existence and Bliss and it cannot be numbered.

25. Because of being veiled by creative energy (yoga maya), I am not manifest to all. This deluded world does not know me who is birthless and changeless.

Yogamaya is nature or the process which is constituted, as mentioned earlier, by the union (yoga) of the three constituents (gunas) of sattva, rajas and tamas.

> **26. O Arjuna! I know all the beings which are past and present and which are to come, but no one knows me.**

> **27. All beings, O Arjuna, the Destroyer of Enemies! become deluded at creation by the deceptive dualities born of love and hate.**

> **28. But those doers of meritorious acts, whose sins have ended and who are free from the delusive dualities of love and hate, worship me with steadfastness.**

The spiritual goal of man is the unity beyond the dualities of good and evil, yin and yang, ego and its desires.

> **29. Those who strive for freedom from old age and death by taking refuge in me know Brahman, the Inner Self and all action fully.**

> **30. Those who know me and worship me as present in the material and spiritual aspects and in sacrificial acts will know me, too, at the time of death.**

The last verse above is a prelude to the next chapter which offers explanations of the material, spiritual and sacrificial aspects and which also describes the passage into different worlds at death.

CHAPTER EIGHT

The Yoga of the Imperishable Brahman
(The Imperishable and Cosmic Evolution)

AJUNA SAID:

1. **What is Brahman? What is the embodied self (*adhyatma*) and what is action (karma)? What is the physical realm (*adhibhuta*) and what is the realm of gods (*adhidaivata*)?**

The traditional popular view was that behind the different bodies and the different gods were different ruling principles. This popular notion of pluralistic principles is rejected by the Gita, according to which the Supreme is the only principle behind every one of the particulars: creatures, gods, sacrifices and actions.

2. O Madhusudana (Krishna)! Who is the ruler of sacrifices in this body (*adhiyajna*) and how does he dwell there? And how again at death would the self-subjugated one know you?

THE BLESSED LORD SAID:

3. The Imperishable (Spirit) is the Supreme Brahman; nature (the embodied spirit) is the inner self (adhyatma); the emission (*visarga*) which is the origin of beings is called karma (action).

Creation is called emission of the power of Brahman. The Neoplatonists speak of creation as emission. Their highest principle is the Good, which is the same as Brahman. "This production is not a physical process, but an emission of force ..." (*Encyclopedia Brittanica,* 13th ed., s.v. "Neoplatonism").

In the oldest Veda, in the famous hymn on creation, creation is called emission (visarga) of the Divine.

Both Plato and Plotinus, the founder of Neoplatonism, expressed Vedantic truths, which has been noticed by a few Western scholars, including B.L. Urwick and H.G. Rawlinson.

Plotinus was a student of Ammonias Saccas in Alexandria, where Buddhist monks, Brahmins and Indian religion and philosophy flourished for centuries. Plotinus was so interested in the religions of the East that he joined the expedition of a Roman emperor to Persia to learn about them at first hand. The expedition failed and Plotinus had to return before he reached Persia.

Plotinus's account of the evolution of cosmos from the One recalls the Samkhya-Vedanta account. Plotinus's disciple Porphyry knew Brahmins in Alexandria.

Plotinus influenced St. Augustine. Neoplatonism became a great theoretical buttress of the Christian religion.

In old days, philosophy was largely a search for moral and spiritual truths, and the method was one of contemplation. Later in the history of Europe, philosophy became more and more a purely intellectual enterprise for the interpretation of nature and for justification of moral truths.

It is, therefore, no surprise that modern philosophy has surrendered its effort to understand nature to science, and that its earlier attempts to find the basis of morality through reason have been reduced to trivial discussions of relativity of ethics and cultural patterns.

Karma has many meanings; its usual meaning is action. The words karma and creation are derived from a common Indo-European root.

4. O the Best of the Embodied (Arjuna)! The mutable bodies constitute physical existence (adhibhuta),

the Cosmic Person is the indwelling spirit (adhidaivata), and I am the Lord of sacrifices in the body
(adhiyajna).

The Cosmic Person or the Ruler of the Universe or Personal God is
the first manifestation of Brahman. The above verse indicates anew
that creation is an emanation. The Personal God is the Ruler of creation; all existent things and beings are the play of His power.

**5. He who leaves the body at death and departs
remembering me unites with me without a doubt.**

Remembrance of God at the time of death presupposes life-long
practice of the presence of God, worship and meditation. Civilized life is indeed a preparation for death. Gandhi died with the
name of Rama, a Divine Incarnation, on his lips when he was
felled by the bullet of the assassin.

**6. O Son of Kunti (Arjuna)! When a person leaves
the body at death he attains to the state or feeling
which grips his mind at that time as a result of his
constant occupation with it.**

The law of karma dictates that the dominant interests of a person
grip the mind of an individual at the time of death and carry him
to a situation where they can find fulfillment.

**7. Therefore remember me always and fight. If you
surrender your mind and understanding to me, you
will come to me without a doubt.**

This is the practice of the presence of God, always and in all
activities.

**8. Dwelling on the Supreme Divine Person, with an
unwavering mind made steady through the practice
of yoga, one goes to him.**

**9-10. Dwelling on the all-knowing, ancient Ruler,
who is smaller than the smallest atom, who is the**

> Protector of all, who is inconceivable, who is efful-
> gent like the sun and beyond darkness; a person of
> devotion, holding with unwavering mind through the
> power of yoga the life force between the eyebrows at
> the time of death, goes to the Supreme Person.

The Sanskrit word for "all knowing" is Kavi which means a poet.
The creator is called an artist. An artist uses sensuous images to
reflect the Beauty of Reality. He acts out of a feeling of delight and
freedom and is not constrained by practical concerns.

God's creation is the expression of his playfulness and delight
of existence. He is Love and Beauty. Creation of the universe is like
the artist's expression of delight in language and form.

> 11. I am going to tell you briefly that state which the
> knowers of Veda (Wisdom) speak of as Imperish-
> able, which desireless mendicants (renouncers)
> enter, and seeking which they live a life of conti-
> nence and purity (*brahmacharya*).

> 12-13. Closing all the gates of the senses, arresting
> the mind in the heart, holding the life-force (prana)
> between the eye-brows, established in yoga of con-
> templation, reciting the monosyllable Om (the
> sound Brahman) and thinking of me, he who departs
> leaving the body attains the Supreme Goal.

> 14. O Partha (Arjuna)! I am easily attainable by the
> yogi who is ever devoted, and who remembers me
> daily and constantly without any other thought.

> 15. Having come to me, the great-souled ones who
> have attained the supreme state of perfection are not
> born again in this transient and miserable world.

> 16. O Arjuna! All worlds from the domain of Brahma
> to this are subject to return, but, O Son of Kunti
> (Arjuna)! there is no rebirth after attaining me.

There are many universes, all of which come and go in cycles of creation and dissolution (the systole and diastole of the cosmic heart).

17. Those who know that a day of Brahma is made up of a thousand aeons (yugas) and his night of another thousand aeons are knowers of day and night (time).

An article in the British science magazine *Nature* states, "The Indian astronomers established an epoch when the sun, the moon and all the planets were last present in zero longitude: that was in 3102 B.C. The period from one such epoch to the next, according to Aryabhatta (fifth century A.D.) is 10,080,000 years and is called a yuga. Four yugas, the Krita-yuga, Treta-yuga, Dwapara-yuga and Kali-yuga make a Mahayuga; and 1,008 yugas make a Kalpa. The current quarter is Kali yuga, assumed to have begun at sunrise at Lanka (a hypothetical place where the meridians of Ujjain, a town in N. India, intersect the equator) on Friday, February 18, 3102 B.C."

According to *Vishnu Purana* (circa fourth century A.D.) four thousand yugas make a day of Brahma.

18. At daybreak (of Brahma), all manifestations proceed from the unmanifest, and at nightfall, they merge into that unmanifest again.

According to a scholiast on Shankara's commentary, the unmanifest above means the night of Brahma, the Demiurge (Creator).

19. All these beings, O Partha (Arjuna)! being born again and again merge helplessly into the unmanifest at the approach of night and are born anew at daybreak.

To the modern mind creation and dissolution of universes can be represented as follows: creation is emission of cosmic energy, subtle and gross. Dissolution is return of material energies through 'singularity' into finer energies of the universal mind which again attaining 'singularity' lapse back into complete dissolution — the unmanifest.

20. But beyond that unmanifest there is a different eternal Unmanifest which is not destroyed when all the beings are destroyed.

21. That Unmanifest which is called the Imperishable is said to be the final goal, reaching which one does not return (is not born again); this is my Supreme Abode.

Modern physical science holds that the amount of energy in the universe remains constant during transfer from one condition to another, and also that all of it may collapse into nothingness. It is also conceivable to mathematician-physicists that innumerable universes may burst forth from that limitless nothingness, the reservoir of all creations (the ether of Plato).

Physical science has trouble dealing with mental phenomena, however. Is knowledge a movement of molecules of the brain? The ideas of space and time are then molecular movements. Then if you should ask, "Where is the brain?" The answer should be, "In the brain since space is in the brain." Physical knowledge is practical, but surrounded by doubt and impenetrable walls.

22. O Partha (Arjuna)! That Supreme Person in whom are all the beings and who pervades all of this can be attained by unswerving devotion.

23. Now, O Best of the Bharata Race! I will tell you of the time, when departing, the yogis are born again and also when departing they do not return.

The "time" here means the paths the departed ones travel. The exact meaning of the two paths is not known. A knower of Brahman does not travel.

24. Fire, light, day, the bright fortnight of the moon and the six months of the sun's northern course; departing at such time, the knowers of Brahman go to Brahman.

25. Smoke, night, the dark fortnight of the moon and the six months of the sun's southern course; departing at such time the yogi returns after receiving the lunar light.

26. These two paths, bright and dark, are considered to be eternal. Going by the one, the yogi attains Freedom, by the other, he returns again.

27. No yogi knowing these paths, O Partha (Arjuna)! is ever deluded. Therefore be devoted to yoga at all times.

28. Knowing all this, the yogi attains the primeval Supreme State reaching beyond all the fruits of meritorious actions, the promised reward of the study of the Vedas, of sacrifices, of austerities and of charitable gifts.

CHAPTER NINE

The Royal Yoga

RELUDE: The foregoing chapters, 7 and 8, describe the nature of the Imperishable and the Unmanifest and the yogic way of departing from the world for attaining union with the Divine. These are difficult to grasp and practice for common aspirants. So the Lord is describing in chapters 9 through 12 the easier path of devotion and the visible manifestations of God. They are, of course, part of karma yoga.

THE BLESSED LORD SAID:

1. I shall now tell you who is without cavil, this most secret wisdom together with its realization, knowing which you will be free from evil.

2. This is the king of knowledge, king of secrets, pure and best, and directly perceptible. It is canonical, easy to practice and imperishable.

The various methods of realizing the Divine have been called "secret knowledge" in the Upanishads (cf. Greek mysteries). Of these, the path of devotion has been called the king of secrets. It is also a fact that kings and noblemen of the past practiced this path, so it is also kingly knowledge.

3. O Tormentor of Enemies (Arjuna)! Persons who are without faith in this path return without finding me into the paths of mortal existence.

There is no relief for a human being till he has wisdom. The Christian dogma of eternal hell probably stands for everlasting mortal existence due to ignorance. Wisdom frees the individual.

4. The whole universe is pervaded by my unmanifested form; all beings abide in me, I do not dwell in them.

The manifested beings represent the mysterious emission from the Godhead, they are not the substance.

5. Look at my divine power (yoga); the beings are not in my eternal nature. My Self is the origin and upholder of beings but is not in them.

The world is maya. It has no real existence. It is, and it is not. Its appearance and disappearance are due to the mysterious power of Brahman, the Substance which creates and dissolves the changing universe by opening and closing its eyes. The mystery of non-duality, or the Real, is being hinted at by language born in the world of duality.

In our experience, the maker of things, things themselves and the objects produced are separate and different. Also if we fashion a thing out of some material, the material disappears in the product. But in creation, the cause is never exhausted nor is it one bit diminished. There can be creations without cease from the inexhaustible Emptiness of Reality.

Our ideas of existence relate to time. If, as today's science speculates, the universe came out of timeless nothingness, can we apply our dualistic imagination to this mystery? Something coming out of nothing — and has that nothing disappeared, or is it still existing? It will be an eternal rigmarole of words meaning nothing to our minds accustomed to dualistic thinking.

Truth of religion becomes revealed as the ego becomes diluted. A raw man becomes a gentleman through chastening of the ego. A gentleman becomes a holy man through further dilution of the little self. And a holy man becomes No-man, or All-man, through complete dissolution of the ego. Religion is everything that helps dilution of the ego.

6. As the air which moves everywhere is in the sky, so know that all beings are in me.

Air is in space, but one cannot say that it is touching space. This is an analogy to express the truth that pure Spirit is transcendent to change, but not to deny that nature is emission of its power. Upon realization of Truth, all is seen as Brahman, change and the changeless; the universe exists as the play of Brahman's Power.

Some commentators have tried to explain this verse dualistically, maintaining a radical distinction between the Creator and the created. But this is not the view of the Gita or the Upanishads. Truth is beyond reason; the resolute, rational pursuit of which leads one to its brink.

The two marks of civilization are knowledge and gentleness. The gentleman is a civilized man who recognizes the same spiritual essence and dignity in all, not only in the members of the political club where he belongs, but everywhere.

Pursuit of the ideal of the gentleman leads to sainthood when one recognizes the same spiritual presence everywhere, in "the Brahmin, the cow, the elephant, the dog and the outcaste," as the Gita declares.

This spiritual drive is constitutional in man. It is arduous and difficult to pursue without faith in the spiritual Essence of all existence. Religion is assertion of the spiritual Reality of existence.

7. O Son of Kunti (Arjuna)! At the end of a cycle all beings dissolve into my nature; I project them again at the beginning of another.

See chapter 8, verses 16-17 and accompanying comments.

8. Ruling my own nature, I project this vast multitude of beings which are helplessly under its control.

9. But, O Winner of Wealth (Arjuna)! these actions do not bind me because I stay detached and indifferent.

The ultimate philosophical Truth, hard to grasp and risky to pursue without the help or grace of the Guru or Teacher, is that in Reality there is no bondage; it is only a nightmarish imagination. It is for the realization of this Truth that the different yogas are prescribed. Karma yoga is the common way which everyone can practice. Error and knowledge exist in consciousness. When error is gone, knowledge establishes itself.

10. O Son of Kunti (Arjuna)! Under my supervision nature produces the living and the non-living. The world goes in cycles of creation and destruction by reason of this.

According to Samkhya, natural process or creation begins when Spirit views nature, just as a dancing girl begins to perform in the presence of the spectator. Vedanta makes nature the power of Spirit and not an independent thing.

The world goes in cycles. Aristotle said that the ideal motion is circular. It was often ridiculed by professors of philosophy. But look at the world and the heavens. The planets, stars, galaxies, etc., all move in cycles. In life, too, we move in cycles though often like a broken record.

11. The dull-witted, without knowledge of my supreme status as the Great Lord of beings, disregard me incarnated in human form.

It is only rare individuals of high spiritual perception who can recognize a Divine Incarnation. Ramakrishna said that only a few among the many saints (rishis) recognized Rama as an Incarnation. With common people of extreme attachment to materialism and the pleasure principle, even good-heartedness, not to speak of high spiritual quality, is suspect.

12. They are of vain hopes, of vain deeds, of vain knowledge and without sense. They are possessed of ghoulish and demoniac natures.

In chapter 16 Krishna describes in detail two broad classes of human beings, the divine and the demoniac.

13. But, O Partha (Arjuna)! the great-souled ones who have the divine nature, knowing me, the Imperishable Source of beings, worship me with single-minded devotion.

Our faith and devotion keep wavering in the beginning of spiritual life, but through persistent effort and doggedness, they become stable and firm by the grace of the Divine. Ramakrishna says that a boatman has to steer his boat out of a narrow and winding creek slowly and carefully, sometimes by pulling it with a rope, but once it reaches open waters, he unfurls the sail and sits in repose at the hull smoking a pipe. Stability in character requires steady and long practice. This is indicated in the next verse.

14. Singing my name always, striving with firm vows and bowing down to me with devotion, they worship me constantly.

15. And others worship me, the all-facing, with the sacrifice of knowledge. Some worship me as the One, some as the Distinct, and some as the Manifold.

The different meanings of sacrifice have been noted earlier in comments on chapter 4. Some worship the Divine as one's own Self; some worship the different forms of the Divine outside (various gods), and some worship the presence of the Divinity everywhere.

16. I am Vedic sacrifice, I am ceremonial sacrifice, I am the offering for the benefit of the departed ancestors; I am medicinal herbs, I am the sacred hymn, I am the oblation, I am the fire, and I am the act of sacrifice.

In the above verse and also in many others, Krishna says that he is everything. The ultimate perception is perception of God in everything. In a lecture under the title "God in Everything," Vivekananda said, "The Vedanta does not in reality denounce the world. The ideal of renunciation nowhere attains such a height as in the teachings of the Vedanta. But at the same time, dry suicidal advice is not intended; it really means deification of the world — giving up the world as we think of it, as we know it, as it appears to us — and to know what it really is and Deify it; it is God alone. We read at the commencement of one of the oldest of the Upanishads, 'Whatever exists in this universe is to be covered with the Lord.'"

> **17. I am the father of this world, its mother, protector and grandfather. I am also all that is to be known, all that is pure, the Om, Rig Veda, Sama Veda and also Yajur Veda.**

> **18. I am the way, the sustainer, the Lord, the witness, the abode, the refuge, the friend, the origin, the dissolution, the ground, the death and the eternal seed.**

> **19. O Arjuna! I give heat, I hold back rain and also pour it. I am immortality and also death, and I am both the existent and the nonexistent.**

Divinity is both the changeless Reality and the flow of changes, birth and death. All actions are the play of the Divine Power.

> **20. Soma-imbibing, sinless performers of sacrifices enjoined in the three Vedas (Rik, Sama, Yajus) pray for passage to heaven and having reached the holy domain enjoy there the celestial pleasure of the gods.**

The Vedic sacrifices and rituals were performed by those who desired results. Soma was an herb.

The Vedas, the original literature of the Indo-Aryans, were divided into three parts in the beginning, Rik, Sama and Yajus, to which a fourth was added later, the Atharva.

The followers of the three Vedas mentioned above meant

those who were believers in ritualistic religion and whose worship was motivated by desire for enjoyment of power and pleasure.

The Vedas contain, besides prescriptions of rituals, portions on wisdom (religion of freedom) known as the Upanishads or Vedanta (end portion of the Vedas).

> **21. Having enjoyed the vast world of heaven, they return to the world of mortals upon exhaustion of the merit of their deeds. Thus, the followers of the religion of the three Vedas who crave enjoyment experience coming and going.**

There is no end to transmigration for persons with desire. Good deeds have pleasant results, bad unpleasant. Freedom is for those alone who take refuge in God and work without desire.

> **22. Those who worship me think of me as their own. For them who are thus always united with me, I bring what they need and secure what they have.**

God takes care of all the needs of the devotee who relies on him completely. Swami Shivananda wrote in a letter to a disciple, "Take the Lord's name without end. Let the heart be filled with His name; you will not in that case feel any kind of want — whether it is material or moral or spiritual. It is only due to lack of faith in the Lord and of devotion and love for Him that the above-mentioned wants are felt."

> **23. O Son of Kunti (Arjuna)! Even those devotees who worship other gods with faith worship me alone, though without knowledge.**

The many different divinities are powers of One God though their worshippers do no know it.

> **24. I am alone the enjoyer and Lord of all the sacrifices, and because they, the worshippers of other gods, do not know me in truth, they fall (return to earth).**

In religion, in worship, devotion is primary, the image or the symbol is secondary. All sincere worship reaches God, but worshippers get results according to their beliefs. In this verse, those who worship Krishna as the Indwelling Spirit of all become free.

> 25. The worshippers of gods go to gods, the worshippers of the ancestors go to the ancestors, the worshippers of spirits go to spirits, while my worshippers come to me.

"Those who worship Krishna are not born again" (*Narada Purana*).

> 26. A leaf, a flower, a fruit or water which a devotee offers me with love, I accept that love offering of the pure-hearted.

Who can offer anything to God who is everything and who has everything? He is satisfied with love alone.

> 27. O Son of Kunti (Arjuna)! Whatever you do, whatever you eat, whatever you sacrifice, whatever you donate and whatever austerity you practice, offer it to me.

> 28. You will thus be free from the bondage of action, its good and bad results, and being free because of renunciation of the results of action, you will come to me.

All worship is sacrifice of the ego. As stated in the beginning of this chapter, the path of devotion is easier to practice than the path of wisdom or the path of pure contemplation. All actions of life can be turned into worship in this path, through remembrance of God and offering everything to God. Through such remembrance actions and character become progressively purified and the heart is drawn toward the Divine as if by a magnet.

The spiritual literature of India is full of examples of persons in all walks of life who became saints by living the life which fell to their lot without running away from it.

The redeeming nature of devotion is proclaimed emphatically in the verses that follow.

29. I am the same to all beings, none is hateful or dear to me. But those who worship me with love are in me and I am also in them.

30. Even if a person of the most outrageous conduct worships me with single-minded devotion, he is to be regarded as holy, for he is rightly resolved.

31. He quickly becomes a righteous soul and attains eternal peace. O Son of Kunti (Arjuna)! Know for certain a devotee of mine never perishes.

God is the Redeemer and this redeeming power is manifested also in God's Incarnations. Spiritual history of mankind is replete with examples of redemption of persons whom civilized society condemned and shunned as its worst sinners and criminals.

The fallen became saints and devotees by the mercy of Incarnations like Krishna, Buddha, Christ, Chaitanya and Ramakrishna. Muhammad said, "God is infinitely merciful and forgiving." Prostitutes, robbers, murderers, drunkards became saints and holy by their love and devotion to Incarnations and their disciples.

Buddha bestowed his grace on the prostitute Amrapali and the thief Agulimal. Christ said to the prostitute (Luke 7:50) who worshipped and anointed him with love, "Thy faith has saved thee, go in peace." And one of the criminals hanging near Christ on the cross had faith in him and was promised salvation (Luke 23:42-43).

A person becomes pure by loving God and the Incarnation of God. Incarnations of God and their disciples purify others by their love.

The truth is that all are children of Immortal Bliss, as the Upanishads declare, but in this world of mysterious maya which is a game of the Divine, some individuals have a very thick coating of ignorance over the Pure Self. It is not easy for them to pull themselves out of their dullness and distractions. But through faith, character changes. Faith grows through practice and through faith an individual becomes free. Existence in time becomes like a dream.

Ultimately, as the great teachers say, and as the Upanishads declare, grace comes from the Self, and only those who open themselves up to the grace of the Great Self within become free. Intellectual knowledge and good upbringing may incline one to belief, but without prayer and appeal to the deeper Truth in the heart, the Great Mother, no one can advance by sheer power of individual will. The ego needs to be completely humbled. The best ego is the dead ego.

This is the religion of bhakti or love of God, and it leads to the same goal as the religion of knowledge. There is only one Truth for all.

In the beginning of this chapter, Krishna says that this path is easy to practice. In this age, when as Krishna remarks in chapter 4, religion has become tarnished and a thick crust of unreality and artificiality has formed over life, the religion of love and service as taught by Krishna based on the Truth of Vedanta, is the yuga dharma, religion of the age, the royal road to Truth. Ramakrishna said that in this dark age devotion as taught by the great sage Narada was the way and that God should be worshipped in man.

The great message of Vedanta, the good news, is continued in the next verses.

32. Even those who are of (so-called) sinful origin, women, Vaishyas and Shudras (businessmen and menial servants), reach the Supreme End by taking refuge in me.

In India businessmen were never credited with the great virtues of life. All groups, organizations, etc., have their principles of operation which are called different dharmas or principles which hold them together. In the Mahabharata it is said that it is the dharma or religion of a businessman to cheat a little on the scale. If he does not he is not a true businessman — the idea is that you cannot survive in the jungle world of money-making without predatory habits. But some may practice business honestly, listing cost and profit exactly.

The Gita and Vedanta are against superstitious distinctions. Ramakrishna said that the devotees of God had no caste distinctions and no sex discrimination.

The Gita has no prejudice. It points out in chapter 5, verse 18, that the enlightened ones look upon the learned Brahmin, cows, elephants, dogs and outcastes with the same eye.

There are always popular prejudices in societies, ancient or modern. What the Gita meant is that even those who are born handicapped and in difficult social situations and who are considered poor by prejudiced and non-spiritual people can, despite lacking the facilities of the high-born, become saints, for the same Truth sleeps in all.

Vedanta teaches the innate divinity of all. Social distinctions and restrictions are no part of religion as the long line of saints from time immemorial to our own day have proclaimed and practiced.

There were women saints in the age of the Upanishads. The Mahabharata and the *Ramayana,* the two great epics of India, mention saints who came from the so-called lower castes. The essential equality of all was never lost sight of in India, though greed and selfishness and lack of education led to terribly corrupt practices in later times for a variety of reasons. But crude caste rules and racial and class ideas are now disappearing in the face of the preaching of Vedantic truths. A lot of things are necessary to spread this truth, but the inspiration has to come from persons who can speak with authority on the great Truth of life.

33. What need to speak of virtuous Brahmins and royal sages (philosopher-kings)? Having come to this transient and unhappy world, worship me.

The first line of the verse above has to be read as a continuation of the previous verse.

The world with its disease, death, violence, hatred, cruelty, injustice and disasters is not a happy place to be in for those who are not drunk with the wine of prosperity and pleasure. The existentialists speak of the tragic reality of human existence which philosophical speculations of a thousand years have not been able to solve. Only the Lord, said Vivekananda, could bear such a world.

The materialistic concept of life as the Bard of Avon said is "a tale told by an idiot full of sound and fury signifying nothing."

Materialistic existence is uncertain and unhappy. It is a nightmare for those who have a conscience and an ideal. Religion is waking up from this dream.

The nightmare ends for those who find refuge in Truth and perceive the untruth of the clash of opposites in the world. Those who become free or are striving to be free try to bring real togetherness in society and life. Moral society is a reflection of a basic spiritual unity. It is the kingdom of heaven come to earth.

Worldly experiences are transient and haunted with pain and anxiety. Only those feelings which have the quality of true and deep love have a touch of eternity in them.

Love of the world without ideals is seen by idealistic persons as a coarse dog-like existence.

Today's world is being generally sucked into violence, disorder and pain due to irrational intellectualism which feeds on the principle of pleasure and greed. Science and psychology have not helped to solve the radical problems of man. Without roots in religion they are only increasing unhappiness in society and the individual.

34. Dwell on me, be my devotee, worship me and bow down to me. Having thus taken refuge in me and uniting your heart with me, you will come to me alone.

Through devotion to the Personal God the devotee finally attains complete union with Him.

CHAPTER TEN

The Yoga of Divine Manifestations

THE BLESSED LORD SAID:

O Mighty-armed One (Arjuna)! Listen again to my supreme word which I will tell you for your own good, for you are pleased to hear me.

2. Neither the gods nor the great sages know my origin; for I am the origin of the gods and the great sages in every way.

The Lord is the origin of time and beings, the uncaused cause of everything.

3. He who knows me to be the Supreme Lord of the world, birthless and beginningless, he among mortals is without delusion and becomes free from all sins.

To know God as birthless and beginningless is to become one with the living and blissful silence beyond change.

Sin here means the bondage of nature, one's identification with change. Some scriptures make too much of sin. Those who keep harping on sin, which is unreal, keep continuing in bondage. That is why Vivekananda once remarked facetiously,

THE YOGA OF DIVINE MANIFESTATIONS

"The Devil is the Hamlet of the *Bible.*"

> 4-5. Intelligence, wisdom, non-delusion, forgiveness, truth, control of senses, external and internal, happiness and sorrow, birth and death, fear and fearlessness, non-injury, equanimity, contentment, austerity, benevolence, fame and infamy — all these different states of creatures arise from me alone.

The above are all processes of nature, manifestations of the Supreme Spirit.

> 6. The seven sages and the four before them, as well as the Manus, are born of my mind, from which comes all these creatures of the world.

The seven sages, the four before them and the Manus are mythical persons. Manu is the name applied to successive mythical progenitors and sovereigns of the earth. One of the Manus, Satyavrata, is regarded as the progenitor of the present generations. He is said to have been preserved, like Noah of the *Bible,* from a great flood by Vishnu (Krishna) in the form of a fish.

> 7. He who knows truly these diverse manifestations of mine, as also the power of projecting them, has unshakable perception of Truth; of this there is no doubt.

Spiritual knowledge is not the relative, uncertain knowledge of intellect. As Vivekananda told some of his disciples at Thousand Island Park in New York, "A person who has a theory knows nothing." Religion is 'becoming' in the beginning, but finally it is 'being'.

> 8. I am the origin of all, all things originate from me; so knowing, the knowers worship me full of love.
>
> 9. With their heart given to me, their life dedicated to me, and enlightening each other, they feel pleased and take delight by discoursing about me always.

CHAPTER TEN

Constant remembrance, *dhruva smriti*, is the sign of true love.

10. To them who are always united with me and who worship me with love, I give the power of understanding through which they come to me.

11. Out of compassion for them I dwell in their mind and dispel the darkness born of ignorance by the bright lamp of wisdom.

The darkness of ignorance is blindness to Reality. Ignorance (avidya) is defined in the Yoga Aphorisms as egoism, desire, hate and clinging to life. The ego-sense which hides Reality lives on selfish desires; it is eroded by pure love.

ARJUNA SAID:

12-13. You are the Supreme Brahman, the Supreme Abode, the Supreme Purity; you are the all-pervading Eternal Person, divine and birthless, the Primeval Deity; so all the sages and the divine sages Narada, Asita, Devala, Vyasa say of you; and you yourself are also telling me.

Krishna himself declares that he is the Divine Incarnation. This is the best proof of an *Avatara* (Divine Incarnation). The Divine Incarnations reveal their divinity to intimate disciples. Only very pure characters can recognize spiritual greatness. "Blessed are the pure in heart, for they shall see God," said Christ. God is absolute purity.

> Just as a storm
> Blows a clear path across the blue depths
>   of the silent sky
> For the rays of the morning sun,
> So let the mists of the past be lifted from life,
> And the clarion call of spirit
> Herald the beginning of a fresh awakening
> At the dawn of a new birth.
> May the blur of colors be wiped away
>   from the clear light,
> And the futile game of the world come to an end,

And may life through self-surrender
Find its supreme value in selfless love.
As I drift along in the stream of life
Let me not look back to the lights and shadows
    of the past.
The self that is stained with the world's joys
    and sorrows
May I cast it out of myself
And discard it in the heap
Where belong all the trivialities of life;
And with eyes free from fear and desire
Look upon the banished self as alien to my being.
And let this be my last prayer
That Infinite Purity make my life complete.
        (Free translation from Tagore)

The longing for purity is love of God. Spirituality begins with external purity. It develops into mental purity and then into awareness of Pure Spirit, the ultimate simplicty of existence. When the idea of me and mine disappears and wisdom ripens further, all that exists is seen as Brahman, waves on the ocean of pure existence.

14. O Keshava (Krishna)! I regard all you tell me as truth, for neither the gods nor the demons, O Lord! know your manifestation.

15. O Supreme Person! The Origin of Beings! The Lord of Beings! God of Gods and the Lord of the Universe! You alone know yourself by yourself.

16. Do tell me fully of your divine manifestations by which you have pervaded these worlds.

17. O Yogi! How shall I know you by thinking of you always? O Lord! In what aspects am I to meditate on you?

18. O Janardana (Krishna)! Tell me again in detail about your lordly power (yoga) and manifestations, for I am not satisfied with listening to your words of nectar.

CHAPTER TEN

Yoga in the above verse means what Vedanta calls maya, the creative power of the Divine. Thoughts and things which make up the universe of change are no substance. Science tells us that matter has disappeared from the scene leaving behind only its appearance, like "the lingering grin of the Cheshire cat" which has disappeared. The substance of all, thoughts and things, is Spirit. To discover it, man has to turn his gaze within.

THE LORD SAID:

19. Now, O the Best of the Kurus (Arjuna)! I will tell you of my principal divine manifestations, because there is no end to the amplitude of my manifestations.

20. O Conquerer of Sleep (Arjuna)! I am the Self dwelling in the heart of all beings; I am the beginning, the middle and also the end of all beings.

Cp. "I am the Alpha and the Omega." The Lord is the origin and end of all beings.

21. I am Vishnu among the Adityas, the radiant sun among the luminaries; I am Marichi among the winds; among the stars I am the moon.

22. Of the Vedas I am the Sama Veda; I am Vasava (Indra) among the gods; of the senses I am the mind; of the beings I am consciousness.

23. Of the Rudras I am Shankara; of the Yakshas and Rakshasas I am the Lord of Wealth; of the Vasus I am the fire-god; among the peaks I am Meru.

24. And know me, O Partha (Arjuna)! to be Brihaspati, the chief among the priests; of the generals I am Skanda; of the lakes I am the ocean.

25. Of the great sages I am Bhrigu; I am the monosyllable Om among words; of sacrifices I am the sacrifice of repetition of names; I am the Himalayas among the immovables.

26. I am the Aswattha of all trees and Narada among the divine sages, Chitraratha among the Gandharvas and among the perfected ones I am the sage Kapila.

27. Among horses know me to be Uchchaishravas, born of nectar, Airavata among lordly elephants and among men as monarch.

28. Among weapons I am the thunderbolt, among cows I am Kamadhuk, cow of plenty, of the progenitors I am the god of love, and of serpents I am Vasuki.

29. And I am Ananta of the nagas (snakes). I am Varuna (Ouranos) among water-beings; among ancestors I am Aryama; among controllers I am Yama, King of Death.

30. I am Prahlada among the titans; time among the calculators; of beasts I am the king of beasts (lion) and among birds Vainateya.

31. Among the speedy, I am the wind; I am Rama among warriors; of fishes I am the shark; of rivers I am the Ganges.

32. O Arjuna! I am also the beginning, the middle and the end of creations; of the sciences I am the science of Self; of disputants I am the discourse.

Science of Self is neither speculative philosophy nor intellectual knowledge of scriptures.

It is said in the Upanishad that two sciences are to be known, primary (*para*) and secondary (*apara*). The primary science is knowledge of Self. The secondary is intellectual understanding of the many branches of nature, or what is called today the different branches of science, and courses of instruction for the conduct of the practical affairs of life. It also includes studies of scriptures such as the *Bible* and others.

Para vidya or supreme knowledge is knowledge of Reality. "It is knowledge never known" (Vivekananda). It is Self-knowledge, the Pure Subject's knowledge of itself or the Self-awareness of pure, non-dual consciousness. It is said in another Upanishad, "By what can the Knower be known?"

When the Upanishad declares that two sciences are to be known it proclaims that no individual or society can neglect without peril practical knowledge; that is, one has to use reason in practical affairs, though one cannot rely on it for realizing the true and ultimate ends of man, the spiritual, the ethical and the artistic.

It needs to be constantly emphasized that higher knowledge, knowledge of morals and of God and Truth is not an intellectual acquisition, but a possession of the heart. God is felt, He is no theory or logical conclusion. "Some have thought deeply and expressed the meaning of thy truth, and they are great. But I have listened to the music of thy play and I am glad" (Tagore).

India's misfortune in the middle ages and later was due to neglect of physical science and uncritical devotion to irrational practices which masqueraded as spirituality, and were accepted because of the veneration which religion enjoyed in the country.

33. I am A among letters, and of the compounds, the dual; I am imperishable time; I am the all-facing protector.

34. I am all-devouring death and also the origin of all that is to be; and among women (feminine virtues) I am fame, prosperity, speech, memory, intelligence, constancy and forgiveness.

35. Of Vedic hymns I am the Brihat-saman; I am Gayatri of meters; of months I am Margashirsha (the first of months); of seasons I am the flowering Spring.

36. I am gambling among the fraudulent; I am the spirit of the spirited; I am victory; I am perseverence; I am the goodness of the good.

37. Of the Vrishnis I am Vasudeva (Krishna); of the sons of Pandu I am Dhananjaya (Winner of Wealth, Arjuna); among the sages I am Vyasa and of poets I am the poet Ushana.

38. I am the scepter of those who rule; I am the plan of those who campaign for victory; I am also the silence of secrets; I am the wisdom of the wise.

39. O Arjuna! Whatever is the seed of all beings, that also I am. There is nothing, moving or unmoving, that can exist without me.

40. O Tormentor of Enemies (Arjuna)! There is no limit to my divine manifestations. These diverse manifestations of mine of which I have spoken are but a token.

41. Whatever exists that is endowed with lordliness, wealth and energy, know that to have sprung from a fragment of my power.

42. O Arjuna! What is your need to know so much? I pervade the whole universe with a portion of my being.

In the *Rig Veda* and also in a later Upanishad it is stated that one step of Brahman pervades the entire existence, while the three other steps are in heaven.

The new physics of our time leads mathematicians to imagine the possibility of many, in fact, innumerable universes. We have mentioned earlier that Hindu spiritual thinkers assert in the ancient religious literature of India, the Puranas, that endless universes come into being from the Supreme Godhead, Vishnu.

One day while meditating under the Bel Tree in Dakshineswar, Vivekananda, then a young student, had a vision of a bright red triangle. He reported this to Ramakrishna who said that he had a vision of the birthplace of universes *(Brahmayoni)* from which endless universes are being born.

Brahman is the limitless being from which endless universes appear and into which they disappear again in vast aeons of time. The void from which visible creation comes remains limitless compared to the limited creations.

The Yoga
of the Revelation
# of Cosmic Form

P RELUDE: In the last verse of the previous chapter Krishna said that only a fraction of the Divine pervaded the entire universe. Upon hearing this Arjuna expressed his desire to see the Divine Cosmic Form of the Lord.

ARJUNA SAID:

1. Lord! The supreme secret concerning the Self which you have spoken out of grace for me has dispelled my delusion.

2. O Lotus-eyed (Krishna)! I have heard extensively from you of the birth and death of beings and also your imperishable glory.

3. Great Lord! It is just as you have described it. Now, O Supreme Being! I want to see your Divine Form.

"God is everywhere" is a common saying of religion. To knowers of divinity all existence is divine, the temporal as well as the transcendental. Sudden revelation, like the lifting of a curtain before a scene, is sometimes granted to fortunate spiritual aspirants. The

Divine is hidden from us by impurities of mind. Sometimes it happens to devotees that the mask of the commonplace is removed from the face of nature and the Divine glory and beauty stand revealed for a while before their gaze.

4. O Lord! If you think I am worthy of seeing it, then, O Lord of Yoga (Creation)! reveal to me your Imperishable Self.

THE BLESSED LORD SAID:

5. O Partha (Arjuna)! Behold my manifold Divine forms of many colors and shapes by the hundreds and by the thousands.

6. See the Adityas, the Vasus, the Rudras, the Aswins, the Maruts. And, O Descendant of Bharata (Arjuna)! see many wonders never seen before.

7. O Conqueror of Sleep (Arjuna)! See this day in this body of mine the entire universe together, moving and unmoving, and also whatever else you want to see.

8. But you will not be able to see me with these eyes of yours; I am giving you the Divine Sight. See my Divine Power.

SANJAYA SAID:

9. Having spoken thus, O King! Hari (Krishna), the great Lord of yoga (power) revealed to Partha (Arjuna) his supreme divine form.

The above verse and the three following ones make one continuous statement.

10. With many faces and eyes, with many strange forms, with many celestial ornaments and with many divine weapons uplifted;

11. Wearing heavenly garlands and costumes, anointed with divine perfume, most wondrous, infinite and facing everywhere;

12. The splendor of that universal form was like the brilliance of a thousand suns if they were to arise simultaneously in the sky.

13. The son of Pandu (Arjuna) saw there in the body of the God of gods the entire universe with its manifold divisions nesting together.

The religious history of mankind is full of revelations from beyond which graphically represent truths of Spirit. Readers of the Gospel of Ramakrishna will be familiar with many of his visions. Arjuna's vision is revelation on a grand scale.

14. Then struck with wonder, the Winner of Wealth (Arjuna) with hair standing on end bowed down his head to the Deity and with folded hands spoke to him.

ARJUNA SAID:

15. Lord! I see in your body all the gods as also the multitudes of varied beings; the Lord Brahma seated on the lotus throne, all the sages and all the celestial serpents.

16. O Lord of the Universe! I see everywhere your universal form of many arms, bellies, mouths and eyes, boundless on every side, but I do not see the end, the middle or the beginning of you, O Lord of Universal Form!

17. I see you everywhere with crown, mace and discus, glowing everywhere like a man of effulgence, blinding to sight, blazing like roaring fire and sun, and immeasurable.

18. You are the imperishable, the supreme object of knowledge; you are the ultimate resting place of this universe; you are changeless, the protector of the Eternal Religion; and I believe you are the Primal Person.

The Yoga of the Revelation of Cosmic Form

Religion is one and it is eternal. This is the perception of the sages of India. The many different religions are so many different ways of reaching the one common goal of all, which is the realization of the human destiny of freedom and eternal life. Philosophically the innate drive in man for freedom has been called the desire for the Good (shreyas). Religion is idealism. The imagination of today is the realization of tomorrow.

Religion is return to Reality. This return is the goal of history, of evolution, of the universe. Man can have no rest until this drive is realized. Progress in society and civilization is measured by the opportunities they provide for the realization of this supreme value.

Religion is universal; it does not create barriers; it is not tribalism. There are infinite ways for human development. The ways are not the goal and they are not universal. The common ideal of man finds expression in different ways in different societies and cultures. When it is realized that the common goal is Knowledge or super-science, the different approaches to Truth do not create conflict. A religion which lacks love for other religions and is opposed to the principle of togetherness of all is a misguided enterprise.

There is no true religion where there is narrowness of heart. "To the large-hearted the whole world is kin," so goes a Sanskrit saying. At the end of his life and following the dictates of his heart Tolstoy, who was without dogma, made a complete about face. As he wrote, what was behind him came to the front, what was on his right came to the left, and so on. Not many can make that turnabout. People are at different levels of development and need ideals and practices which they can grasp and follow. But religion should be understood in civilized societies as the key to human development and prized as super-science. Knowledge or Truth is the goal of all.

The Gita, the sermon of Krishna, emphasizes the eternal character of the common human drive for fulfillment, though it recognizes that different people need different approaches to the same Truth. Arjuna therefore addresses Krishna as the Protector of the Eternal Religion.

19. I see you as without beginning, middle or end, of infinite power, of endless arms, with the sun and moon as your eyes; your mouth as blazing fire and as scorching this universe with your own flame.

20. By you alone, O Great Soul! the space between heaven and earth and the ten quarters is pervaded. Seeing this strange and fearful form of yours, the three worlds are stricken with fear.

21. Those hosts of gods yonder are entering into you; some, frightened, are praising you with folded hands, while the host of great sages and perfected ones saying, "Peace be with you," (svasti) are singing your praise with myriads of hymns.

22. The Rudras and the Adityas, the Vasus and the Sadhyas, the Vishvadevas and the Aswinis, the Maruts and the Manes, the Gandharvas, the Yakshas, the Asuras and the Siddhas are all looking at you struck with wonder.

23. O Mighty-armed (Krishna)! Seeing your colossal form of many mouths and eyes, with many arms, thighs and feet, with many loins and fearful with many large teeth, the worlds as well as I are stricken with terror.

24. O Vishnu (Krishna)! Seeing your many colored, fiery form touching the sky, with mouths wide open and shining large eyes, my heart is stricken with fear, and I find neither stability nor peace.

25. O Lord of Gods! Seeing your mouths looking terrible with fearsome teeth and blazing like fires at the end of time, I am losing my sense of direction and find no peace. O Refuge of the World! Be gracious.

The Stoics who had a great influence on the Roman Empire and who had many famous followers including the emperor Marcus Aurelius believed in cycles of creation and in a great conflagration at the end of a cycle. There is no question that the Stoics like many others were influenced by Indian thought.

> 26-27. Yonder all the sons of Dhritarashtra together with the multitude of kings, as well as Bhishma, Drona, and the son of Suta (Karna) along with the principal warriors on our side are speedily entering your mouths, looking terrible with crushed heads hanging from frightful teeth.

> 28. As the many tides of rivers rush toward the ocean, so also are these heroes among men entering your mouths blazing fiercely on all sides.

> 29. As moths rush with headlong speed into the blazing fire to destruction, so also are these men rushing speedily into your mouths only to perish.

The Lord is the governor of history, the ruler of peoples' minds. It is by surrendering to His will, that is, by not acting selfishly but by giving up through assiduous practice the ideas of me and mine, that one becomes free and learns to play the game of the world without bondage and as an instrument of the Divine. Then the game does not hurt or turn into drudgery. Otherwise life is driblets of pleasure and pain and haunted with anxiety and fear.

> 30. O Vishnu (Krishna)! Devouring all the worlds with your flaming mouths, you are licking all around. Your fierce rays filling the whole universe with radiance are scorching them.

> 31. Tell me, who are you in this terrible form? Salutation to you, O the Best among Gods! be propitious. I want to know you, O Primeval One! for I do not know your purpose.

THE BLESSED LORD SAID:

> 32. I am hoary time, the destroyer of worlds. I am now engaged in the destruction of the world. Even

**without you none of these warriors who are arrayed
in the opposing armies will live.**

As indicated earlier, God rules everything. An individual gains
freedom by obeying God's will through sacrifice of narrow self-
will. An individual's feeling of freedom increases through observance of moral law.

**33. Therefore arise, acquire glory, and conquering
the enemies enjoy the undisputed kingdom. They
have all been slain by me already; be you, O Savyasa-
chin (Arjuna)! only an instrument.**

The theological doctrines of predestination and individual freedom create insoluble problems. Vedanta proclaims on the basis
of the ultimate realization that there is only one person who is
the Ruler of all nature. The many and different individuals are
not real but apparent existents. The Supreme Person is reflected
in the many egos and creates the notion of individuality. The
goal of life, of spirituality and religion, is to attain this realization
by surrendering ego, self-will, to God. This attainment comes
through practice of self-lessness in thought and action. It may
take a long time; it may not. It depends on the grace of the Lord
within.

Realization of freedom is like waking from a dream. Modern
science also makes the plural universes of time a contingent experience. This is the gist of religion, the meaning in history and civilization. The Gita points out in diverse ways how the goal is to be
reached and freedom secured.

**34. Slay Drona, Bhishma, Jayadratha, Karna as well
as the other heroes of war who already have been
slain by me. Do not be afraid; fight, you will conquer
the enemies in battle.**

SANJAYA SAID:

**35. Having heard these words of Keshava (Krishna),
the crowned one (Arjuna) was very much terrified.**

Trembling and saluting and prostrating himself, he spoke again to Krishna in choked voice.

36. It is right, O Hrishikesha (Krishna)! that the world rejoices and becomes devoted by the singing of your glory. Frightened, the Rakshasas are fleeing in different directions and all the hosts of the perfected ones (siddhas) are bowing down to you.

37. O Great-souled One! The Infinite Being! The Lord of Gods and Refuge of the World! You are even the origin of Brahma. Why should they not salute you who is the imperishable, the existent and the non-existent and also that which is beyond.

The dualities of being and non-being belong in the world of maya, the world of temporal existence, while Reality is beyond temporal being and non-being.

38. You are the Primal Deity, the Ancient Person. You are the Supreme Refuge of this universe. You are the Knower and the one to be known and the Supreme Abode. The world is pervaded by you, O One of Boundless Form!

39. You are Vayu (the wind), Yama (the King of Death), Agni (fire), Varuna (ocean), Shashanka (moon); you are the Lord of creatures and the Great Grandsire. Salutation to you a thousand times. Salutation again and over again, salutations to you.

40. Salutation to you in front and salutation to you from behind and salutation to you on all sides. O All! You are infinite in power and immeasurable in prowess. You pervade everything; therefore you are all.

41-42. Not knowing this greatness of yours, and thinking of you as my friend, whatever I have spoken

presumptuously out of either carelessness or fond-
ness, addressing you as, O Krishna! O Yadava! O
Friend! and O Changeless One! in whatever manner
I have been disrespectful to you either in jest or at
play, in bed or while sitting, at meals or alone or in
the presence of others, I pray, O Unfathomable One!
for forgiveness from you.

43. O One of Incomparable Prowess! You are the
father of this world of the moving and the unmoving;
you are its object of worship, the Teacher of teachers. There is no one equal to you in the three worlds;
where is one who excels you?

44. O Adorable Lord! I therefore salute you by prostrating myself and seek forgiveness. Please, O God!
forgive me just as a father forgives his son, a friend
his companion, and a lover his beloved.

God is all in all. This idea has been variously repeated in the
Gita.

God is the creator and the created. In Vedanta timeless Reality is called Nirguna Brahman and the universe Saguna Brahman,
i.e. Brahman with qualities. Vedanta accepts Samkhyan cosmology but rejects its philosophical dualism. In the Gita we find that
the two aspects of Brahman, the transcendent and the immanent,
are called *purusha* (person) and prakriti (nature, procreatrix) after
the Samkhyas; they are the same as Nirguna and Saguna Brahman.
We also find the word "prakriti" used for maya in an earlier Upanishad (*Shvetashwatara Upanishad*).

In later spiritual literature which emphasizes the creative
aspect of Reality for purposes of worship and prayer, prakriti is
called kali (time) and purusha is called mahakala (super-time).
The creative feminine energy became an object of worship as
Durga, Kali and Tara (among the Buddhists) and as Mary (among
Christians) because of the need for a personal spiritual ideal who
loves and cares for all. We find a hymn to the Deity as Goddess
even in the earliest Vedic literature.

The Yoga of the Revelation of Cosmic Form

The Gita emphasizes the personal aspect of the Deity for purposes of worship. God is all in all, mother, father, friend, lover, Lord and so on. He can be worshipped in any form.

45. O God! I am delighted to have seen your form never before seen, but my heart is laden with fear. O God of Gods! O Refuge of the World! Have mercy and show me your other form.

46. I want to see you even as before with crown, mace and discus in hand. O Thousand-Armed Universal Form! Please assume your four-armed form again.

The Blessed Lord spoke:

47. O Arjuna! Pleased with you I have shown you by my Divine Power the effulgent, infinite, primeval great universal form of mine which no one else has seen before you.

48. O Hero among Kurus! Neither by the study of the Vedas nor by sacrifice, nor by charity or rituals, nor by severe austerities am I visible in the world of men to any one other than you.

49. Do not be frightened or bewildered by the sight of this terrible form of mine. Now look at my former form, free from fear and glad at heart.

Sanjaya said:

50. Having thus spoken to Arjuna, Vasudeva (Krishna) showed him again his form and assuming his graceful mien, again consoled him who had been so frightened.

Arjuna said:

51. O Janardana (Krishna)! Seeing this graceful human form again my thoughts are collected and I have recovered myself.

52. Even the gods are ever desirous of seeing this form of mine which you have just seen and which is so difficult to see.

53. Neither by the Vedas, nor by austerity, nor by charity, nor by rites is it possible to see me just as you have seen me.

54. O Tormentor of Enemies (Arjuna)! But by single-minded devotion alone is it possible to know me, to see me and enter me thus.

55. O Son of Pandu (Arjuna)! One who works for me, regards me as his goal, is devoted to me and is non-attached and who has no enmity toward any creature enters me.

The last verse above of chapter 11 is regarded by commentators of great spiritual attainments as a key utterance of the Gita, where work, love and knowledge are combined and the character of a truly spiritual person is indicated.

One cannot love all or find God without going beyond the dualities of love and hate, the ambivalent emotions of little egos. A person who reaches the Truth beyond dualities loves all, for God is in all.

CHAPTER TWELVE

The Yoga of Love
(Bhakti Yoga)

RELUDE: The worship of unqualified, Imperishable Brahman (Absolute) as also the worship of the all-powerful and all-knowing Deity has been described in chapters 2 to 10. In chapter 11 Krishna revealed to Arjuna his Universal Form and enjoined him to do his work and be devoted to him, etc. Arjuna now wants to know which is better: the worship of indescribable Brahman or the worship of the personal aspect of Divinity.

ARJUNA ASKED:

1. Of those devotees who thus worship you steadfastly and those who worship the Imperishable and the Unmanifest, who knows yoga the best?

"Who knows yoga the best" means the best yogis or the best worshippers of Truth.

THE BLESSED LORD SAID:

2. Fixing their minds on me, those who worship me constantly without a break, being endowed with supreme faith, are in my view perfect in yoga.

3-4. But those who contemplate the Imperishable, the Undefinable, the Unmanifest, the Omnipresent, the Unthinkable, the Unchanging, the Immobile, the Eternal, subduing all the senses, even-minded toward all and engaged in the welfare of all the beings, they come to me also.

A long line of Indian saints of the highest spiritual realization dating back from the earliest of times have been active in relieving the suffering of man. In our time Vivekananda, the enlightened hero and leader, who felt he had a mission for the new age wrote the following in a letter to an American friend in 1897 from the Himalayan town of Almora in India:

... and may I be born again and again, and suffer thousands of miseries so that I may worship the only God that exists, the only God I believe in, the sum total of all souls; and above all, my God the wicked, my God the miserable, my God the poor of all races, of all species, is the special object of my worship.

He who is in you and outside of you, who works through every hand, who walks through every foot, whose body you are, Him worship and break all other idols.

In whom there is neither past life, nor future birth, nor death nor going nor coming, in whom we always have been and always will be one, Him worship, break all other idols.

Ay, fools, neglecting the living Gods and His infinite reflection with which the world is full, and running after imaginary shadows, Him worship, the only visible, and break all other idols (*Letters of Swami Vivekananda*, 3rd ed., p. 348).

And in another letter to an English disciple he wrote:

If I did not break my heart over people I was born amongst, I would do it for somebody else. I am sure of that. This is the way of some, I am coming to see it. We are all after happiness, true, but that some are only happy, in being unhappy — queer, is it not? There is no harm in it either, except that happiness and unhappiness are both infectious. Ingersoll said once that if he were God, he would make health catching, instead of disease, little dreaming that health is quite as catching as disease, if not more! That is the only danger. No harm in the world in my being happy, in being miserable, but others must not catch it. This is the great fad. No sooner a prophet feels miserable for the state of man than he sours his face, beats his breast, and calls upon everyone to drink tartaric acid, munch charcoal, sit upon a dung-heap covered with ashes and speak only in groans and tears! — I find they all have been wanting. Yes, they have. If you are really ready to take the world's burden, take it by all means. But do not let us hear your groans and curses. Do not frighten us with your sufferings, so that we come to feel we were better off with our own burdens. The man who really takes the burden blesses the world and goes his own way. He has not a word of condemnation, a word of criticism, not because there was no evil, but that he has taken it on his own shoulders willingly, voluntarily. It is the Saviour who should "go his way rejoicing, and not the saved."

This is the only light I have caught this morning. This is enough if it has come to live with me and permeate my life.

Come ye that are heavily laden and lay all your burden on me, and do whatever you like and be happy and forget that I ever existed ... (*Letters of Swami Vivekananda,* 3rd ed., p. 404).

5. Greater is the difficulty of those whose minds are set upon the Unmanifest for it is arduous for the embodied to attain the Unmanifest.

6-7. But I quickly save those from the ocean of mortal existence, O Partha (Arjuna)! whose hearts are set upon me, who surrender all their actions to me and are devoted to me and who worship me meditating on me with single-minded devotion.

8. Settle your mind in me alone, steady your understanding in me, you will dwell in me alone hereafter, no doubt of this.

9. O Winner of Wealth (Arjuna)! If you are unable to concentrate your mind steadily on me then seek to find me through repeated practice (Abhyasa).

Abhyasa in the verse above means practice; in spiritual literature practice means repeated efforts at concentration of mind
on the spiritual idea.

> **10. If you are unable to practice concentration, be a
> worker for my sake alone; by doing work for my
> sake, you will attain perfection.**

Vivekananda started the Ramakrishna Mission in his Master's
name with the idea of serving God in man *(nara narayana)*, God in
the poor, the ignorant, the sick and the troubled.

The above verse also bears a narrower interpretation as meaning ritualistic worship of God according to scriptural injunctions.

> **11. And if you are still unable to practice this, then
> taking refuge in me and controlling your mind, sur-
> render the results of all actions.**

> **12. Knowledge is indeed better than practice of
> concentration. Meditation is better than knowl-
> edge. Renunciation of the results of action is supe-
> rior to meditation. Peace follows immediately after
> renunciation.**

"Knowledge" (jnana) above means intellectual conviction of the
reality of Self gained through scriptural study (knowledge) and
reasoning. The different practices are matters of emphasis and
choice but Krishna here eulogizes renunciation of the fruits of
action.

> **13-14. He who has no hatred for any being, who is
> friendly and kind, who is without possessiveness
> and egoism, who is equal in pain and pleasure and is
> forgiving, who is ever content and meditative, self-
> subjugated and of firm conviction, who has surren-
> dered his mind and intellect to me and who is thus
> devoted to me is dear to me.**

15. He by whom the world is not troubled and who is not troubled by the world and who is free from elation and depression, fear and anxiety is dear to me.

16. He, my devotee, who is independent, pure, energetic, unconcerned, fearless and who has given up all selfish undertaking, is dear to me.

17. He who neither rejoices nor hates, neither grieves nor desires, he who has renounced good and evil and is full of devotion is dear to me.

18-19. He who is the same to enemy and friend, the same also in honor and dishonor, the same in heat and cold, pain and pleasure and free from attachment, who is the same in praise and blame, restrained in speech, content with anything whatsoever, without any fixed abode, steady-minded and devoted, is dear to me.

20. The devotees who practice this immortal discipline (dharma) thus described, with faith and complete dependence on me, are exceedingly dear to me.

In the above chapter and those which follow Krishna emphasizes selfless action with devotion to the personal aspect of the Deity based upon the advaitic conviction of the non-dual unity of existence.

Faith is the beginning of spiritual life and spiritual realization. This is emphasized in all the religions. Even mundane life in the world is based on faith and uncritical belief. The precariousness of such a life is obvious to all who spend a little time thinking about it.

The Yoga
of the Division of the Field
and Its Knower

P RELUDE: Chapter 7 indicated the evolution of the universe from the two aspects of the Divine, the perishable and the imperishable. This chapter indicates the nature of the Deity by a determination of the two natures. For a comprehensive grasp of the nature of the Divine it is necessary to understand not only the evolution and dissolution of universes but also the psycho-physical complex, the body, the field and the Conscious Principle, the Knower of the field, that lights it up.

ARJUNA SAID:

1. O Keshava (Krishna)! I want to know prakriti (nature) and Purusha (the Person), the field and the Knower of the field, knowledge and that which is to be known.

The above verse is not found in all editions of the Gita.

THE BLESSED LORD SAID:

2. O Son of Kunti (Arjuna)! This body is called the field and he who knows it is called Knower of the field by the wise.

The Yoga of Division of the Field and its Knower

The body is a constellation of the elements of nature or prakriti. The body is of two kinds, gross and subtle. The subtle body includes mind, intellect and ego-sense. They are all constituted by the three elements of prakriti, sattva, rajas and tamas.

The body is the known, the field of knowledge or the object. Pure Consciousness which lights up the field is the Knower.

The Real Man is the Knower of the field. But there is also the apparent man, consciousness limited by the elements of nature. This limitation is a false perception, which is the cause of bondage.

This gross part of man, this body in which are the external instruments, is called in Sanskrit, *sthula sharira,* the gross body; behind it comes the series, beginning with the organs, the mind, the intellect, the egoism. These and the vital forces form a compound which is called the fine body, the *shukshma sharira.* These forces are composed of very fine elements, so fine that no amount of injury to this body can destroy them; they survive all the shocks given to this body. The gross body we see is composed of gross material, and as such it is always being renewed and changing continuously. But the internal organs, the mind, the intellect, and the egoism are composed of the finest material, so fine that they will endure for aeons and aeons. They are so fine that they cannot be resisted by anything; they can get through any obstruction. The gross body is non-intelligent, so is the fine, being composed of fine matter. Although one part is called mind, another the intellect, and the third egoism, yet we see at a glance that no one of them can be the 'Knower'.

None of them can be the perceiver, the witness, the one for whom action is made and who is the seer of action. All these movements in the mind, or the faculty of intellection, or egoism, must be for someone else. These being composed of fine matter cannot be self-effulgent. Their luminosity cannot be in themselves. This manifestation of the table, for instance, cannot be due to any material thing. Therefore there must be some one behind them all, who is the real manifester, the real seer, the real enjoyer and He in Sanskrit is called the Atman, the Soul of man, the real Self of man (*Complete Works of Swami Vivekananda,* 10th ed., vol. 2, p. 424-25).

The *Mundaka Upanishad* gives, in beautiful imagery, the distinction between the Real actionless Self of man and the individualized consciousness of the apparent man:

Two birds of beautiful plumage, close companions to each other, cling to the self-same tree (the body). Of these one eats the sweet and bitter berries, while the other sitting on top watches its companion eating. The lower bird is bewildered and sorrowful because of eating bitter fruits. It looks up at its companion and sees it sitting serene and majestic. It hops up and as it approaches its companion it vanishes into it, becoming pure and free from all sin and sorrow. The lower bird was a reflection.

> 3. O Descendant of Bharata! Know me to be the Knower of the field and also as present in all the fields. The knowledge of the field and of the Knower of the field is to my mind true knowledge. What the field is, of what nature, what its modifications are, from what and how it arises, and also the nature of the Knower and His powers — about all of these hear from me briefly.

> 4. This has been sung variously by the sages in many different hymns and also ascertained convincingly by the aphorisms on Brahman with rational arguments.

The aphorisms on Brahman (*Brahma Sutras*) are one of the three pillars of Vedanta, the other two being the Upanishads and the Gita.

> 5-6. The fine elements, ego-sense, intellect, the unmanifest, the ten sense-organs, mind and the five objects of sense; desire and aversion, pleasure and pain, the aggregate, consciousness and fortitude — thus the field has been described briefly with its modifications.

Roughly what we call the body-mind complex is the field or nature. Consciousness mentioned in the foregoing verse is the reflection of pure Self-consciousness on the inner organ of the embodied self, like the heat absorbed by a ball of iron placed near fire.

The nature of the Knower of the field or Pure Consciousness is indicated in the following verses, 13-18.

The spiritual practices leading to that knowledge are described in verses 7-11. The phrase "this is declared to be knowledge" at the end of verse 11 includes all the verses from 7-11.

7. Humility, non-arrogance, non-violence, forgiveness, straightforwardness, service to the teacher, purity, steadiness, self control,

8. Renunciation of sense-objects as well as absence of egoism, perception of the evils of birth, death, old age and suffering,

9. Non-attachment, non-possessiveness in regard to son, wife, home and the rest, equal mindedness in regard to all desirable and undesirable happenings,

10. Unwavering love for me through single-minded constancy, resort to secluded areas, dislike for crowds,

11. Constant devotion to Self-knowledge, contemplation of the meaning of the knowledge of Truth — this is declared to be knowledge; its opposite is ignorance.

Religion is character. The ethical goal is the Good; the goal of religion is God. God is Good. Modern philosophy and science in the West have both retreated from their ambitious goal of finding Truth. Modern philosophical discussions focus on ethical questions of choices and commitments in life without reference to an absolute standard.

Religion is quest for Truth and its realization. Truth and the Good are one. One cannot reach Truth through false conduct. Absolute integrity is the price for spiritual illumination.

It is necessary to instill into young children some good rules of conduct, and develop in them good taste so that a life of integrity and moral power becomes easy for them later on. Religion is good taste.

When a short-sighted psychology views ethical conduct as an irksome imposition necessary for the pursuit of pleasure, disintegration of the individual and the society begins.

12. I will now tell you that which is to be known, knowing which one attains immortality. It is the Supreme Brahman without beginning, which is said to be neither existent nor non-existent.

Existence and non-existence are terms used in regard to objects in the world of duality. Reality is that which is beyond speech and from which speech comes (*Kena Upanishad*).

13. With hands and feet everywhere, with eyes, head and mouth everywhere, with ears everywhere, it exists covering everything in the universe.

14. It is expressed through the actions of all the organs but is without any organ. It is non-attached yet it supports all. It is devoid of modes yet it experiences the modes.

The modes (gunas) are the elements of nature, sattva, rajas and tamas.

15. It dwells within and without all beings. It is moving and unmoving. It is incomprehensible because of subtlety. It is far and also it is near.

The inscrutable Spirit is far from the ignorant, but near to the Knower.

16. Indivisible it exists as if it were divided in beings. It is to be known as the protector, the end and origin of all beings.

17. It is the light even of all the lights and is said to be beyond darkness. It dwells in the hearts of all as knowledge, as that to be known and as the Known.

Knowledge in the above verse means the moral qualities mentioned earlier in the chapter (verses 7 to 11). "That to be known" means Brahman which is to be known and when known it becomes "the Known."

> 18. Thus the field and knowledge and that which is to be known have been mentioned briefly; knowing this my devotee is fit for attaining my status.

The Upanishads declare that the Knower of Brahman becomes Brahman. This is no mere partaking of Divine nature or relative knowledge. In the language of Plotinus it is the flight of the Alone (One) to the Alone (One).

> 19. Know both Purusha (the Person) and prakriti (procreatrix, nature) to be without beginning and also know that the modifications and the qualities (constituents of nature) are born of nature.

Nature, to recall what has been indicated earlier, is the creative energy of Spirit, a kind of feminine energy producing, or giving birth to this universe and endless others. There is only one Person, one mind and one body, but there are limitless parts of these. She is the object of our worship, call her father, mother, friend or whatever. Through her grace one goes beyond the delusion of bondage, of fear and pain, and gains the Absolute.

Purusha or the Person is pure Spirit. The androgynous character of Reality and its creative power is reflected in Platonic myths about man and woman being physically joined together before they were bisected.

> 20. Nature is said to be the origin of body and the organs, while the Person (Purusha) is said to be the cause of experience of pleasure and pain.

It is the reflection of Spirit in the body-mind complex, like the reflection of the sun in a vessel of water, which creates the appearance of the individual agent and enjoyer of experience.

21. The Person situated in nature experiences the constituents born of nature. It is this contact with the constituents (sattva, rajas, and tamas) which is the cause of its incarnation in good and evil wombs.

Situated in nature means reflected in nature or limited by nature, apparently. This seeming limitation is the cause of the human experience of pleasure and pain or of bondage. As awareness of the Spirit's independence develops, one begins to experience true freedom, character and independence, large-heartedness, etc.

22. The Supreme Person who is in the body is called the witness, the approver, the sustainer, the experiencer, the Great Lord, the Supreme Self.

The Supreme Self is the Lord, support and substance of all from the intellect to the body.

23. He who thus knows the Person (Spirit) and nature with the elements is not born again, whatever he may do.

24. Some see the Self in the self by the self by means of meditation, others by the path of wisdom, still others by the yoga of action.

25. Others again without knowing this (Self) worship it after hearing of it from others. They also overcome death by following what they have heard.

26. O Bull of the Descendants of Bharata (Arjuna)! Whatever living and non-living beings come into existence know them to be born of the union of the field and the Knower of the field.

27. He who sees the Supreme Lord dwelling the same in all, not perishing when they perish, sees truly.

Creatures of maya are forms; birth and death are changes of form. Substance is like water, waves are the forms.

28. Seeing the Lord dwelling the same equally everywhere he does not hurt the self by the self and so he attains the Supreme end.

Vivekananda said that the above two verses contained the essence of Krishna's teachings — the presence of indwelling spirit everywhere.

29. He who sees all actions being performed by nature alone without exception and the Self as the non-agent sees truly.

30. When he sees the separate existence of beings as established in One and also their manifestation from that One, then he becomes Brahman.

31. O Son of Kunti (Arjuna)! Being beginningless and non-elemental, the Supreme Self is imperishable; therefore it neither acts nor is tainted though dwelling in the body.

32. As the all-pervading space (akasha) is not tainted because of its subtlety, similarly the Self though dwelling in all the bodies is not tainted.

33. O Descendant of Bharata (Arjuna)! Just as the single sun lights up the entire world even so the Dweller in the field reveals the entire field.

34. Those who thus know the distinction between the field and the Knower of the field, as also the liberation of beings from nature, attain to the Supreme.

CHAPTER FOURTEEN

The Yoga of the Division of the Three Gunas of Nature

THE BLESSED LORD SAID:

I will tell you again the supreme wisdom, the best of all wisdom, knowing which all the sages have reached the highest perfection after departing from this world.

2. Betaking to themselves this wisdom and having attained to my nature they are neither born at creation nor are they troubled at dissolution.

The highest wisdom is knowledge of Reality. Truth is the Reality of man, the untrammelled existence of pure, unalloyed bliss. Vedanta recognizes also existences superior to the earthly ones, but they are not the highest.

> 3. O Descendant of Bharata (Arjuna)! The great Brahma (nature) is my womb. I cast my seed into it, from which all beings originate.

Creation is a mysterious expression of the inexpressible Reality which projects the universe. The Divine Personality is the first expression, and it comprehends all that exists.

4. O Son of Kunti (Arjuna)! Mahat Brahma (nature) is the mother of all the forms which are born in all the wombs, and I am the father who casts the seed.

Mahat is the great principle. Vedanta rejects the dualism of Samkhya which makes a radical distinction between nature (mahat) and Spirit. Creation is the play of the living conscious divine energy. Nature is God in time.

5. O Mighty-armed One (Arjuna)! The three constituents of sattva, rajas and tamas (sentience, activity, dullness) born of nature (prakriti) bind the immutable dweller in the body.

For an understanding of the constituents of nature see the Introduction. Accustomed as we are with unphilosophical concepts of nature, it is not easy to grasp the meaning of the principles of sattva, rajas and tamas. As regards the above verse, sattva, rajas and tamas can be rendered into pleasant, exciting or stimulating and dull. These are feelings or moods which characterize nature. The gunas or constituents are always together in endless combinations and therefore create endless varieties of moods and feelings. The preponderance of the sattva element produces feelings of calmness, peacefulness, happiness, steadiness, for the sattva principle reflects Reality which is blissful and steady — the one and only fact.

6. O Sinless One! Of these, sattva being transparent is revealing and is free from trouble. It binds the embodied one through attachment to happiness and knowledge.

Sattva comes from the root *sat* which means Being or Truth. It is the quality or mood in nature which reflects the unchangeable nature of pure Being. Sattva is balance. Happy, calm feelings and love of science are steady feelings reflecting the steady blissful Spirit. Serenity is close to Reality, but it is not yet Reality. Since the moods are in combination they follow one another and there is no freedom for the person attached to any one of them. But the sattva mood is close to Reality which is only a step away from it. The following story by Ramakrishna of the rich man and the three robbers illustrates this:

Under the spell of God's maya man forgets his true nature. He forgets that he is heir to the infinite glories of his Father. This divine maya is made of three gunas. And all three are robbers, for they rob man of all his treasures and make him forget his true nature. The three gunas are sattva, rajas and tamas. Of these, sattva alone points the way to God. But even sattva cannot take a man to God.

Let me tell you a story. Once a rich man was passing through a forest, when three robbers surrounded him and robbed him of all his wealth. After snatching all his possessions from him, one of the robbers said, "What's the use of keeping the man alive? Kill him!" Saying this, he was about to strike the victim with his sword, when the second robber interrupted and said, "There is no use in killing him. Let us bind him fast and leave him here. Then he won't be able to tell the police." Accordingly the robbers tied him with a rope, left him and went away.

After a while the third robber returned to the rich man and said, "Ah! You're badly hurt, aren't you? Come, I'm going to release you." The third robber set the man free and led him out of the forest. When they came near the highway, the robber said, "Follow this road and you will reach home easily." "But you must come with me, too," said the man. "You have done so much for me. We shall be happy to see you at our home." "No," said the robber, "it is not possible for me to go there. The police will arrest me." So saying, he left the rich man after pointing out the way (*Gospel of Sri Ramakrishna*, 5th ed., p. 218-9).

7. Know rajas, O Son of Kunti (Arjuna)! to be of the nature of passion which creates thirst and attachment. It binds the embodied one by attachment to action.

Sattva is represented by white color, rajas by red and tamas by black.

8. But know, O Descendant of Bharata (Arjuna)! tamas (dullness) to be born of ignorance, the cause of delusion in all beings. It binds by false perception, indolence and sleep.

9. O Descendant of Bharata (Arjuna)! Sattva (intelligence) creates attachment to happiness, rajas (activity) to action, while tamas (dullness) veils understanding and attaches one to indolence.

10. O Descendant of Bharata (Arjuna)! Overcoming rajas and tamas, sattva sometimes becomes dominant; and rajas becomes dominant, overcoming sattva and tamas; and so likewise tamas becomes dominant, overcoming sattva and rajas.

As will be remembered, the three modes or constituents of nature are always united and they manifest themselves in an infinite variety of combinations in different objects. Some individuals who are loving and kind, and who are interested in knowledge and spiritual ideas, manifest the dominance of the sattva element; others who are energetic and ambitious about success manifest rajas; while dull and selfish characters reveal more of tamas.

Development of character proceeds from the dull to the active and then to the spiritual. Even the tamasic element of anger and violence, the rajasic element of passionate longing are used by the sattvic seekers of spiritual perfection to promote spiritual growth. This is what Ramakrishna meant when he said to some followers that instead of suppressing their negative tendencies, they should turn their inclinations to make positive use of them, like getting angry with oneself for doing something unethical.

It is said that a devotee with a violent disposition may have quicker success than one of mild temperament if the rage is rightly directed, even if it is against God and Guru.

11. When all the gates (senses) of this body are illumined by knowledge, know then that the sattva element has increased.

Sattva element is revealing. Perceptibility and manifestation of an object are due to sattva. Clear reception of information by the senses is due to their healthy, unagitated state.

12. O Bull among the Descendants of Bharata (Arjuna)! Greed, enterprise, undertaking, insatiable desire — all these arise when rajas becomes predominant.

13. O Descendant of Kuru (Arjuna)! Darkness, indolence, negligence of duty and delusion — these arise when tamas becomes predominant.

14. If an embodied being dies when sattva is predominant then he attains the spotless regions of the Knowers of the highest.

15. Dying while rajas is dominant he is born among men attached to action, and dying while tamas is dominant he is born in the wombs of the sluggish (animals, birds, etc.).

16. It is said that the fruit of good deeds is pure and of the nature of sattva (pleasant), the fruit of rajas (passionate deeds) is pain, while the fruit of tamas (dullness) is ignorance.

17. Knowledge is born of sattva; greed alone is born of rajas; negligence, delusion and ignorance are born from tamas.

18. Persons established in sattva go upwards; those who dwell in rajas stay in the middle; the dull established in tamas and engaged in the worst occupations go downwards.

The verses 5 to 18 in this chapter describe the nature of the gunas (constituents of nature), their actions, their binding character and the migration of individuals bound by them. These all belong to maya or have their origin in ignorance. In the next verse the Lord describes the nature of ultimate perception which is the means of freedom.

19. The seer, who perceives no other agent besides the gunas (the constituents of nature) and knows also that which is beyond them, attains to my being.

20. Going beyond these three modes (gunas), in which bodies originate, the embodied spirit becomes free from birth and death, old age and pain and attains immortality.

ARJUNA SAID:

21. Lord! What are the marks of the person who goes beyond the three modes; what is his conduct and how does he go beyond these three gunas (modes of nature)?

Arjuna's question is similar to the one he asked toward the end of chapter 2, inquiring about the marks of a person established in wisdom.

The person who is beyond the three modes of nature is the same as the person who is established in wisdom (end of chapter 2). Both are one with Brahman and free.

The words "he is said to be beyond the modes" at the end of verse 25 should be conjugated with each of the verses from 22 to 25.

Verse 26 mentions the means of attaining to the status beyond the modes.

THE BLESSED LORD SAID:

22. O Son of Pandu (Arjuna)! He who does not hate when the modes of manifestation, activity and dullness arise or desire them when they cease,

23. He who sits like one unconcerned and is not moved by the modes and who stays and does not waver knowing that the modes only are acting,

24. He who is the same in pleasure and pain, who is self-established, who views alike a clod, a stone and a piece of gold, who views the pleasant and the

unpleasant as the same, who is steady and equal in praise and blame,

25. He who is the same in honor and dishonor, the same among friends and foes, and who has given up all undertakings, is said to be beyond the modes.

26. He who worships me with the unswerving yoga of devotion becomes fit for the realization of Brahman after transcending the modes.

27. I am the haven of Brahman, the immortal, the imperishable, the eternal religion, and absolute bliss.

CHAPTER FIFTEEN

The Yoga
of the
Supreme Person

 RELUDE: In the previous chapter in verse 26 it was declared that those who approach the Divine on the path of love (bhakti yoga) gain wisdom through his grace and become liberated by going beyond the three modes of nature. In the present chapter Krishna without being asked continues to elaborate on the truth of Self.

The universe of many things has been described in ancient Vedic and Sanskrit literature variously as a tree or a forest with roots in heaven and branches below.

THE BLESSED LORD SAID:

1. They speak of an eternal peepal tree with roots above and branches below. Its leaves are the Vedas. He who knows it is the Knower of the Vedas.

The Gita recalls the description of the *Katha Upanishad* (3:1), "This peepal tree with it roots above and branches below is eternal."

The Mahabharata also describes the universe as the eternal tree or forest of Brahman where Brahman is always present.

"They" in the first verse stands for scriptures.

**2. Its branches, nourished by the modes (gunas) and
with sense objects as the buds, are spread above and
below. Its roots stretch down below in the world of
men producing the chain of actions.**

The first verse speaks of Brahman as the root of the universe; the
second verse characterizes the other roots below as desires result-
ing from actions.

**3-4. But its form is not experienced in that manner
here; it is without beginning, without end and without basis. Having cut down this peepal tree of
strong roots by the firm weapon of detachment,
then that destination has to be sought reaching
which one does not return any more. I take refuge
in the Pristine Person from whom flows the primor-
dial events.**

**5. Those who are without pride and delusion, who
have conquered the weakness of attachment, who
are ever occupied with spirituality, whose desires are
dead, who have been liberated from the dualities
termed pleasure and pain — these without delusion
attain that imperishable goal.**

**6. The sun does not illumine it, nor the moon, nor
fire. That is my supreme abode, going where they do
not return.**

**7-8. A portion of myself, eternal, has become the
individual self in the world of living beings. When
the governing spirit obtains a body and when it
leaves one, it draws the six senses including mind
which are in nature, and departs, taking them along
like wind carrying perfume from its source.**

"Them" in the last sentence above indicates the subtle organs.

Verses 7 and 8 describe the passage of the subtle body at
death to another body. The subtle body includes the mind, the
intellect, the ego sense and the five subtle organs.

The Ruler (Ishwara) is the individual self, a reflected portion of the Eternal Spirit.

In the sixties of this century *Life* magazine published an article about a medical and psychological experiment. The head of a decapitated monkey was under observation for a while for detection of consciousness till life departed from the brain. The doctor-psychologist wrote that after a while consciousness left the brain "like perfume" being spirited away from a flower. This reminded me when I read it of the above verse where exactly the same simile, about fragrance leaving a flower, is employed when the subtle body leaves the corpse at death.

> **9. Presiding over the ear, eye, skin, tongue and nose as well as the mind, the individual spirit experiences objects of sense.**

> **10. The deluded do not see it transmigrating or residing, or experiencing or united with the modes, but those who have the eyes of wisdom see it.**

The subtle spirit is not perceptible to dull minds, but can be seen by those alone whose sight has been turned within.

> **11. Diligent sages (yogis) see it dwelling in themselves, while the unintelligent ones of impure heart do not see it despite striving.**

> **12. The light that is in the sun which illumines the whole world and which is also in the moon and in fire — know that light to be mine.**

> **13. Entering the world I support the beings by my power and nourish all herbs by becoming the watery moon.**

> **14. Dwelling in the body of living beings as fire I, being united with prana and apana, digest food of four kinds.**

Prana and *apana* are nerve currents involved in assimilation of food. The four kinds of food are those which are masticated, sucked, licked, and drunk — just food and drink in simple language.

15. I am seated in the hearts of all. From me memory and knowledge arise and in me they disappear. I am the creator of Vedanta and the knower of the Veda also.

Vedanta is literally the end of the Vedas (Veda + anta) and means the last, the part dealing with wisdom in the vast literature known as the Vedas.

Creator of Vedanta also means the originator of the tradition and order that upholds the truths of the Upanishads. The Lord as the invisible source as well as the Incarnation (Son of God) in human form is the originator of schools of Vedanta, ascetic and non-ascetic.

16. There are in this world two persons, perishable and imperishable. The imperishable is one who is changeless.

This is a difficult verse. As has been noted before the Gita uses Samkhyan cosmology but does not maintain a radical distinction between Spirit and nature as Samkhya does. In Vedanta nature is the power or maya of Spirit. Being in maya, the individual is both perishable and imperishable because until knowledge dawns, the individual continues its transmigrations endlessly in time.

Scientists today imagine timelessness before the universe came into being and then again when it is supposed to roll back into 'singularity' and non-existence. But the scientists themselves are in time and are imagining something which is beyond imagination. This sort of imagination will continue endlessly unless the scientist stops thinking and delves into real timelessness in the depths of his heart and reaches the Silence from which all creations, scientists and their observations, emerge. Then it will be known that timelessness is the Reality of all — the timelessness which is not barren, but the limitless, inexpressible fund of bliss, consciousness and immortality.

17. But the Super Person is another and is called the Supreme Self. He is the imperishable Lord (Brahman) who upholds the three worlds entering into them.

The Super Person rules both the perishable nature and the transmigrating self which is a curious mixture of nature and Self.

The above verses have created difficulties for commentators. The fundamental facts of existence cannot be comprehended by knowledge based on non-fundamentals. Truth in the final analysis can only be indicated.

However, the essential and important fact is that there is the human condition of bondage, of fear and pain and also of some pleasure and of ignorance about the origin and goal of life. On the other hand there is the state of knowledge and freedom when no questions are asked for there are no problems anymore, while in conditions of pseudo-knowledge there are endless questions and problems and no final answers and solutions, and these go on without cease.

It is a fact that prayer opens the gate to Truth. Believe and you advance toward Truth. If you don't you will always be beset with problems. Merciful and loving Reality sends messengers when we are in desperate trouble and pray for help.

> **18. Because I am beyond the perishable and superior even to the imperishable, I am known in the world and in the Vedas as the Supreme Person.**

> **19. O Descendant of Bharata (Arjuna)! He who, free from delusion, thus knows me as the Supreme Person is all-knowing and worships me with all his heart.**

> **20. O Sinless One (Arjuna)! This most secret scripture (truth) has been spoken by me. Understanding it one will become wise and will have achieved all goals.**

The Sanskrit word *shastra* is translated as scripture. Shastra literally means the rules or injunctions that govern conduct or life. It also means revelation — the revealed Truth before being spoken or written.

The Yoga
of the Division of Divine
and Demoniac

P RELUDE: The divine and the demoniac are two broad divisions of human nature. In one of his letters Vivekananda classified people into two groups of tough and tender. William James, the American philosopher and psychologist, also made a similar division between the tough and the tender minded that has become famous.

The above divisions are never absolute. The two natures are found in all individuals in different strengths. Shankaracharya, the great scholar and saint, wrote that two opposite forces were always battling within us for mastery and that this struggle was mythically represented as the battle between the immortals and the titans.

In this chapter the division between the divine and the demoniac natures has been drawn in sharp contrast. There would not be a world or history without these divisions. In myths and history the demons often become powerful and destructive and seem to overpower the gods, but the gods pray for help from the Divine Mother and with her help overcome the demons. This is the perpetual see-saw of history; civilizations rise and fall and advance again to new heights.

However the true destiny of man is beyond time and history. Individuals are only phantoms who play the Mother's game and when the dream-play becomes a task they seek freedom and wake up from the nightmare.

The gods and the demons, according to the Brihadaranyaka Upanishad, are descended from a common ancestor.

This chapter describes elaborately the natures of the two, which were hinted at earlier in chapters nine, twelve and thirteen.

Some characterizations of the demoniac nature are quite modern.

THE BLESSED LORD SAID:

1. Fearlessness, purity of mind, steadfastness in the yoga of knowledge, charity, self-control, sacrifice, austerity, straight-forwardness,

2. Non-violence, truthfulness, absence of anger, renunciation, peace, overlooking faults of others, compassion for living beings, non-covetousness, gentleness, modesty, non-capriciousness,

3. Vigor, forgiveness, fortitude, purity, non-enmity, absence of pride are, O Descendant of Bharata (Arjuna)! the traits of those born with divine endowments.

4. Ostentation, arrogance, pride, anger, abrasiveness and ignorance, O Partha (Arjuna)! are the endowments of those born with the demoniac nature.

5. The divine endowments are cause for liberation, the demoniac ones cause bondage; do not grieve, O Son of Pandu (Arjuna)! you are born with divine endowments.

6. Two types of beings have been created in the world, divine and demoniac. The divine has been described at length, now hear, O Partha (Arjuna)! the demoniac.

7. The demoniac do not know what to practice and what to refrain from. There is neither purity, nor right conduct nor truth in them.

8. They say that the world is without truth, without a basis, without God, not born of anything; what else can it be except for satisfaction of desire?

The materialistic view is that there is no moral governance of the world; it has no roots, no goals, and has meaning only as a place where desires can be satisfied.

9. Holding to this view these depraved souls of little understanding and of outrageous conduct are born as enemies of the world.

10. Entertaining insatiable desires, filled with arrogance, pride and insolence and holding on to evil designs through delusion, these men work with unholy resolve.

11. Filled with limitless desires till death and given to the enjoyment of sensual desires as the supreme end and so convinced,

12. Bound by a hundred ties of hope, subject to lust and anger, they try by unjust means to amass wealth, for the enjoyment of sense-pleasures.

13. "This I have gained today, and I will gain this my heart's desire; this is already mine, and this wealth, too, will be mine again.

14. "This enemy I have slain and I shall slay others, too; I am the lord, I am the enjoyer, I am successful, strong and happy.

15. "I am rich and high born, who else is there like me? I will sacrifice, I will give and I will rejoice."

16. So, deluded by ignorance, and with minds distracted by many desires, entangled in the net of delusion and addicted to the enjoyment of pleasure, they fall into a foul hell.

17. Conceited, haughty, intoxicated with the wine of wealth and vanity, they perform sacrifices merely

in name with ostentation and without regard to
injunctions.

18. Given over to egotism, force, insolence, lust and
anger, these malicious detractors hate me who lives
in their bodies as well as in the bodies of others.

19. I hurl these malignant, hateful and cruel dregs of
men over and over again into the wombs of the
demoniac beings.

20. Entering into demoniac wombs birth after birth,
O Son of Kunti (Arjuna)! the deluded ones, without
ever finding me, descend into still lower states.

21. The gates to this hell are three: lust, anger and
greed, destroyers of soul; therefore, one should
renounce these three.

22. O Son of Kunti (Arjuna)! Free from these three
gates to dark hell, man strives for the good of self
and thereafter attains the supreme end.

23. Disobeying scriptural laws, he who conducts
himself impulsively attains neither perfection nor
happiness, nor the supreme end.

Freedom is beyond law, but as long as we are in the realm of maya
we have to observe laws in order to be beyond law.

There are rules in every department of life which need to be
observed to attain perfection in it. There are rules for doing things
to achieve success in a field, and there are rules of conduct, ethics,
to achieve harmony in family, society and international relations.
But that does not exhaust the scope of relationships and law.

Our goal is freedom, to be spontaneous in our life. This is
achieved by following the religious or moral law. We call it God's
law or scriptural injunction. Our goal is Spirit which is the only
fact and our Supreme Goal as human beings. We reach it by obeying the moral law laid down by messengers of God, by those who
have attained freedom.

CHAPTER SIXTEEN

The moral law is for elimination of the superstition of egoistic and multiple existence and for reaching the height of undivided and self-subsistent Reality. We need a ladder to climb to the roof; when we reach the roof we do not have any use for the ladder.

When a person reaches perfection in any field of activity he does not need any regulations. In fact his performance becomes the source of regulations. So also in life, one who reaches Truth is beyond law. His words and actions become our guide to perfection. His words are scripture. We have to follow them, obey them, respect them to find meaning and peace and fulfillment in life.

Civilization is really "A Slow Boat to China." The ideal has been represented in different cultures in forms suited to the understanding of common people. Great Truth is mystery and is called mysticism. Today, thanks to science and general education, the higher ideal of religion can be brought to the comprehension of many. There is no reason today for humanity to cling to primitive ideas of religion which create barriers between men and men, and which cater to the needs and interests of a particular community, or which condemn man. Even a person like Bertrand Russell who did not believe in religious dogmas said that the aim of higher religions was to extend love to other human beings beyond the limits of one's community.

It should also be noted here to remove a possible misapprehension that the Gita does not teach predestination or a radical division of good and evil beings. All are children of God and all are perfect in essence. Evil tendencies, which can be conquered, hide the original freedom and purity of Self of all.

Great scriptures like the Gita do not condemn any method or type of worship or religious idea, recognizing the different needs of individuals, but seek to eliminate ignorant fanaticism and hatred among the various sects which foolishly claim "absolute truth."

24. Therefore scripture is your authority in regard to the determination of duty and non-duty. You should act in the world knowing what has been sanctioned by scripture.

CHAPTER SEVENTEEN

The Yoga
of Division of Three
Kinds of Faith

RELUDE: This chapter divides a person's character and actions into three kinds according to the three modes of nature (sattva, rajas and tamas). The ideal character and action are those which belong to people of sattvic nature. The aim of spiritual life is to build up character. All possibilities are within us. They can be realized through faith and practice.

ARJUNA SAID:

1. O Krishna! What is the nature of the belief of those who worship (sacrifice) with faith, disregarding scriptural injunctions. Is it good (sattva), indifferent (rajas) or bad (tamas)?

THE BLESSED LORD SAID:

2. The faith of the embodied ones is of three kinds born of their nature: sattvic (pure), rajasic (mixed) and tamasic (impure). Listen to these.

3. O Descendant of Bharata (Arjuna)! The faith of persons is according to their nature. Man is made of faith; he is truly what his faith is.

Faith in the broadest sense is universal. Every moment of our life is based on faith. In religion faith means belief in God or freedom, i.e., in a higher destiny than the mundane.

Faith is in the constitution of man. The history of civilization may be viewed as development and clarification of man's faith. Even in the most primitive societies people have faith in powers and spirits which rule nature. Though such faith stands opposed to rational understanding of nature, it has a kernel of truth which is missed by those whose outlook is materialistic. Still, those who reject religion or belief in a higher truth than that found in nature pay homage to some ideal of faith in man's nature. None can live without faith.

In religion faith varies according to the character, or development of individuals in moral perceptions and intellectual attainments. In developed societies reason clarifies faith. Those who have subtle perception and can reason enough see no opposition between reason and faith. Contradiction between faith and reason rests upon a misperception of the scope of reason and of the meaning of faith.

Faith varies according to the moral character and intelligence of people. People also have faith without allegiance to a set of dogmas or creed.

Good company, good examples, are means of creating and developing faith in us. In our time of widespread knowledge of science, popular faith has to come to terms with reason. Messengers from beyond appear from time to time in history to assure men in declining times of their inalienable spiritual destiny.

4. Good people (sattvic) worship gods, the passionate (rajasika) ones worship demigods and demons, while others of dull nature worship ghosts and goblins.

Cults are to be found in all ages. Men of cruel and violent natures create cults of demons and satans.

5-6. Those non-discriminating persons, insolent and conceited, given over to desire, passion and violence, who practice terrible austerities not sanctioned by

scriptures, torturing the senses and also me who dwells in the body — know them to be of demoniac persuasion.

7. Food dear to all these people of different natures is also of three kinds; so also are worship, austerity and gifts. Listen to their differences.

8. Foods which enhance longevity, stability, strength, health, happiness, cheerfulness and which are sweet, mild, nourishing and agreeable are dear to persons of sattvic nature.

9. Foods which are bitter, sour, salty, very hot, pungent, dry and burning and which produce pain, grief and disease are dear to persons of rajasic nature.

10. The food that is cold, insipid, putrid, stale, left-over and unclean is dear to persons of tamasic nature.

11. The sacrifice that is performed by worshippers without desire for reward, thinking that it has to be done as enjoined by scriptures is sattvic (excellent).

12. But the sacrifice which is performed with the desire for reward and for the sake of ostentation, know that sacrifice, O Best among the Descendants of Bharata! to be rajasic (pompous).

13. The sacrifice which is without sanction of scripture, without distribution of food, without chanting of sacred formulas and without remuneration (to priests) is said to be tamasic (perverted).

The word sacrifice (*yajna*) in the Gita has a wider application than the performance of ritualistic, ceremonial sacrifices and oblations of the Vedic times. In the Gita, yajna means an act of worship in the widest sense.

It must have been seen from what has been said in earlier chapters that the Gita wants all life to be turned into an act of worship if one wants God, freedom and peace.

The words of men like Vivekananda and his brother disciples

are illuminating commentaries on the Gita. Vivekananda said to his disciples, "Cut out the word help from your minds. You cannot help, it is blasphemy! You worship when you give a morsel of food to a dog, you worship the dog as God. He is all and is in all."

It is the inspiration from the children of God alone which can turn the tide of history.

God works through them whose hearts have been purified by the practice of love.

> **14. Worship of the gods, of the twice-born, of teachers, of the wise, purity, continence and non-injury are called austerity of the body.**

> **15. Speech which does not cause anxiety, which is true and beneficial, and regular study of the scriptures are called the austerity of speech.**

Among the moral practices which the *Yoga Aphorisms of Patanjali* enjoin for yogis striving for perfection, ahimsa or non-injury comes first. Next is truthfulness. Commentator Vyasa says that truthful speech "instead of hurting any being should be beneficial because if spoken words hurt beings they do not become meritorious acts or virtue, but become vice. Such vicious truths lead to painful consequences; therefore, one should ponder and speak truth which is beneficial to all beings." It is a far cry from politics and self-serving truthfulness. Those who want to climb high in moral purity and fearlessness have to follow the rules enjoined by those who know the map of the spiritual world.

> **16. Cheerfulness, gentleness, silence, self-control and purity of heart — this is called austerity of the mind.**

> **17. These three austerities practiced with the best faith by devoted men without desire for rewards are called sattvic.**

> **18. The austerity which is practiced with the object of earning praise, honor and worship and with ostentation is unstable and fleeting in this world and is called rajasic (commercial).**

19. The austerity that is practiced with foolish determination and self-mortification, or for the purpose of
annihilating others is said to be tamasic (violent).

Austerity is penance if the morbid and self-degrading associations
that often go with it are left out.

20. The gift that is given at the proper time and place
to the proper person from a sense of duty and without thought of return is known as sattvic.

21. But that which is given reluctantly with the hope
of return or desiring some reward is known as a rajasic (tainted) gift.

22. The gift which is given with disrespect and con-
tempt in the wrong place, at the wrong time, to an
undeserving person is called tamasic (degrading).

23. *Om-Tat-Sat* are the three indications of Brahman.
Brahmins, Vedas and the sacrifices of old were made
of this.

24. For this reason the acts of sacrifice, gift-giving and
austerity mentioned in the scriptures are always begun
by the followers of the Vedas after the uttering of Om.

25. Uttering the word Tat and without desire for
reward, the aspirants after freedom perform various
acts of sacrifice, austerity and gift-giving.

26. O Partha (Arjuna)! The word Sat is used in the
sense of reality and goodness. Thus it is also used for
auspicious acts.

27. Steadfastness in sacrifice, austerity and gift-giving is called Sat, so also is the act performed for the
sake of the Supreme Lord called Sat.

28. O Partha (Arjuna)! Whatever is sacrificed or
given, whatever austerity is practiced or whatever is
done without faith is said to be unreal. It is no good
either here or hereafter.

CHAPTER SEVENTEEN

Sat-Chit-Ananda and Om-Tat-Sat are both indications of Brahman, of which Om-Tat-Sat (pronounced Ohm-tut-sut) is earlier.

Om is the most sacred sound symbol of Divinity among the followers of Sanatana Dharma (Eternal Religion) from the earliest of times.

An aphorism in the *Yoga Sutras of Patanjali* states that it is the manifesting word of Divinity.

Commenting on it, Vivekananda says:

The idea 'God' is connected with hundreds of words, and each one stands as a symbol for God. Very good. But there must be a generalization among all these words, some substratum, some common ground of all the symbols, and that which is the common symbol will be the best, and will really represent them all. In making a sound we use the larynx and the palate as a sounding board. Is there any material sound of which all other sounds must be manifestations, one which is the most natural sound? Om (Aum) is such a sound, the basis of all sounds. The first letter A is the root sound, the key, pronounced without touching any part of the tongue or palate. M represents the last sound in the series, being pronounced by the closed lips, and the U rolls from the very root to the end of the sounding board of the mouth. Thus Om represents the whole phenomena of sound production. As such it must be the natural symbol, the matrix of all various sounds. It denotes the whole range and possibility of all the words that can be made. ...

Om has around it all the various significances of divinity which cannot be said of the word God or other similar words signifying Divinity. Om has around it all the various significances of Divinity, Personal, Impersonal or Absolute God. As such it is the universal sound symbol of Divinity (*The Complete Works of Swami Vivekananda*, Mayavati Memorial ed., vol. 1, p. 218-19).

Tat and Sat mean the visible and invisible aspects of Reality or Brahman. Sat-Chit-Ananda as mentioned earlier means Existence-Consciousness-Bliss — the trinity of Brahman.

Om is called *Nada-Brahman* or the original sound of creation. "All things are created by Om" (Kabir, medieval Hindu saint).

The Yoga
of Liberation

RELUDE: This last chapter of the Gita summarizes its teachings. The Gita is a book of conduct. Life is a matter of conduct in all the various branches of its expression as well as in the orientation to its ultimate goal. Ethics and religion are not separate as it has been thought by many thinkers in the West including theologians. God is Good. The ideal of morality is never realized fully in action in the relative world. It is, however, realized within, in feeling as the height of spiritual experience. Ethics points to this goal.

A civilized society with its various functions and relationships has the ideal of duty. However its correct performance is not easy unless duty is greased with love and becomes true dedication. As we advance in civilization we feel a strong obligation to Truth. This duty does not cancel other duties; it includes them but excludes pursuits which hurt integrity. When all activities are performed with dedication to Truth, life becomes religious. When it is realized that Truth is the essence of our personality which is also love, freedom and bliss, the concept of duty melts into the spirit of worship. It is through erosion of the shadow-self that we advance toward our true Self which is eternal life.

CHAPTER EIGHTEEN

The ancient Greeks had the ideal of the unity of human conduct. Aristotle made politics a branch of ethics. Indeed all branches of human action have Truth as their ultimate goal, which in essence is religion.

Such a transformation of life happens through faith and worship. The Gita delivers this perennial message in an unparalleled manner.

ARJUNA SAID:

1. O Mighty-armed One! O Lord of the Senses and O Destroyer of Keshi (a demon)! I want to know respectively the truth about abandonment of works and also of renunciation.

THE BLESSED LORD SAID:

2. The learned declare the renunciation of actions with desire to be abandonment (sannyasa); the sagacious say that renunciation of results of all works is relinquishment.

3. Action should be given up as an evil say some philosophers; while others say acts of sacrifice, gift and austerity should never be given up.

4. O Best among the Descendants of Bharata (Arjuna) and Tiger among Men! Hear from me the final truth about renunciation, for renunciation has been declared to be threefold.

5. Acts of sacrifice, charity and austerity should not be given up but ought to be performed, for sacrifice, gift and austerity are purifying for the discerning.

6. Even these acts are to be performed giving up attachment and the desire for results — this is my certain and mature conviction.

The above verses and the following emphasize the path of self-less action as the method of Self-realization.

7. Renunciation of duty that has been enjoined is not proper; its relinquishment through delusion is declared to be tamasic (stupid).

8. He who gives up work out of fear of physical hardship, thus performing rajasic (tainted) renunciation only, will not reap the fruit of renunciation.

9. O Arjuna! When a prescribed action is performed without attachment and the desire for results, that renunciation is called sattvic (pure).

10. The man of renunciation endowed with sattva (serenity of mind), wise and with his doubts dispelled, does not hate a disagreeable action nor is he attached to an agreeable one.

11. Because it is not possible for an embodied being to give up action altogether, he who gives up the results of action is called a man of renunciation.

12. Good, evil and mixed are the three kinds of results of action which accrue to the non-renouncers after death, but never to those who have renounced.

13. O Mighty-armed One! Now learn from me these five causes which Samkhya philosophy declares for the success of all actions.

Some interpret Samkhya in the above verse as Vedanta; it does not make any difference.

14-15. The body, the agent, the senses of different kinds, many separate functions and fate; whatever action a man performs with his body, speech and mind, both that which is right and its opposite — these five are its causes.

Fate implies that there is an uncertain factor in the process called the world. We begin life with the belief that we are free to choose and act. Then we find that our freedom is limited and discover that despite our hopes and dreams and efforts our lives, individual

CHAPTER EIGHTEEN

and collective, reach conclusions we did not anticipate. The question is are we free agents or is nature, which includes ourselves, governed by some inscrutable power?

The question of man's freedom to choose and act has been debated endlessly and fruitlessly.

Vedanta gives the following answer, which can be grasped with the help of the findings of modern science. The idea of determinism has disappeared from modern science. Nature is chaotic at heart. Events are basically uncertain. It is possible, they say, that a steel bullet fired at a flower may sometime recoil after hitting it. One does not know when it may happen, but it may happen some time though such chances are extremely rare. Science cannot grasp the unknown factor in nature.

Vedanta says that nature is the power play of a personality whose will governs everything. Physical nature is expression of that will. The following lines are from a poem by Viveknanda entitled, "Who Knows How Mother Plays!":

> What law would freedom bind?
> What merit guide Her will,
> Whose freak is greatest order,
> Whose will resistless law?
> (*The Complete Works of Swami Vivekananda*,
> Mayavati Memorial ed., vol. 5, p. 439).

Human freedom is a glimpse of the Freedom which is man's real nature and which we all seek knowingly or unknowingly for it is our goal in life. We move toward that Freedom through renunciation of the little self and its agency and by acting without a sense of me and mine. When actions are selfless they are acts of God.

Contemplation of energies by modern science reveals a small part of the underlying truth of nature. Physical theories do not explain nature.

16. This being the case, he who sees the self as the only agent, because of impure understanding and a perverse mind does not see the Truth.

"Self" here means the ego, the feeling of agency of an unenlightened person.

17. He who has no egotism and whose understanding is not sullied does not slay even after slaying all the people, nor is he bound by action.

18. The knowledge, the knowable and the knower are the threefold cause of action; the instrument, the action and the agent are the threefold source of action.

19. Knowledge, action and agent are said to be threefold by the Samkhya philosophy, according to differences in the modes. Listen to them as they are.

Since all the differences in nature are due to differences in the preponderance of a particular mode over the other two, an object is characterized by its dominant mode, either as sattvic, rajasic or tamasic, which are generally best translated as steady, active and dull.

20. The knowledge by which one immutable existence is seen in all beings, the undivided among the divided, know that to be sattvic or pure.

21. But know that knowledge which sees many existents of distinct nature separately in all beings to be rajasic or tainted.

22. But that which is unreasonably attached to one object, as if it were all in all, is unreal and trivial and is called tamasic or deluded.

23. The action which is enjoined and which is performed by one without desire for results, without attachment and without love or hate is called sattvic or pure.

24. But an action involving great exertion which is performed with desire for results and with egotism is called rajasic or tainted.

25. The action which is undertaken through delusion, without heed to results, loss or injury (to others) or one's ability, is called tamasic or stupid.

26. The agent who is detached, non-egoistic, persevering and enthusiastic and who is unaffected by success or failure is called sattvic or good.

27. The agent who is passionate, desirous of results of action, greedy, cruel, impure and given to elation and depression is declared to be rajasic or indifferent.

28. The agent who is unsteady, vulgar, conceited, dishonest, malicious, lazy, morose and procrastinating is called tamasic or bad.

29. O Winner of Wealth (Arjuna)! Hear the threefold division of understanding and fortitude according to the modes, being described exhaustively and separately.

30. The understanding, O Partha (Arjuna)! which knows when to act and when not to, what is duty and what is not, what is to be feared and what is not, and what is bondage and what is freedom is sattvic or pure.

31. The understanding, O Partha (Arjuna)! by which right and wrong, duty and non-duty are known in a wrong manner is rajasic or confused.

32. The understanding, O Partha (Arjuna)! which is covered with darkness and which views unrighteousness as righteousness and everything in the opposite manner is tamasic or perverted.

33. The steadiness by which the actions of mind, life and the organs are controlled through the unwavering practice of yoga (control) is called sattvic or superior.

34. But, O Partha (Arjuna)! the steadiness by which one holds on to duty, desire and wealth through attachment and with desire for rewards is called rajasic or indifferent.

35. The steadiness by which, O Partha (Arjuna)! the dull-witted do not give up sleep, fear, sorrow, sadness and vanity is called tamasic or destructive.

36-37. O Bull among the Descendents of Bharata (Arjuna)! Now hear from me the three kinds of happiness. That happiness which comes through practice and which ends all pain; that which at first is like poison and like nectar at the end is called sattvic or pure; it is born of the serenity of self-knowledge.

This happiness has been described earlier in verse 21 of chapter 6.

38. The happiness which is born of the contact of sense-organs with sense-objects and which is like nectar in the beginning and like poison in the end is known as rajasic or passionate.

39. That happiness which deludes one in the beginning and also at the end and which arises from sleep, indolence and false perception is known as tamasic or delusive.

Pleasures from dullness and passion are tamasic and rajasic for they cloud consciousness, while intellectual and spiritual interests produce pleasure which is enduring being of a pure nature. However, as the Upanishad declares, even in the dullest pleasure there is intimation of the Bliss of Brahman. The *Taittiriya Upanishad* proclaims, "Who could ever breathe or live if there were no Bliss of Brahman in the heart?" The truth is that the limitless Bliss of Brahman is within all. When it is discovered through inwardness a person does not look outside for happiness.

In tamasic and rajasic pleasures happiness comes from periodic relief of dullness and tension, producing momentary calmness and peace revealing somewhat the inner tranquillity of Spirit. Between two fits of passion it is calm of the heart.

40. There is no being on earth or among the gods in heaven who is free from the three modes born of nature.

41. O Tormentor of Enemies (Arjuna)! The duties of Brahmins, Kshatriyas, Vaishyas and Shudras have been divided in accordance with their inborn qualities.

The four classes of Brahmins, Kshatriyas, Vaishyas and Shudras correspond roughly to the classes of philosophers, guardians, artisans and menials in Plato's *Republic*. These are divisions of members of society based on different vocations. They became caste distinctions and as society became more complex many sub-castes were formed. These social distinctions are against the spirit of Vedanta. In the long course of India's history true religious leaders have fought against the privileges of caste and wealth. The social prejudices lingered due to priestcraft, greed and lack of education. In modern times the distinctions are on their way to disappearance.

In a lecture on "Vedanta and Privilege" delivered in London at the end of the last century, Vivekananda said that the work of Vedanta was to break down all privileges of birth and wealth and he mentioned the gigantic attempt of Buddha to preach Vedanta ethics. "Some of the best epithets addressed to Buddha," he said, "are 'Thou breaker of castes, destroyer of privilege, preacher of equality to all beings!' So he preached this one idea of equality" (*Complete Works of Swami Vivekananda*, 16th ed., vol. 1, p. 424-25).

Vivekananda also said, "We read in the Mahabharata that the whole world was in the beginning peopled with Brahmins, and that as they began to degenerate, they became divided into different castes and that when the cycle turns round, they will all go back to that Brahminical origin" (*Complete Works of Swami Vivekananda*, 13th ed., vol. 3, p. 147-48).

Many passages in the Gita, the careful reader must have noticed, assert the equality of all beings.

The task of religion is to break down all privileges. In an enlightened civilization man finds his vocation dictated by his nature, but has equal rights with all.

Ramakrishna said, "All distinctions of caste may disappear in one way. That way is faith (love of God). The person of faith has no caste. The body, mind and spirit all become pure as soon as one has faith. Gaur and Nitai preached the name of the Lord and embraced everybody including the outcaste. The outcaste is no outcaste if he has faith. The untouchables become clean and pure if they have faith" (Translation from Bengali *Kathamrita* by S.K.M.).

> **42. Control of mind and the senses, austerity, purity, forgiveness, sincerity, wisdom, knowledge and faith in God are the duties of Brahmins born of their nature.**
>
> **43. Heroism, spiritedness, steadfastness, skill, not retreating in battle, generosity and lordliness are the duties of the Kshatriyas, born of their nature.**
>
> **44. Agriculture, rearing of cattle and trade are the duties of Vaishyas born of their nature, while service is the duty of Shudras born of their character.**
>
> **45. Man attains perfection by being devoted each to his duty. Hear now how man occupied with his duty attains perfection.**
>
> **46. From whom come the living beings' impulse to work, by whom all this is pervaded — by worshipping Him with his duty man attains perfection.**

One does not have to retire from work to develop spiritually. "Work is worship" is the teaching of what Vivekananda called practical Vedanta. "To labor is to pray."

Work for the good of the world (lokasamgraha) is the teaching of the Gita. The spirit of work characterizes the quality of an individual and society. When civilizations lose sight of the divine intention in history and make pleasure the paramount motive, the moral feeling of togetherness which holds family and society together is eroded and decline sets in. The disintegration caused by selfishness is the cause of fear and anxiety in economically developed societies which have lost sight of the moral purpose of life and which have surrendered their souls to the pleasure principle.

Each is great in his own place. In the epic Mahabharata, of which the Gita is a part, there are many examples of common men and women working in families who reached the height of spiritual realization. A society which forgets the ideal and is dominated by commerce or narrow-minded priests invites the wrath of history.

47. Better is one's duty, though imperfectly done, than another's well-performed. A man does not incur sin by doing work ordained by his nature.

The Mahabharata points out that Aryans and non-Aryans, men and women, all have the right to the knowledge of Brahman. Raikva, Vachaknavi, Samvarta and others attained perfection though they were outside the pale of orthodox *varnashrama dharma,* that is, duties prescribed by caste and the ages of man.

48. O Son of Kunti (Arjuna)! One should not give up the duty to which one is born even if it is defective, for all undertakings are covered with faults as fire with smoke.

49. He who is without attachment to anything, who is self-subjugated and who is without craving attains the supreme perfection of non-action through renunciation.

50. O Son of Kunti (Arjuna)! Now know from me briefly how after reaching perfection one attains to Brahman, the supreme state of wisdom.

The supreme state of wisdom has already been indicated in several verses in previous chapters. This supreme state of wisdom which is attained by one who has achieved perfection through worship of the Lord by following his vocation is described in the following verses 51-53, which are to be conjugated together.

51. Joined with pure understanding, controlling self firmly, relinquishing sound and other sense-objects, rejecting longing and aversion,

52. Resorting to a secluded spot, eating lightly, controlling speech, body and mind, devoted to meditation always, and practicing renunciation,

53. Renouncing egoism, power, pride, desire, anger and possession, without sense of 'mine' and being tranquil, he earns fitness to become one with Brahman.

54. Becoming one with Brahman, serene in spirit he neither grieves nor desires; the same to all beings, he attains supreme devotion to me.

55. Through devotion he knows me truly, what and who I am; having thus known me truly, he enters me forthwith.

Ramakrishna said that pure devotion takes one to the same goal reached by the followers of the path of knowledge.

56. Ever performing works, he who takes refuge in me attains the eternal, imperishable abode through my grace.

57. Mentally surrendering all actions to me, regarding me as the supreme end and resorting to yoga of understanding (detachment), let your mind dwell on me always.

58. With your mind on me, you will by my grace overcome all difficulties; but if you do not listen to me out of conceit, you will perish.

In all situations of life the word of the expert is the rule for success in work. As regards the goal of life and principles of living, the word of an Incarnation of God or Truth is our sole authority. Disobedience to the word of God is the cause of the fall of individuals and civilizations.

CHAPTER EIGHTEEN

Fate or karma is never conquered by suppression. It is through practice of self-less dedication to duty that we enlarge our sense of freedom and free ourselves from the compulsions of nature.

Ramakrishna points out that the Great Mother who has put us all in her trap has kept open a little door for our escape into Freedom. Unfortunately, most of us do not see it and knock our heads against impenetrable barriers in our search for happiness.

Man is much more than a rational animal. His essential divinity is reflected in his moral will, the sense of obligation and duty.

We cannot escape fate through self-will.

60. O Son of Kunti (Arjuna)! The work that you do not want to do out of delusion you will perform helplessly bound by your own karma born of your nature.

Karma technically means a person's nature formed by past habits of thought and action.

61. O Arjuna! The Lord dwells in the hearts of all beings causing all beings to revolve as if mounted on a machine.

62. O Descendant of Bharata (Arjuna)! Take refuge in him in every way. You will find supreme peace and eternal abode through his grace.

We are moved by two forces of maya; namely, vidya maya, the power of knowledge and avidya maya, the power of ignorance. Mind flows both toward what is good and toward what is evil. Both these forces belong to the Power who dwells in the heart of all beings. The ego is a limitation of Pure Consciousness; it is the creation of Divine Power. This creation is a game. We enjoy it for a while and then get tired and want to escape into Freedom and Reality. When the ego rejects its selfish wishes and interests and surrenders itself to the creator who dwells in the heart, it begins to see itself as an instrument of the Divine. When the ego-sense becomes attenuated it sees itself as a reflection of Pure Consciousness.

THE YOGA OF LIBERATION

The mystery of creation is never explained in terms of the created. But in the realm of maya, the realm of time, space and causation, we can have a description of perceptions leading to the goal which is beyond the dualism of thought and speech, beyond science and mathematics.

Science tells us that the universe evolved from some 'singularity' and will return to it again. 'Singularity' is another name for emptiness. But this is only the imagination of the scientist, or a likely story, or a myth. When the diverse energies of the mind become collected and become a 'singularity' the whole universe collapses along with it into the Reality of Pure Existence-Consciousness-Bliss which dwells, as the Upanishads say, in the cave of the heart.

The knot which ties pure Consciousness and the creature together is in the heart. The *Katha Upanishad* says that the knot of the heart is cut asunder, that all doubts vanish and that all karma ends when the Supreme One is seen. If the scientist can resolve himself into such a 'singularity' by looking within he will know what Reality is. Otherwise the search for Reality outside of consciousness is like the search of a blind man in a dark room for a black cat that is not there. More than fifty-five years ago I read George Bernard Shaw's little book, *A Black Man in Search of God*, where he said something like that.

Today science has given up its search for Reality. Some even doubt like Paul Davies, the mathematician and writer on popular science, whether there is anything which can be called reality.

What the quantum scientists observe today about space-time is so weird that they proclaim it to be like a foam-like substance, ever changing and of capricious and random fluctuation.

Long ago poet Tagore wrote:

> The world is the ever-changing foam
> That floats on the surface of a sea of silence.

Silence is Truth or Reality — the pure Consciousness, the womb of time and of all appearances and values. However we have the idea of the Real against which we check our observations and experiences. The Real is that which is what it is whether observed or not. In the book of Exodus, God said to Moses, "I am that I am." It is an honest self-proclamation of Reality. The idea of the Real comes from within us but we can never locate or grasp it however fine our analysis is. It is the primary datum of all experience, yet it is beyond all search, being the intangible ground of all observation and experience.

63. This is the wisdom which is more secret than the secret that has been spoken by me. Pondering over it thoroughly do as you like.

There is no logic which will explain doctrinal difficulties about free will and predestination. The world is a game of maya. When we like the game we continue in maya, when we feel tired we want to go home and find that it is grace from within which breaks the dream of our conditioned existence. As long as we are in maya and have the sense of individuality we have to pray and ask for grace from the One Person who is the supreme manifestation of the Power of Reality.

In the above verse the phrase, "do as you like," has to be understood properly. Krishna asks Arjuna to ponder thoroughly his statement that God dwells in the hearts of all and makes them move like machines. When a person thoroughly understands it, he has become enlightened. An enlightened person, says Ramakrishna, does not take a false step. Whatever he wills or does is an expression of God's purpose. In other words his action is born of freedom. Krishna's words are no counsel for hasty, wilful action.

There is a grain of freedom in all created beings. In civilized man who fashions ideals of truth, beauty and goodness, the feeling of freedom is enhanced and he acts less with the feeling of constraint. As a person pursues the spiritual goal his life falls into order with the demands for self-expression in others. In higher societies the constitution which applies to all clearly reflects religious truths. In spiritual organizations this is more manifest. In the life of the saint, the Self or Consciousness steps beyond all order into the limitless expanse of freedom.

By pondering over Krishna's "secret" one begins to see life's and civilization's true direction; faith grows, love of truth increases and a man's journey toward Reality becomes steady and pleasant.

64. Hear again my supreme word, the most secret of all. You are well-beloved of me; therefore I shall speak of what is good for you.

65. Let your mind dwell on me, be my devotee, worship me and bow down to me. You will come to me I promise you truly, for you are dear to me.

Krishna here emphasizes the personal aspect of the Godhead. The Impersonal is difficult to contemplate (chapter 12) and sometimes such contemplation becomes dry and there is a reaction. It is easier to melt the ego in love. Indian spiritual literature indicates that perfect, selfless love of any object reveals the Divine within.

A lover of God arrives at feelings of freedom and bliss toward the end of life.

> Today my mind refuses to strike a balance sheet
> of what I got and what I did not;
> For in the lights and shadows of the heart I hear
> today the notes of a glad music.
> (Free translation from Tagore)

66. Giving up all rules and regulations take refuge in me alone. I shall free you from all sins, do not grieve.

The Divine Ruler, the Redeemer, is in the hearts of all. Who can be more merciful than the mother to her child?

In this uncertain world of doubt and disaster only one can speak with authority: one who is one with Truth, one who can say I am the goal and I am the way. As the demons in chapter 16 declare, there is no truth in the world; it is the very same conclusion of modern science, according to which our observation does not and cannot reveal anything that is objective. Truth is not accessible to thought or contemplation of physical energies.

But there is Truth; we could not live or have any hope or ideal without it, though we do not find it outside. Truth is not the quality of a statement as some philosophers define it. It is the basis of all statements. Tagore once wrote, "Words well up from the depths of Truth."

CHAPTER EIGHTEEN

Sins are mistakes, falsehoods, which hide the Truth from us. We move toward Truth and Reality through practice of manliness. Manliness is virtue, which comes from the old Vedic word for man, *vira*. Socrates said virtue is knowledge. This is Vedanta; for super-science, which it is, is the knowledge of Self, the real Man, the self-knowledge of the Knower. Such knowledge is character. A wise man does not do foolish things.

The ancient Pythagorean, Socratic, Platonic tradition of philosophy sought to find Truth by looking within, through contemplation (know thyself). Modern intellectual attempts of philosophers in the West have not advanced philosophy a bit. Professor Alfred N. Whitehead wrote that the history of Western philosophy is a series of footnotes on Plato.

Surrender is the easiest way for gaining Freedom. However it is not without a struggle. But in this path no scholarship, no scriptural knowledge, no rules and no regulations, no elaborate ceremonies are necessary to reach God. The only thing needed is holding on to faith — belief in the words of God.

This verse underlines that religion is not ritualism. Religion is obedience to moral law, law of conduct of life, the law of love which leads finally to the entire elimination of the little self of desire.

Priests often reduce religion to petty observance of insignificant rituals, as was frequently the trouble in India at different periods of her history. Vivekananda said in rebuke that religion had entered the kitchen when he saw masses of people in India following ridiculous rules about eating and caste.

But the spirit of true religion was kept alive by prophets and monks, men of complete renunciation who had no axes to grind and who were not beholden to anybody.

Speaking about religion ruled by priestcraft, Vivekananda said in a lecture in America, "In every religion it is the priest who is conservative, for two reasons — because it is his bread and because he can only move with the people. All priests are not strong. If the people say, 'Preach two thousand gods,' the priests will do it. They are the servants of the congregation who pay them. God does not pay them."

Martin Luther who preached against indulgences and priest-craft and who claimed that man can go straight to God without the intermediary of priests was hailed by Vivekananda as the George Washington of religion.

There are numerous instances in history of great spiritual transformation of persons who seemed to be lost beyond all hope, because of their faith, in the mercy of Incarnations and their disciples.

Tolstoy pulled himself out of his youthful, passionate wilderness through faith and I have the feeling from reading some of his stories that his mantra or sacred formula was, "Have mercy on me."

Swami Premananda, another intimate disciple of Ramakrishna, wrote to a monk, quoting from a song sung by Ramakrishna:

Let us go with our load to Ajodhya where Rama is going
    to be crowned king.
We will give it back to Him and take refuge in Him.

As Christ said, "Come unto me, all ye that labor and are heavy laden, and I will give you rest" (Matt. 11:28.).

Many commentators of the highest spiritual attainments regard this verse as the ultimate in spiritual counsel for the realization of Truth or God; namely, the complete surrender of the ego, the scene of the warring dualities of nature. It is the counsel for those who seek freedom from the shackles of karma.

Religion or spiritual life or love of Truth has many levels. First, there is the ritualistic religion, which Vivekananda termed the kindergarten of religion — a beginner. If it does not lead to the higher religion of love it is unsteady. Ramakrishna said that it was not real faith, but a kind of hearsay devotion which could disappear as quickly as it came. In times of stress it vanishes. A Myna bird can be taught to take the name of the Lord, Rama and Krishna, but when a cat catches it, it only shrieks.

Love of God is a rare thing and has to be cultivated through spiritual studies and contact with holy people, personally or through their biographies. When the religion of love ripens it attains its ideal of complete surrender and ends in wisdom, the Truth beyond all relationships, when the lover and the beloved, the worshipper and the worshipped merge into the unity of ineffable Bliss and Truth.

"All sins" means all karma, the duality and conflicts of existence, which is the fall from heaven.

A person of total surrender has no fear. Others fear and anxiety in different degrees are the lot of all, though they are relieved by holy company for a while.

It is the ego which carries the burden of karma. The ultimate spiritual effort is complete surrender of the ego to Reality. All thinking, all study, philosophy and theology have to be left behind and the aspirant after Truth must plunge into the depths of Reality with utter abandon just as one dreams of doing in true love, of which a dim reflection is found in romance.

In this pedestrian age of economics and individualistic psychology the hint of truth in romance has been lost and what passes for love generally is a nervous condition.

The Upanishad declares that Truth is that from which all thoughts recoil along with the mind without reaching it." Truth is beyond formula and discipline. All self striving ends finally in complete resignation and effortlessness.

> **67. This should never be spoken by one who is devoid of austerity, who is not a devotee, who does not want to hear, nor to one who speaks ill of me.**

Verse 66 can be easily misunderstood, so Krishna warns Arjuna against casting seeds on stony soil.

> **68. He who will relate this supreme secret to my devotees will, because of his excellent devotion to me, come to me without doubt.**

> **69. There is none among men who does dearer service to me than he; nor will there be another dearer to me in the world.**

Here Krishna describes true evangelism. Lovers of God, those who are established in faith, bring the Truth to those

who are piring after knowledge and freedom. Their inspiration
is love a compassion; they are the agents of the merciful God,
said Ramrishna.

70. ill be worshipped with the sacrifice of knowl-
edg him who will study this sacred dialogue
betn us. This is my view.

71. even the man who only listens to this, who
has and who is without cavil, will be freed from
evi reach the holy regions of the righteous.

Even th no listen to the recitation of the Gita with faith will
benefit ally though they may not grasp the meaning.

Ramna told the story of a man who was weeping when
the Gita ing recited though he was without learning. When
asked wept he said that he did not understand the verses
but he shna and Arjuna seated in the chariot.

72 ha (Arjuna)! Have you listened to this with
a cated mind? O Winner of Wealth (Arjuna)!
Ha elusion born of ignorance been dispelled?

ARJUNA SAID:

73 geless One (Krishna)! My delusion is
de nd I have recovered my memory through
yo stand firm with doubts gone; I will fol-
lo rd.

We do edom or peace of mind by flight from our obligation ssibilities. Our problems can be solved and freedom ea y facing them boldly with detachment and by
surren lves to the will of God. Rousseau's theory of
genera ource of law in society is a faint indication of
the wil ns the universe.

F nxiety and all the rest in the basket of our
weakn m lack of faith in the innate strength of man.
It is fe the root of all weakness. Vivekananda said,
"Let fe t is more to the point than the noble statement, we have to fear is fear itself."

CHAPTER EIGHTEEN

"Memory" means remembrance of Self, the essence of our personality, the Divine in our heart.

In the *Brihadaranyaka Upanishad* the Spirit is described as *abhaya*, the fearless. This is the fearlessness of Socrates who drank hemlock obeying the law of Athens.

SANJAYA SAID:

74. Thus have I heard the wonderful and hair-raising dialogue between Vasudeva (Krishna) and Partha (Arjuna) of noble spirit.

75. Through the grace of Vyasa I have heard the supreme secret of yoga directly from Krishna, the Lord of Yoga, who was speaking himself.

Sanjaya had the gift of distant vision from Vyasa, the author of the Mahabharata.

76. O King (Dhritarashtra)! I rejoice again and again as I keep recalling over and over again this wonderful and holy dialogue between Keshava (Krishna) and Arjuna.

77. And, O King! recalling repeatedly the most wondrous form of the Lord Hari, great is my amazement and I rejoice over and over again.

"Wondrous form" is the cosmic form, chapter 11.

78. Wherever is the Lord Krishna, with Partha (Arjuna) the archer, there will prevail prosperity, victory, progress and immutable law. This is my conviction.

Both wisdom and power are necessary for an ideal society. An idea lives and marches on them both.

The Gita ends with the counsel for the preservation of the world order of peace and prosperity. A civilized society needs strength and wisdom for its preservation and progress. A society without the ideal of renunciation, i.e., the ideal of love and non-violence, slides back to primitive and self-destructive violence — the ultimate death of a materialistic culture. While non-violence and wisdom are the true ends of culture, a community with individuals on different levels of self-development needs for the sake of its preservation an ideal hero, such as Arjuna, for deterring violence from outside. Such use of violence in a civilized society is without hatred and is lawful. A mother lioness chastises her young ones when they become too troublesome and frolicking.

An arrogant society which puts its trust in violence as the means for attaining and maintaining peace and which has no ideal of selfless love is doomed to a violent death. No lasting and great work is achieved through violence and cunning.

An ancient Sanskrit saying in the Mahabharata proclaims, "By injustice men prosper, gain what they desire, and triumph over their enemies, but finally they are destroyed at their very roots." Societies based on violence and war, cruelty and hatred have disappeared.

"Immutable law" is the law by which one gains wisdom, freedom and bliss. This is Sanatana Dharma, the Eternal Principle, the Truth that upholds the universe. It is the law of continual sacrifice of the little self till the true Self of man stands revealed to his sight. The little self of man is like a tiny speck in the eye which blots out the vision of the entire universe.

The ethics of the materialists who pursue power and pleasure are the ethics that the Mahabharata calls "fish ethics" where the big fish eat up the small ones. A civilization which remains loyal to the ideal of love and strength never perishes.

Glossary

Abhaya — Fearless.

Abhyasa — Practice, repeated effort.

Adhibhuta — The physical realm.

Adhidaivata — Indwelling spirit.

Adhiyajna — Lord of sacrifice.

Adhyatma — The embodied self.

Advaita — Non-dualism.

Ahimsa — Non-violence, non-injury.

Akasha — Space.

Apana — Nerve current involved in food assimilation and elimination.

Apara — Inferior, other.

Ashtavakra Samhita — Scripture of highest wisdom.

Atma — Self, mind.

Atman — Spirit, the soul of man, self.

Atmanam biddhi — Know thyself. (Gk., *gnothi se auton*)

Avatara — Divine Incarnation.

Avidya — Ignorance, misunderstanding.

Avidya maya — Delusive, tempting illusion; appetite for selfish enjoyment.

Bhagavad — Divine.

Bhakti yoga — The path of love.

Bodhi — Wisdom.

Brahma — Creator, God.

Brahmacharya — A life of continence and purity.

Brahman — One self-existent Spirit, the Godhead, the Self, Existence-Consciousness-Bliss, Reality.

Brahmayoni — Birthplace of universes.

Brahmin — Priest.

Buddhahridaya — The heart of the Buddha, the enlightened.

Buddhi — Pure intellect, understanding.

Chidakasha — The space of Consciousness.

Chitta — Mind as a whole.

GLOSSARY

Darshan — Vision.

Desha-kala-nimitta — Time-space-causation.

Dharma — Law, discipline, principles of conduct in organizations, professions, etc.

Dhruva smriti — Constant remembrance.

Dhyana yoga — The way of meditation.

Durga — Creative feminine energy, Redeemer.

Dvanda — Dualities in nature.

Ganita — Numbers or mathematics.

Gunas — Three constituents of nature.

Guru — Spiritual teacher.

Ishwara — Ruler, God.

Jagadamba — Mother of the universe.

Jivanmukta — The free living person.

Jivatman — The transmigrating self.

Jnana — Knowledge, wisdom.

Jnana yoga — Path of wisdom.

Kaivalya — Aloneness, the state of freedom.

Kali — Creative feminine energy, Time.

Kali yuga — The dark age.

Karana salila — Causal waters, the waters of creation.

Karma — Action, fate.

Karma yoga — Path of action.

Kavi — Creator or artist, the All-knowing One.

Kshatriyas — Warriors, guardians of Plato.

Lokasamgraha — Welfare of the world.

Mahakala— Spirit, super-time.

Mahamaya — Mother of universes, great enchantress.

Mahat — The Great, the first manifestation of prakriti.

Manas — Mind.

Maya — The mystery, the magic of creation, illusion.

Nada-Brahman — The original sound of Brahman.

Nara Narayana — God in man.

Nirguna — Without gunas (the three principles of nature).

Nirguna Brahman — Pure Spirit, timeless Reality without gunas.

Nirvana — Enlightenment, extinction of the ego (used especially by Buddhists).

Om (Aum) — The original sound of creation, the sacred monosyllable.

Om-Tat-Sat — An early indication of Brahman.

Para — Primary, superior.

Paramatman— The Supreme Self.

Paravidya — Super-science, supreme knowledge, knowledge of Reality, Self-knowledge.

Prakriti — Nature, procreatrix.

Prana — Life-force, energy.

Pranayaman — Breath control, control of nerve currents.

Preyas — The pleasant.

Puranas — Ancient religious literature of India.

Purusha — The Person.

Rahasya — Mystery.

Rajas — One of the three gunas, the principle of activity, change.

Rajasika — Passionate.

Rishis — Saints.

Sachchidananda — Truth-Consciousness-Bliss.

Saguna Brahman — Brahman with qualities, the universe, the manifested Reality.

Saguna — With gunas.

Samadhi — Super-conscious experience.

Samghata — Constellation of forces.

Samhitas — Vedic hymns.

Samkhya — A basic philosophy, numbers.

Samsara — The universal process.

Sanatana Dharma — The Eternal Religion.

Sannyasa — Renunciation.

Sannyasin — Monk.

Sat — Truth, invisible aspect of Brahman.

Sat-Chit-Ananda — Truth (Existence)-Consciousness-Bliss.

Sattva — One of the three gunas, principle of balance and intelligence, pure, revealing the existence of objects serenity.

GLOSSARY

Shastra — Revealed truth, scripture, rules governing the conduct of life.

Shiva— Beneficent aspect of Reality.

Shreyas — The highest good, summum bonum.

Shudras — Menials.

Shukshma sharira — The fine body.

Shunya —Emptiness

Sthula sharira — The gross body.

Swatantra — Self-governed, autarch (Greek).

Tamas — One of the three gunas, the principle of inertia, resistance, obscurity, dullness.

Tara — Creative feminine energy (Hindu-Buddhist), Redeemer.

Tat — Visible aspect of Brahman.

Upanishads — Final sections of Vedic literature.

Upasana — Worship.

Vaishyas — Businessmen, tradesmen.

Varnashrama dharma — Duties prescribed by caste and age.

Veda — Wisdom, literature of wisdom.

Vedanta — Religion of knowledge and freedom, wisdom, literal meaning "the end of the Vedas."

Vedas — Earliest literature of the Indo-Aryan people.

Vidya maya — The drive for freedom, the power of knowledge.

Vijnana — Knowledge of the principles of nature, special knowledge.

Vikalpas — Empty concepts, imaginations.

Vira — Vedic word for man.

Visarga — Emission.

Vyadha — Hunter, butcher.

Yajna — Worshipful sacrifice.

Yoga — Contemplation, the way of union with Spirit, to bind, yoke.

Yogamaya — Creative energy.

Yogi — One who practices yoga.

Yuga — An epoch.

Yuga dharma — Religion of the age.

Index

INDEX

Bodhisattva, 23

Body, tamas 29, subtle 31, control 44, freedom 45, in time 65, incarnated 65 2.18:20-22, 66 2.26, transmigration 66, gross 67, the spirit in 68 2.30, nature 89, hunger 92, chariot 95, unreal 118, conquest of 118 5.7, the yogi 119 5.11, 122 5.23, the wise 123, ruler of 148 8.2, physical 150 8.4, at death 150 8.5-6, leaving 151 8.12-13, God 177 11.13:15, knowledge of 191, the field 191 13.2, 192, the tree 193, nature 196 13.20, Self and 197 13.22, 198 13.31-32, gunas 200 14.5. senses 202 14.11, spirit leaves 207, 207 15.7-8, hatred 214 16.18, demoniac 218 17.6, austerity 219 17.14, action 224 18.14-15, pure 229, control 231 18.52

Brahma, 80 3.10:15, 151 8.16, 152 8.17-18, 152, 177 11.15, 182 11.37, 199 14.3

Brahma sutras (aphorisms), 193

Brahmayoni, 174

Brahmacharya, 151 8.11

Brahman, Reality 20, experience of 31, the third eye 37, all is 39, difficult 41, knowledge 62, bliss 68, Reality 69, indivisible 76, poise 77 2.72, 78, with and without gunas 80, pure Spirit 81, united 104 4.10, wise person 108, all is 109 4.24, sacrifice 110 4.25, 111 4.30-3l, Reality 118, karma yoga 118 5.6, wisdom 120 5.16, established 121 5.19, Self 122 5.20-21, nirvana 122 5.24-25, unity 123 5.26, bliss 131, becomes one 133 6.27-28, failure 135 6.38, all is 138, "I am ..." 143, maya 145, infinite 146, Inner Self 147 7.29, what is? 148 8.1, power 149, personal God 150, sound of 151 8.12-13, knower 153, 153 8.24, maya 156, Truth 157, Supreme 169 10.12-13, all is 170, limitless 174, imperishable 186,

three pillars 193, aphorisms 193 13.4, Supreme 195 13.12, knower 196, becoming 198 13.30, free 204, realization 205 14.26-27, forest of 206, root of 207, imperishable 209 15.17, three signs 220 17.23, Om 221, intimation 228, for all 231, to attain 231 18.50-53, one with 232 18.54

Brahmin, 5, 12, 19, 25-26, 71 2.46, 72, 93, 106, 120 5.18, 149, 157, 165, 165 9.33. 220 17.23, 229, 229 18.41, 230 18.42

Brahmo Samaj, 143

Brahui, 28

Brigandet, Bishop, his *Life of Buddha* 23

Brihadaranyaka Upanishad, 146, 212, 241

Brook, Peter, 2

Brown, Malcolm, 40

Buber, Martin, 73

Buddha, 12, 15, 17, 21-25, 27, 46, 76, 86, 99-100, 110, (his *Awakening of Faith* 114), 114, 122-23, 127, 130-31, 149, 163, 229

Buddhahridaya, 123

Buddhi, 26, 34, 69, 119, 133

Buddhism, 21-22, 24

Buddhist, monastery 23, monks 149

Burke, Marie Louise, her *Swami Vivekananda, New Discoveries* 23

Caesar, 14

Campbell, Joseph, 13, 37

Carlyle, Thomas, 5

Catholic, church 22, saints 23, religion 23

Chaitanya, 163

Chandrasekhar, 42

Chaos, 2, 16, 39, 100, 225

Chidakasha, 40

Chitta, 40

Christ, Jesus, 2, 13, 21-24, 83, 86, 100, 106, 163, 169, 238

Christian, thinkers 23, religion 24, philosophy 31, missionaries 68, 87, communion 128, church 143, religion 149, hell 156, worship 183

INDEX

INDEX

INDEX

religion 97, failure of reason 102, movement to 104, good ego 105, Brahman 109, non-dual 113, one with 114, reveals 115, Brahman 118, in all hearts 119, knowledge 120, Self 120 5.17, 121 peace, Brahman 121 5.19, many roads 125, physical love 129, pleasure 130, distinctions, pure intellect 133, consciousness 137, the sound of 139, eternal 140, ego diluted 142, Brahman 143, mathematical image 146, art 151, emptiness 156, religion 157, birth and death 160, blind towards 169, Supreme Knowledge 172, Einstein 173, return 178, beyond being and non-being 182, Vedanta 183, Self 189, beyond speech 195, Platonic myth 196, wisdom 199, serenity 200, sattva close to 201, timeless 209, messengers from 210, moral law 215, Sat 220 17.26, Brahman 221, escape ego 233, 'singularity' 234, power of 235, manliness 237, surrender 238-39

Religion, is Truth 2, books 3, Gita 4-5, historical 9, without servitude 10, me and mine 11, Eternal 13, Vivekananda 14, Vedanta 15, science 16, search 17, dualistic 18, Vedanta 19, of love 21, Christ 22, Catholic 23, Incarnation 24-25, Western 26, Indian influence 28, recovery 32, in the heart 33, science 38, ethics 41, scientists and 42, action 43, freedom 45, sectarian 55, Einstein 72, leap into the dark 73, ritualistic 75, Reality 82, selfish 84, ethical 86, caricature 87, rid of ego 91, eternity 92, Eternal 97, tarnished 100, 101 4.7, Kali yuga 101-02, Toynbee 103, incarnate 104 4.8, Reality 105, ways 106, sacrifice 110,114, misconceptions 117, Gita 123, not philosophy 126, celibacy 129, two kinds of 136, dharma 139,

higher law 140, love 142, Indian 149, Truth 156, Vedas 161, devotion 162, bhakti 164, divinity in all 165, waking up 166, India 173, God is everywhere 175, history 177, Eternal 178, surrender 181, faith 190, character 194, moral law 214, ideal 215, faith 217, ethics and 222, Truth 223, equality 229, moral law 237, many levels 238

Renunciation, 13, 116 5.1, 117-18, 117 5.2-3, 118 5.6, 119 5.12-13, 121, 126-27, 126 6.1-2, 127 6.3, 134, 134 6.35, 160, 162 9.28, 189, 189 12.12, 194 13.8, 223 18.1-2:4, 224 18.7-11, 231 18.49, 232 18.52, 237, 241

Rishis, 158

Rolland, Romain, 12, 14

Roman Church, 23

Roman Empire, 21, 149, 179

Rousseau, Jean Jacques, 240

Russell, Bertrand, his *Free Man's Worship* 142, 215

Saccas, Ammonias, 149

Sachchidananda, 83

Sacrifice, 80, 80 3.9-15, 106 4.12, 109-10, 110 4.25, 111 4.28:33, 124 5.29,148, 154 8.28, 159, 159 9.16, 160, 160 9.20, 161 9.24, 162 9.27, 218, 218 17.11-13, 220 17.23-25:27-28, 223 18 3:5, 240 18.70

Saguna, 80

Saguna Brahman, 183

Saint Augustine, 130, 149

Saint Paul, 13, 77, 145

Samadhi, 32, 132

Samghata, 37

Samhitas, 19

Samkhya, 25, 27-31, 35, 63, 69, 81, 117 5.4, 118 5.5, 119, 128, 131, 138, 149, 158, 183, 200, 209, 224, 224 18.13, 226 18.19

Samsara, 17

Samvarta, 231

Sanatana Dharma, 1, 3, 13-14, 22, 24,

INDEX

INDEX

way 118 5.5, Brahman 118 5.6, of
Meditation (Dhyana Yoga) 125,
meaning of 126, renunciation 126
6.2, 127, settled in 127 6.4, contemplation 128, the yogi 128 6.8,
concentration 129, the practice of
129 6.12, meditation 131 6.16-17,
ascetic practice and pain 131,
united with Truth 132, the still
mind 132 6.20, non-attachment
132 6.23, Self 133 6.29, equanimity
134 6.33, difficult 135 6.36, failing
135 6.37-38, reborn 135 6.41,
action 136, perfection 136 6.44,
action 136, of Spirit and Nature
137, 137 7.1, veiled 146 7.25,
yogamaya 147, of Imperishable
Brahman 148, steady mind 150
8.8-10, gates closed 151 8.12-13,
paths 154 8.27, Royal Yoga 155,
Self 156 8.5, karma yoga 158, of
Divine Manifestations 167, ignorance, ego, etc. 169, manifestations
170 10.18, maya 171, of Revelation
of Cosmic Form 175, Self 176 11.4,
the Divine Form 176 11.9, of Love
of God 186, who is best 186 12.1,
worship 186 12.2, of Division of
Field and Its Knower 191, the ways
197 13.24, of Division of the Three
Constituents of Nature 199, worship 205 14.26, of the Supreme
Person 206, of the Division of the
Divine and Demoniac 211, knowl-

edge 212 16.1, of the Three Kinds
of Faith 216, of Liberation 222,
sattvic action 227 18.33, detachment 232 18.57, secret of 241
18.75

Yogamaya, 146 7.25, 147

Yogi, meditation 17, devotion 76 2.61,
karma 80, 87, desireless 108, sacrifice 110 4.25, self-purification 119
5.11, renunciation 119 5.12, contain impulses 122 5.23, Brahman
122 5.24, the Lord 124 5.29,
renunciation 126 6.1-2, same-
sighted 128 6.8-10, solitude 129,
meditation 129 6.13-14, truth and
chastity 130, freedom 130 6.15,
sorrow 131, moderation 131 6.17,
Self 131 6.18, concentration 132
6.18-21, Self 133 6.26-27, welfare
134, an equal eye 134 6.32, failure
135 6.38, rebirth 136 6.42, karma
yoga 136, yogi is highest 136 6.46-
47, attainable 151 8.14, rebirth and
Brahman 153 8.23-25, two paths
154 8.26-28, a prayer 170 10.17,
subtle spirit 208 15.11, non-
injury 219

Yuga, 152

Yuga dharma, 102, 164

Zeitgeist, 102
Zero, 146
Zoroaster, 27